Wisdom
Walking
PILGRIMAGE AS A WAY OF LIFE

GIL W. STAFFORD

Church Publishing
NEW YORK

Church Publishing
19 East 34th Street
New York, NY 10016

www.churchpublishing.org

Cover design by Jennifer Kopec, 2Pug Design
Typeset by Denise Hoff

Library of Congress Cataloging-in-Publication Data
Names: Stafford, Gil W., 1953- author.
Title: Wisdom walking : pilgrimage as a way of life / Gil W. Stafford.
Description: New York : Church Publishing, 2017. |
Includes bibliographical references.
Identifiers: LCCN 2016052947 (print) | LCCN 2017006582 (ebook) |
ISBN 9780819233493 (pbk.) | ISBN 9780819233509 (ebook)
Subjects: LCSH: Pilgrims and pilgrimages.
Classification: LCC BL619.P5 S73 2017 (print) |
LCC BL619.P5 (ebook) | DDC 203/.51--dc23
LC record available at https://lccn.loc.gov/2016052947

Printed in the United States of America

The pilgrimage of this book is dedicated to those in my family
who have walked Ireland with me:
Catherine Ann Stafford, my anam cara
Neil Stafford, Alicia Stafford Escobar, and Phil Escobar
Without your love there would be no adventure.

Contents

Acknowledgments

While walking Ireland solo, I was never alone. There was always someone paying attention to my progress, making sure I arrived safely every night. Writing is also a solitary process, but the author is never alone. And the production of this book would not have been possible without the many people who cared enough to make sure I completed it, always better with their help than alone.

This book would not exist without the stories of those who have been on walking pilgrimage with me, especially my family, the Saint Brigid's group, and Vox Peregrini. Their stories have made this book come alive. And special thanks to Dr. John Wiles for inviting me to be a part of that crazy idea you had of putting together a singing pilgrimage. I am deeply indebted to those who have been so gracious and vulnerable to share their intimate pilgrimage stories of personal tragedy and illness. These stories have shaped my soul. And without my parents and my sister, Dinah, there would be no "first steps" of the pilgrimage of storytelling.

I am extraordinarily grateful to Beth Gaede, my writing coach and editor. She has been a guiding light and mentor through two books. And finally, I am thankful for the Church Publishing team. They have been very attentive and always encouraging, making sure I have indeed made it safely to the finish line.

:

Introduction

Your search is who you are. . . .
Your search is your gift.
And your search never ends.

Steven Charleston[1]

Have you had one of those moments when you were driving down the freeway and decided to change lanes, so you checked all your mirrors, turned on your blinker, started to move into the other lane—and suddenly, in a flash, out of nowhere, there was a car right next to you, the car that had been hiding in your blind spot? You jerked your car back into your lane, now disorientated from an abrupt realization, jarred out of your comfort zone, relieved that you didn't collide into a disastrous future.

I have had several of those moments while writing this book. One of them was a month after I thought I had finished it. I had met the publisher's deadline and thirty days later was headed to a writer's workshop at the Collegeville Institute on the campus of Saint John's University, northwest of Minneapolis.

I arrived at the Minneapolis–Saint Paul airport with the instructions needed to find the fun van that would take me to the Collegeville Institute for a week of writing. I'm not the best of travelers. I get lost easily and turned around quite often. When I reached the spot where I thought I was supposed to meet my ride, there were vans from hotels, car rental companies, shuttles to other terminals, but no fun van. I panicked. I read the instructions for the fourth time.

And then I saw her, a woman wearing a Chicago Theological Seminary t-shirt. I just knew in my heart that she had to be going to the same workshop. Before asking her, I had to overcome my profound introversion—admittedly, I have problems striking up conversations with people I know.

"Um, are you going to the Collegeville Institute?"

I gave her a bit of a start. Still, she offered this over-sixty white guy with long hair a kind but curious look.

"Oh, sorry, I didn't mean to startle you. I'm Gil."

"Hi. I'm Renee." She was holding her phone in one hand and a small bag in the other with her carry-on propped against her leg. She was calm. Her brilliant brown eyes crackled with energy. This African American woman exuded presence and that was reassuring to me in my moment of anxiety.

I kept talking. "I'm going to the Collegeville Institute. I saw your t-shirt and just thought maybe you were going there as well."

Her smile was warm. "Oh, yes, my t-shirt, of course. Yes, I'm going to Collegeville."

She told me she had already received a text from the van driver, who was waiting for all the passengers to arrive before heading to our pre-arranged pickup. I was relieved. I wasn't lost and I had met someone who confidently knew where she was, and that's what I needed.

The van arrived and we boarded. We sat down next to each other. Made introductions with our fellow passengers and started off on what turned out to be a long, sweltering ride. I came to learn that my new colleague was the Rev. Dr. Renee C. Jackson, a United Church of Christ pastor. Renee and I, weary travelers and possibly two introverts, dozed off while the other passengers chatted pleasantly.

I had been looking forward to this workshop for months and I was confident my hopes to learn something valuable would not be disappointed. Our workshop officially began the next morning. It was all I had hoped. Karen Hering, author of *Writing to Wake the Soul*,[2] was our facilitator. She made the space feel safe and at the same time creative. Karen quickly engaged us in her writing process of "contemplative correspondence."

Then the afternoon session began. Karen had instructed us that before arriving we needed to choose a metaphor that we had been using in our writing, a word we would be willing to share with the group. When my turn came, I said I had chosen the metaphor "pilgrimage" and that I would use alchemical language to unpack its meaning. One of our classmates asked me if I would say a bit more about alchemy.

I gathered my thoughts. I had read nearly a hundred books and spent thousands of hours studying alchemy. Now I had to boil it down to an elevator ride explanation. "We begin in the chaos and confusion of blackness and through the many shades of darkness we eventually move into the burning of the white ash, which gives rise to the multicolored phase of the raven with the peacock tail, who eventually becomes the rising Phoenix who flies into the sun of the healing red tincture for the sake of other's healing."

Karen then said, "Your language is very poetic. However, we need to be mindful of the baggage our words carry. Words like 'black' and 'white' can be very heavy words packed with racial associations. How we use them in relationship to what is good and bad is important to our awareness of racism functioning in society and our language—especially in these charged days of heightened racial tension following the death of so many black men."

Chaos and panic fell over my soul. The stormy clouds of shame rushed into my heart with lusty vengeance. I thought I had searched through all the secret corners of my life looking for latent racism. I had been open in the past that in 1850 my great-great-grandfather had enslaved a black man and woman, and their baby. My great-great-grandfather died in 1860 in Alabama at the age of forty-one, a year before the Civil War broke out. He left behind a wife, four children, and the three people he had enslaved. One of his sons became my great-grandfather, but I have no idea what happened to those three souls who had been liberated from his subjection. I have tried mightily to extract the DNA of enslavement out of my life.

My parents moved our family from Oklahoma to Arizona when I was five years old. One of my good friends and teammates in high school lived two doors down the street. Clyde Cunningham was one of a dozen African American kids in our school of five thousand. My high school baseball coach was Gil Trejo, a Hispanic man and the best coach I had ever played for. He didn't tolerate racism of any kind and he would become the model for my twenty years of coaching college baseball. After high school, the Houston Astros drafted me and my five-year professional baseball career began. In almost every team I played on, caucasians were the minority. The teams were filled with Latin players of every shade of black and brown, then African American players, and then the rest of us. In 1973, my third year of professional baseball, our manager was Bernie Smith, the first African American minor league manager in the history of professional baseball. I loved playing for him. When my playing career was over, my wife and I took teaching jobs in Coolidge, Arizona. The collective minorities were the majority in that town. The Black, Hispanic, and Native kids wove their way deep into my heart. Twenty years later, when my sister-in-law and her two-year-old African American son were in desperate straits, they moved in with us. For five years we provided a safe and loving place for them to heal. I thought I had worked through the ancestral DNA of racism that had lurked in my life. Evidently not.

Karen Hering's words felt like she had shoved a rusty railroad spike into my heart, cracking open the stone egg of my soul—and from it oozed the putrid smell of an unconscious blind spot. At that moment, this book was sitting on Richard Bass's desk, my editor at Church Publishing. I had spent four years writing it. I had studied Carl Jung inside out. (And yes, I know he was a racist, a sexist, and a philanderer, but his ideas on alchemy, pilgrimage, and individuation helped make sense of my life.) Somehow, though, the names of the phases of alchemy, the words *black, white, yellow,* and *red,* hid in my unconscious blind spot. How could that have happened? How did I not see the weight of those words?

Sitting in that conference room at the Collegeville Institute, I wanted to run and hide. I felt like I was going to vomit. Synchronicity, however, had brought me to that moment of suspended timelessness. Months before, I had been notified that I had not been selected as one of the twelve who were invited to attend the workshop. I was, however, asked if I would be an alternate in the rare case that someone else would decline. A month later, I was notified that a slot had opened and asked if I would accept. Synchronicity had brought me to that moment, for that workshop with Renee, Karen, and my blind spot. I could not run. If there is one solitary thing I have learned from pilgrimage it is that when I feel like I can't take another step forward, I must keep walking for any chance of transmutation to emerge in my life.

That evening, as our group went to dinner, I walked alongside Renee. I said a few inane things about the weather. Then I apologized. I told her I didn't mean to offend her or hurt her in any way. I was simply using alchemical language. She told me she wasn't offended. She understood the context.

Gently and graciously, but firmly, she said, "But I did have a reaction. I wish we could find other words so that black isn't always bad and white is always good."

I knew what I had to do. I told my editor I needed to make a major revision to the book. I wanted to take any color language that smacked of racism out of the alchemical metaphors. I would need to create new names for the alchemical phases, replacing them with more expressive words, void of the baggage of racism.

The next day I was walking toward the Saint John campus and Renee was walking in the opposite direction back toward the Institute. Synchronicity was working overtime. We stopped under a large oak tree for needed shade and more conversation. I asked for her permission to tell this story. Renee said she'd think about it and then quickly got to the heart of the matter. She told me that our conversations were building racial and cultural bridges. "Our work is about more than a book. It is about more than you or me. I believe this is God's work, truly a marvel to behold." Then she asked me a question that would further pry open the egg of my soul.

"So Gil, where are you on your pilgrimage?"

I told her that I am still on pilgrimage. I am still experiencing the surprising, yet confusing, moments of synchronicity that turn up the heat in my life. I am still being transmuted by the pilgrimage of writing and living as a pilgrim. I am still returning again and again back to the beginning, back to the chaos of the alchemical process—still doing the dangerous work of turning up the heat, phase by phase. And why do I do this—because, consciously or unconsciously, I never want to enslave another soul with my words. I have to keep searching for all the blind spots in my life.

Jungian therapist and author James Hillman (1926–2011) wrote in his book *Alchemical Psychology,*[3] "The stuff of which we write becomes the stuff with which we write and we are affected by the material we work with." Writing is a pilgrimage of transmutation and the pilgrimage never ends. What you are about to read are the many stories that have affected, transmuted, my life— and the stories just keep coming.

Back to the Beginning, Again and Again

Let's go for walk. A very long walk. A journey down the pilgrim's path. Traipsing through the forest of life. Climbing over the mountains of adversity. Enduring the climate of challenge. Over the course of countless miles and numerous days, we will mine the golden wisdom hidden within our pilgrimage experience.

I once walked Ireland, coast-to-coast, alone. I've walked the Wicklow Way in Ireland with several pilgrim groups. I have also journeyed with my sister through the physical and mental handicaps of Prader-Willi Syndrome. I've walked to death's doorway with my mom. I failed at being the president of a university. I changed careers in midlife. Each of these life experiences held in common the primary characteristics of a walking pilgrimage; the exterior trials created within me an interior transmutation. The wisdom walking of a pilgrimage takes on many forms.

A pilgrimage is a living metaphor, a journey with the purpose of deepening the wisdom of the mind, body, soul, and spirit. Our mind is the vessel in which we experience our inner and outer journeys. Our body is the vehicle for the pilgrimage. Our soul is the totality of our psychic process. And our spirit is the presence of the "ground of all being" within us that holds mind, body, and soul together in a loving embrace. The work that it requires to transmute the mind, body, soul, and spirit into a new being will be the most painful, yet rewarding, experience of our life. This, I believe, happens by living as a wisdom walker on the pilgrimage of life.

A wisdom walker engages the world around them in anticipation that a profound transformation of life is about to happen. Each step of the quest carries potential for an awakening, something unique that will add a tiny bit of truth that we need about our self. If we are willing to go on a wisdom walk, we will become fully aware of the experiences that bombard the senses, stretch the thoughts, evoke the feelings, and expand the imagination. Our complete awareness will fuel the fire that brews this golden wisdom. The ingredients with which we make our sacred elixir, however, can be fragile, and while we might feel we are doing the work alone, in truth, we're never truly walking by our self—we are in the stream of nature, the ancients, sages, fellow pilgrims, and the cosmos of the divine.

For years, I thought my mentors were wise simply because they were uniquely gifted and had lived longer and had more experience than I did. I assumed their wisdom came easily. These wise sages have assured me this is not the case. While age and experience gave them the opportunity to become wiser, they have told me that without the hard work of fully embracing their journeys, both good and bad, successes and failures, they would have little advice and counsel to offer. You must walk the miles to gain the wisdom, they assured me.

By good fortune, or as psychiatrist Carl Jung (1875–1961) would say, through synchronicity, twenty years ago I met Scott Haasarud. He has spent most of his life studying Jung and has shared his ideas and interpretations of depth psychology and alchemy through his spiritual direction practice. I have been one of his clients for the past twelve years, and he has become a wisdom walker companion in my life. Through study and practice, I too have become a spiritual companion for those walking the wisdom way. Through Scott's guidance and my own reading, study, and research, I have become steeped in Jungian alchemical thought and practice. The thinking of Robert Bosnack, Edward Edinger, James Hillman, Bill Plotkin, Eligio Stephen Gallegos, and several other depth psychologists whose work has been significantly shaped by Jung is woven into my life and this book.

Few could study Jung without paying close attention to his work on archetypes and alchemy. Archetypes are the universal symbols and images of the unconscious shared by all cultures—father/mother, king/queen, warrior/shaman, and countless others. Alchemy, in psychological terms, is the ancient art of exploring these unconscious symbols in order to expand the consciousness of the mind, body, soul, and spirit. Jung spent his life laying bare the riches of the imagination sparked by the collective unconscious. *Psychology and Alchemy, Alchemical Studies, The Archetypes and the Collective Unconscious, Aion, Mysterium Coniunctionis, The Red Book,*[4] and many other volumes bear witness to Jung's ability to explore, translate, and give meaning to the ancient archetypal symbols and their expressions through alchemy. The purpose of the complete oeuvre of Jung was to delve into the human experience of individuation, the evolution of becoming wholly conscious through the integration of the unconscious.

Jung was a soul pilgrim, a world traveler. He took several epic journeys in his lifetime. He was always seeking to learn about the universality of cultural archetypes, while at the same time, confronting his own unconscious—where the anima, the soul, resides. He has provided me with a framework for unpacking what has happened to my mind, body, soul, and spirit in the aftermath of having been on multiple pilgrimages. Jung's perspectives of archetypes and alchemy expanded my awareness as I walked with the dual purpose of experiencing my inner world while simultaneously encountering the divine in nature. I know I've gained some wisdom. For sure, I see all of life as a pilgrimage

—a wisdom walk. Some of that wisdom has come from surprising people and places.

My sister Dinah and I were having lunch three months after our mother died. Dinah has Prader-Willi Syndrome (I'll explain more later in the book). Despite her limitations, she is a wise crone and connected to God like a mystical saint.

Conversations with Dinah are slow and halting. She asks how my children are doing. She simply names them. I know she wants to hear every detail of their lives. Dinah is most interested in our grandsons and my dog, Jesus.

She tells me her stories, stringing a few words together, then silence. I ask a question. More silence. She ponders the next word. Somewhere in the little strands of conversation she told me she had washed her hair that day.

"Do you wash your hair every day?" I asked.

She nodded an affirmative yes, as if to say, "Yes, idiot brother, don't you?"

I suffered the older brother chagrin. "Do you style your own hair? It looks nice." I was struggling to recover.

"No. Joey," she said, referencing her beloved caregiver.

"You have beautiful silver hair, Dinah," I said in truth.

She said without hesitation, "My momma's hair."

I wanted to cry, but stuffed my emotions.

Then she said to no one in particular except herself, "My momma's hair."

Long silence.

Then she said, "Momma no more."

I looked away. Our mother was no more. We sat in pristine silence. It was as if the entire restaurant, the outside world, and God herself had stopped breathing in communal grief, waiting to hear what Dinah would say next.

Then she shook her head as if to drive the thought of our mother being dead out of her memory. She looked at me and changed the subject back to the dog. Time to move on to our new reality. I must face every pilgrimage that comes my way with a new imagination. I must keep walking, gathering wisdom from unexpected people and places.

Wisdom Walking

Wisdom walking is the alchemical, four-stage spiral process of pilgrimage. Let me unpack that sentence. In my experience, wisdom seems to come through a series of life's trials and painful events. After reflecting on my own tests of life,

I've noticed some patterns from the experiences that have yielded the most knowledge and wisdom. Typically, during trying circumstances, I have had the sense that something keeps turning up my psychic heat. These life events create the heat of dis-ease and discomfort that's hot enough to bring about a systemic change in our interior world. Psychic heat is the unstable, but useful, energy created by the daily grind of living through these trials. I have struggled to know if this was something potentially creative or terribly dangerous. Jung tells us that the increasing feeling of rising heat during these painful events is both the creative potential and the dangerous labor of alchemy.

For Jung, the alchemist's chemical experimentation of trying to turn lead into gold is a metaphor for the maturation process of individuation, which is most often initiated by life's struggles. In laymen's terms, he believed that to become a fully mature person, we must integrate the elements of our life, the pairs of opposites—the good and bad, dark and light, the hot and the cold, the female and the male. We do this seemingly impossible work by holding together the tension of the opposites using the volatile energy realized from their intimate bond. In Jungian terms, the integration, or the union of opposites, is the primary goal of individuation. The process of psychological alchemy utilizes the heat in our life to create psychic gold through a healthy lifetime of deep personal reflection found in the exercise of imagination. I am suggesting that the metaphor of pilgrimage is the container where life's elements are transmuted into alchemy's psychological gold.

The alchemical process, what I call "wisdom walking," is based on Jung's personality typology, most commonly encountered in the Myers-Briggs Type Indicator. Jung named these interior functions sensing, intuition, thinking, and feeling. According to Jung, we gather data through the functions of sensing and intuition. We make decisions through the opposing functions of thinking and feeling. While everyone has and uses each of the four functions, we typically prefer to use one of the paired functions over the other. I might naturally use my five senses to gather data and use my feelings to make decisions, while you might prefer to use your intuition to gather data and your thinking to make decisions.

In wisdom walking, the objective is to access both sides of the pairs as fully as possible, a 360-degree view. Using each pair in this manner is what Jung thought of as the union of opposites—each function uniquely identifiable as opposites, but functioning as one. Utilizing all four of the functions to their fullest extent creates the alchemical environment for developing mature wisdom in our life. Whether we're walking through a forest or waiting for treatment in a hospital, by processing the experience through the complete range of the interior functions, we can uncover a deeper level of wisdom in our life.

The process starts with sensing, moves to thinking, then feeling, and finally imagining (I'll explain a bit later why I use the term "imagination" instead of "intuition"). Obviously, it's very difficult to distinguish the functions from one another. We cannot sense without thinking, or feel without sensing, or imagine without relying on all the senses. But I believe we can afford each function its fullest opportunity to inform our pilgrimage experience. Psychiatrist Daniel Siegel, in his book *Mind: A Journey to the Heart of Being Human*, says that sensing perception "can be trained."[5] The purpose of wisdom walking is to train ourselves to focus our energy on each function, one at a time, for as long as possible. We might be able to hold our attention on the function of sensing for only a few minutes, even just a moment, before our thinking takes over (this often happens in meditation). Or we might be in the depths of thinking through the experience when our feelings emerge. The goal of the wisdom walk is to open ourselves, first to the experience of sensing, then to focus on thinking (reflecting), then to explore our feelings, and finally to imagine what wisdom is emerging from the pilgrimage. This whole process might take a few minutes, maybe a few hours, possibly years.

Alchemy, pilgrimage, and wisdom walking are not linear in design. Carl Jung believed the alchemical process is spiral in nature—simultaneously upward and downward. While I might reach the end of the journey, the experience of wisdom walking—sensing, thinking, feeling, and imagination—continues to repeat itself many times in my life. Each time I go through the four-stage process I've gained new insights and more experience. I carry this new wisdom with me when I take my next pilgrimage—starting each new journey with an expanded wealth of wisdom, looking to gain more with every next step.

Hopefully, as we are walking up the spiral we will be gaining wisdom. The farther we walk up the spiral of consciousness, the deeper we will also be walking down the spiral of our unconscious. That is one of the reasons people on pilgrimage have such profound dreams. The more they are consciously aware of the pilgrimage, the more the unconscious world of their dreams has something to say. The downward spiral can be experienced in dreaming, but also through meditation and imagination exercises. Correspondingly, the deeper we go down into the unconscious spiral, the higher we will be able to explore our conscious awareness. Jung believed this spiraling upward and downward is a necessary part of our holistic maturation as adults.

The Phases of Wisdom Walking

Let me take you through the spiral phases of wisdom walking, their definitions, and why I have organized them in this order. Before we begin, let me say that these phases are not to be limiting or confining in any way. It's like walking through a foggy rain, then the clouds break for a moment, and then oddly it's raining while the sun is shining, then you're back in the fog again. Siegel, in his book *Mind*, describes this way of receiving energy and information as "flow": an experience that happens "between our bodily selves and the larger world in which we live."[6] "Flow" is change across time or space, a change brought about by the intentional work of the integration of our interior and exterior world. And while we take up this work in order to bring about transformation, we must suspend, Siegel says, our notion that a "blueprint" for the process exists.[7] These facets of alchemy are typically sequential in nature, but without the time necessary for the maturing of the experience of each event, or phase, we can get stuck in any one aspect of the process. We might enjoy it when the clouds break for a moment, and we must take in the moment fully, but we can't stay there forever, we must keep walking. My explanation of wisdom walking as a process is not to infer that it is a map for well-being, nor that it is a procedure that guarantees success. The uncertainty and complexity of life exist to defy the notion that any process or procedure will lead to a golden life. I'm simply offering a metaphorical way to walk in the world.

Let's start with a basic reality: we live in our bodies and through our sensations we first encounter the world. The entry point of wisdom walking, then, is to become aware of what we are sensing. During a wisdom walk, we'll use our five or six senses to gather data about our experience. We see, hear, touch, taste, and smell the world of the seen and, at times, the unseen. Our senses are the first active agents in our interpretation of what's happening in front of us. We have to slow down our pace and quiet our mind in order to sense without any distraction. At this point, it doesn't matter what I think or feel about what I am sensing. I am just taking it all in. Focusing solely on our senses can be exhilarating. For instance, though I've walked the Wicklow Way several times, by being keenly aware of my senses, I can walk each journey as if I've never experienced the path before. Yet, paradoxically, I will be walking with all the wisdom I've gained from my previous walks.

A unique tree grows just south of Knockree Hostel on the Wicklow Way. Starting from the north in Dublin, I've passed this tree three times on the second day of the walk. The tree is a giant oak, hundreds of years old. At the base of the tree is a large rectangular stone, six feet long and three feet high. The tree has grown around the stone, leaving a gaping hole in the center, large enough that I can stand on the stone and reach high up into the interior of the oak. Stepping up onto the stone and into the tree is like disappearing into another dimension of time and space. The last time I walked the Way, however, I started from the south. That time the tree was at the end of the next-to-last day of the trip. I knew where the tree was, but from the south side, I couldn't see the opening in the tree. For a bit, I thought the tree had died and fallen over. At one point, I thought I must have walked past it. Not until I was right next to it did I recognize my favorite tree in all of Ireland. I was walking the same trail, but my perspective changed my sensing experience. My senses were encountering the tree as if it were the first time I had seen it—like I was meeting an old friend for the first time.

Maintaining our attention on the senses, while avoiding thinking and feeling, can be very difficult. When I was looking for my old tree friend and thought I had walked by him, my thoughts and feelings were overwhelming me. I had to stay with my senses so that I could see the tree. And I did, but in a new way. By remaining with the sensing phase long enough, we are preparing to learn from our experience at another higher level on the spiral of wisdom—like seeing something we're very familiar with for the very first time. Of course, when we stay in the sensing phase for a prolonged period, a tiny bit of disturbance is created, maybe impatience, boredom, or frustration. Disturbance of any kind creates alchemical heat, which is necessary in order to incubate the alchemy of transformation on the pilgrimage trail.

In addition to focusing our senses on our surroundings, we can train them on the unconscious—the downward counterpart of the upward spiral. We will discover the unconscious is trying to communicate with us through our dreams, liminal experiences like daydreaming, and our unfettered imagination. In the senses of our imagination, we can ask ourselves questions like, "What did that demon in my dream smell like? Was he green or was he translucent? Did I shudder in my dream because I was cold?" And what about those waking imagination experiences? "Was that raven talking to me in my imagination? Or was she really talking to me?" When I can activate my senses in the world of my imagination, I am expanding my conscious awareness. When I stepped inside my favorite tree, I smelled it, tasted a piece of its bark. I touched its delicate insides and could see the inner makings of this ancient tree, and in my imagination I could hear her speak to me. This is the first phase of wisdom walking, to sense both the conscious and the unconscious—what the alchemist referred to as being in touch with the chaos of life, or fully sensing everything around us. In this phase we can see, hear, smell, taste, and touch the dark storm rising within us.

In the second phase, we allow our thinking—our intellectual reflection— to engage. In phase one, we tried to allow our senses to completely experience an event without actively interpreting or thinking about what we were taking in. We tried to quiet the mind, so that when we move into phase two, we can begin to intellectually interpret what we have seen, heard, tasted, touched, and smelled. By being consciously aware of our thinking, the process of reflection turns up the psychic heat, like stepping into a very hot bath. While we are slow to enter it, we know we have to drop down into the steamy water to enjoy its benefits. Waiting to think improves the quality of the reflection.

My son-in-law is a business executive and he walked the Wicklow Way with me. At the end of our pilgrimage, he told me that after the third day he realized at one point he wasn't thinking about anything. His mind had reached a point of meditative nothingness. And then, without thinking about a business problem he had been faced with, the solution began to unfold before him. The space of not thinking opened a space for creative thinking. These long periods of meditative liminal states of unconscious thinking will free our mind for unencumbered creativity. For the alchemist, this is the phase where the crack in the egg of the soul appears—the slow emergence out of the dark womb into the air, earth, water, and fire of life.

Phrase three is where we acknowledge our feelings about the data our senses have gathered and what our intellect has reflected upon during the experience. What emotions are being evoked on this long walk? My own experience has taught me to expect the unexpected. Long-forgotten or suppressed emotions can rise to the surface during a wisdom walk. I've found myself weeping in the middle of a long day's walk for no apparent reason. By not being afraid of my feelings and allowing my emotions to be fully expressed, I can begin to work through what I had suppressed for years. The flame under the crucible of the pilgrimage, the long days of walking, has increased the heat significantly enough to cause my pushed-down emotions to float to the top of the psychic soup. The long hours of walking alone with our feelings create a space for the soul to explore the full range of the emotional milieu. The longer the pilgrim can stay present to the interior experience of feelings and not let herself become distracted by what she is sensing or thinking, the more likely her soul will find some suppressed emotional event of the past.

After I had rediscovered my favorite tree in Ireland, I began to think, "what if this was the last time I would see this tree?" That thought released the emotions of missing my granddad, who had died twenty-two years earlier. The wise old tree reminded me of listening to his stories, from which I had learned so much. Staying present to this state of the emotions of the heart is challenging, a place many of us would choose to avoid. But to keep holding our self in the presence of this difficult phase builds the heat for the soul to do her alchemical work.

Wisdom walking makes a place for the type of soul work that acknowledges the validity of our feelings as a path to wisdom. Often, by paying attention to these subtle feelings, we enter the unconscious realm of what I call healthy brooding. Like a hen nestled over her eggs, we patiently, quietly, sit and wait in expectation, knowing these emotional and sometimes mystical experiences cannot be forced. They hatch only if we are present and attentive. We must be patient and gentle with our feelings. By embracing our emotions, we can begin moving through the alchemical phase of transparent vulnerability, the moment when the raven with the peacock tail emerges from the egg; when the imagination has given birth to a new image and language.

Phase four is when our imagination is liberated. Depth psychologist Eligio Stephen Gallegos (b. 1934) has influenced my decision to use "imagination" instead of Jung's term, "intuition." Gallegos used the term "imagery" instead of "intuition" in his book, *Animals of the Four Windows: Integrating Thinking, Sensing, Feeling and Imagery*. He explained, "Deep imagery necessitates a willingness to discover a world that is not yet known, and to allow our own dimensions to grow larger as a result of interaction with this discovered realm."[8] Gallegos's definition mirrors Jung's term "active imagination,"[9] which he used almost entirely to write *The Red Book*[10] and to draw his mandalas. Jung called the imagination, "the mother of human consciousness."[11] I use the term "imagination" because most everyone can remember exercising his or her imagination, which is the creative juice of every child. Our goal is to set free the child that still abides within us. During this stage, we can begin to imagine a new possibility for our life. We can move beyond our perceived personal limitations and into the realms of expanded consciousness.

We begin to see our Self, our maturing consciousness, being influ
our unconscious. This intersection and integration of our conscious life and
unconscious world is the thin place of our imagination, the seat of the soul
and the spirit that resides within us. In the sacred interiority of place, we may
begin to imagine a new way to live, move, and have our being in the world.

Through integration, we can begin to experience individuation, the second
half of life's maturation. In this fourth and most creative phase the heat becomes
intense, much like firing a piece of pottery. By placing the green artwork into
the kiln, we allow something new to emerge. Often, colors and textures appear
that not even the artist could imagine. The work of the fourth phase is difficult and most often avoided. The transformative work of this phase means letting go of our comfort zone and stepping out into the unknown, in order to
risk becoming someone we never imagined possible—the phoenix rising from
the ashes of chaos. According to Jung, few people are willing to walk through
the flame of individuation in order to fully experience higher consciousness,
the realm of true wisdom, because the process is too costly. We must sacrifice
our ideal of normal for a new, yet unknown, normal. In chapter four, I'll tell
the stories of some people who have suffered through trials of the mind, body,
soul, and spirit. They worked through the powerful issues they faced and then
were able to endure the heat of each alchemical phase. These people turned
what seemed to be a hopeless situation into a new soul-consciousness where
they would become healers for others.

This seems to be why Jung so valued alchemy as a process for understanding individuation. Indeed, the medieval alchemists were the forefathers
of modern chemistry. But Jung believed they were also experiencing the emergence of an unconscious collective archetype—the universal unconscious
archetypal figure of the Christ. What follows in this book about the Christ is
not to be confused with the commonly held dogma of the historical figure of
Jesus Christ as an agent of salvation. When I write about the historical human
Jesus, I will not attach Christ to his name. The word Christ will be reserved for
the archetypal figure. The Christ figure is the symbol of complete integration
—the union of all functions and shadows—leading to a non-dual consciousness. The Christ archetype is the model for becoming our true Self. Here, in
the step of active imagination, we must face the demons, dragons, and serpents that live in the shadow of our soul. These are my opposites, which
live within my unconscious as archetypes. I must confront them in my consciousness, embrace them and make them a part of my conscious life. Unless I

embrace the darkness of my light, the light will never shine its brightest. We've been taught to deny, run, avoid, or exorcise our demons, dragons, and serpents, and never allow them to have space in our life. The problem is, they never go away. Jung says that the human Jesus fully embraced the shadow of his Self, thereby modeling the Christ work we all need to do in our life. Jesus did this by adopting the archetype of the serpent. Jesus said he would be lifted up on the cross as a serpent for all to see and receive healing. There in that image, Jesus the Christ, the Life-Giver, and the serpent, whose poison is feared, become one. Jesus, like us, was then set free to be his true Self. The union of the opposites brings wholeness, integration, and the non-duality of thought and practice into our lives. I will use this archetypal image of the union of Jesus and the serpent throughout this book as a model for our own integration.

Jung thought some of the alchemist's work was more about the psychic gold of the true Self than about the religious currency of the conscious economy; in other words, this is not "self-help." This work is for the healing sake of others. In the imagination of the alchemists, the opposites of Jesus the Christ and the Serpent became one. In this union, the alchemists found the gold of the psyche that could be used for healing. Given that they were doing this work, in part during the inquisition of the Roman Catholic Church, their risk was extraordinarily high. But the risk, Jung believed, created enough heat to produce their desired inner transmutation. The risk was worth the product it produced. Such is the nature of a true pilgrimage. Only risk delivers a lasting visible and valuable transmutation of the old into something new.

The Pilgrimage through This Book

I know of several excellent books about pilgrimage. I highly recommend Episcopal priest and professor of theology Sheryl A. Kujawa-Holbrook's book *Pilgrimage—The Sacred Art: Journey to the Center of the Heart.*[12] In addition to reading Kujawa-Holbrook's book, I have heard her speak on retreat, and she offers some excellent background on the religious history of pilgrimage as well as practical ideas about processing our journey. Phil Cousineau's *The Art of Pilgrimage: The Seeker's Guide to Making Travel Sacred*[13] was one of the first books I read about pilgrimage. Cousineau is a professional guide and provides many beautiful stories about a wide range of pilgrimage opportunities around the world.

My book, however, is something different. This is about the soul work of a pilgrim. Whether we're walking down a road in Ireland or walking through the path of life, this book is about gaining wisdom as we live life as a pilgrim. Much like the shepherd in Brazilian-born novelist Paulo Coelho's wonderful story *The Alchemist*,[14] we are all looking to fulfill our dreams and imaginations. By going on pilgrimage, we learn our journey is filled with the wisdom necessary to live the alchemist's imagined life. But no matter how exotic the trail, walking for hours on end can be boring and mundane—just like daily life. We think we'll never see our dream come true. The key to pilgrimage walking is to take every step with an expectation that something around the next corner might be amazing and filled with wisdom. That next corner may be after the walking is done, when the cancer treatments have been completed, when the divorce is final, or years after the funeral of a loved one. We will learn that as a pilgrim, the journey of wisdom begins before we start walking and continues long after we've put our boots away, for the process of wisdom walking is a way of life.

Each chapter of this book contains stories about pilgrims making their risky way through the four alchemical phases of wisdom walking. The stories in this book are from people I know and have walked with on pilgrimages of one sort or another. Some have made walking pilgrimages to Ireland, Spain, and Nepal. Some have journeyed through the trials of disease, addiction, and grief. Knowing these people and being involved in their lives has shaped me deeply, and it has been a privilege to walk with each of them.

The transitions through the phases may be subtle. Sensing, thinking, and feeling may happen within moments of each other. Even though it may only be an instant between each phase, there is that moment, however gray, when we experience a shift. In the quiet moment, something exhilarating and frightening happens. Sometimes, only in the reflection of the experience can we parse out the changes in the steps. The key to recognizing the interior movement is to allow the time needed for the alchemical process of the wisdom walk to have its effect. Otherwise, we're just on a long, painful, wearisome hike or dealing with a trial that can appear to be purposeless.

The first four chapters will be structured somewhat like a walking day. I'll open the chapter with descriptions of some pilgrimage experiences. The story might be about the pilgrimage I've walked alone, or about a pilgrimage with Saint Brigid's Community, or with John and his singing group, Vox Peregrini. In the next section of the chapter, the walking group will be gathered somewhere, along the trail, at a hostel, or in a pub, having a conversation about the day's experience. Finally, the walking is over for the day and now it's time for some reflection. This structure will provide a vessel for the alchemical work of wisdom walking as we make our pilgrimage through this book.

As interludes between some chapters, you will find personal stories about pilgrimage from friends of mine. I have also used the interludes to share some practical tips about making a walking pilgrimage. I do hope you enjoy these interludes. After all, you can't spend your entire pilgrimage carrying your pack.

In chapter 1, we explore the idea that the pilgrimage begins before you start walking. The first phase of pilgrimage is innocent enough. I want to go on a pilgrimage—so I get ready. Sounds simple. I have discovered that in the preparation, we begin to experience what will happen over and over during our walk. What we thought was going to happen doesn't, and what we couldn't have imagined does happen—chaos ensues. Our expectations and preconceptions are cooking in the cauldron, the melancholy of it all.

Chapter 2 is about moving from the first exuberant hours of the pilgrimage into the long, mundane days of walking. During those days we begin to learn what it really means to put one foot in front of the other, especially if one foot or knee is in serious pain. We start naming our blisters, our aches and pains. We begin to let our troubles travel with us like odd friends—even though we would just as soon they magically disappear, we know they'll just keep hanging around. Then our pack gets heavy and we discover the baggage we're carrying is more than just the thirty pounds on our back. We know, though, we must endure and stay steady on the exterior work of the wisdom walk so that we can learn more about our inner world.

Chapter 3 journals the unexpected experiences of walking a long pilgrimage, alone and with other people. After the third or fourth day of walking, and before reaching the halfway mark, the pilgrim is able to become transparent and vulnerable. If she can relax and lightly hold onto what is going to happen next, she can have a life-shaping experience. Many of the alchemists depicted this phase as a raven trying to fly with a peacock's tail. By staying at the difficult work of wisdom walking, the mundane can be transformed into the fantastical—our imagination of a new future begins to take shape and the strange bird begins to rise out of the alchemist's cauldron.

Chapter 4 confronts that moment in life when we think we can't go on. We think we're finished. We're ready to quit. For the alchemists, this is when the flame is the hottest. Here, the alchemist leans over his fragile work and prays fervently for the golden stone of healing to emerge. The process of alchemy, according to Jung, was to create the healing stone in one's own life in order to be a healer for others. I firmly believe that if we take a pilgrimage for our sole benefit, we will never experience the true power of transmutation. We must have a purpose beyond our own personal gains that motivates us to go on a long journey.

Chapter 5 is the story of my sister, Dinah, and my family's walk with her through the pilgrimage of Prader-Willi Syndrome. Living with a person who is mentally and physically handicapped can be maddening, and at the same time transformative. Depth psychologist James Hillman (1926–2011) said that "alchemical soul making is illuminated lunacy."[15] For most of my life, I felt like living with Dinah was a series of cycles that repeated themselves endlessly. I wondered if the painful mundane madness would ever get better, or still worse, come to an end too soon. But by leaning into the difficult work of alchemical psychology, I came to realize that depression has several shades of darkness, and yet, the dark storm has its own illumination. This chapter is the story of a family being transmuted over and over again.

Chapter 6 is dedicated to what I and others have experienced after the pilgrimage is over—a feeling that lies somewhere between a lovely afterglow and a bad hangover. A few of my friends have confessed, "The walking is over but I feel like I'm still on the pilgrimage." Others have told me, "When my friends ask me how it was, I'm at a loss for words." In this chapter, I continue to process the pilgrimage weeks, months, and years after the backpack is gathering dust in the attic. Even when the walking is over, we must continue letting others know what we've discovered on our outer pilgrimage and our inner journey. The story is difficult to tell because it is raw and vulnerable.

While walking across Ireland, I had many dreams, two of which I would describe as epic—meaning long, detailed, graphic, and startling. Those two dreams had important meaning for my life. They inspired this book and my discovery of the process of wisdom walking. I came to understand that both dreams were about the past, present, and future of my life woven together into an ancient/future imagination of timelessness. Through working with those dreams and the process of wisdom walking, I came to understand that pilgrimage is a metaphor for life. Long days of walking. Realizing my expectation of pilgrimage was being replaced with new imaginations. Finding the unexpected. Living into my full purpose of Self—then negotiating, and re-negotiating, with myself about how I would now live into my new way of seeing life. All this personal work was important for my health and well-being. But if the work was for me alone, then I really didn't finish it. The final stage of alchemy concludes with the creation of gold—healing gold—created for the sake of other people. This book is an attempt to share what I have learned.

Let's begin our wisdom walk. We will have to climb over some very high mountains, through the forest, and across streams. In the morning mist and the heat of the day, our back will ache from the weight of the pack. Our feet will most likely blister. But if we can be present to every tree, stone, bird, pool of water, the ancients, and everyone we walk with as much as we are to our aches and pains, I am confident we will find the golden wisdom we seek.

Prologue

*The way to the goal seems chaotic
and interminable at first, and only
gradually do the signs increase that
it is leading anywhere. The way is
not straight but appears to go round
in circles. More accurate knowledge
has proved it to go in spirals.*

—Carl Jung,
Psychology and Alchemy[16]

*Pilgrimage is wandering with a purpose.
Pilgrimage is also to wonder into the
imagination of the soul. Let go of what
you must leave behind. Set down the
burdens that are too heavy. Pick up what
you need this day. Remember, tomorrow
may bring something new to consider.*

—*Pilgrim's Prayer Book*[17]

I was visiting my daughter on a spring holiday. She lives in a suburb just outside Seattle, Washington. The sun was shining. It was a pristine morning, a rare day in the Pacific Northwest. I decided to take a long walk through a park near her house. The destination was her favorite local coffee shop. I love walking through that park—what my wife calls forest bathing—because it reminds me of Ireland.

I was barely into the first mile of the trail when my phone rang. I didn't intend to answer a call unless it was a family member. The name of the son of one my treasured friends appeared on the caller ID. A moment of panic shook me. Was this bad news about my friend? He and I are in our sixties. He wouldn't be the first friend I've lost to a heart attack. I answered the call.

"Dr. Stafford, this is John Wiles."

"Hey, John, how's it going? Everything okay?"

"Yes, things are great. Do you have a few minutes? I want to run a crazy idea by you."

I've known John since he was in the first grade. Now he's an assistant professor of choral conducting at the University of Northern Iowa. My wife and I met John's dad, Tom, when he became the pastor at a Baptist church in Buckeye, Arizona. That was over thirty years ago. For both our families, life has taken many dramatic turns, changes in occupations, religious understandings, and relationships.

Relieved this wasn't the call I had imagined in my moment of panic, I said, "Sure John, now's a great time to talk. I'm on a walk through a lovely forest in Seattle. Walking and talking to you will be awesome. What's going on?"

"Like I said, I've got this crazy idea." Then John began to speed talk with passion. His way of talking is refined and precise, yet laced with a laser-like humor. "You probably haven't heard of John Eliot Gardiner, but in 2000 he created the Bach Cantata Pilgrimage. Gardiner performed all 200-plus of Bach's cantatas in one year. I watched a documentary on the pilgrimage several years ago and became inspired to perform Bach's music with my students. It's been great. A couple of years ago I watched the documentary again and became hooked on the concept of pilgrimage itself. At the same time, something else has been going on for me. I've become more and more disillusioned with the preoccupation for applause, which can become all-consuming.

"I've begun to wonder what it would be like to put together a Pilgrimage Choir. Perhaps we walk the Camino de Santiago, learn Spanish Renaissance music, and sing in churches along the way. We wouldn't have to have audiences.

It would be about the music as a spiritual reality. Or maybe we learn some Tudor cathedral music or humanistic music about light and journey, and walk the Wicklow Way. I don't really know.

"What I do know is that I believe in the power of music to take up physical space and yet remain invisible. I would like to find an opportunity for like-minded people to search for themselves, using the music and the way to symbolize an inner transformation. Anyhow, that's all I've got. I know that you have experience walking the Wicklow Way. Do you think something like this is doable? How do you start to organize a pilgrimage?"

At the point when John said something about using music and walking as a means of transformation, I had stopped walking and started imagining what listening to John's group sing on the Wicklow Way would be like. I hadn't said a word as John laid out his dream.

"Dr. Stafford, are you still there?"

"I'm still here, John. I was just imagining listening to your group sing on top of White Hill, the highest point of the Wicklow Way."

"Dr. Stafford, does that mean you'll help me?"

"Dr. Wiles, I'll help you if you stop calling me Dr. Stafford and start calling me Gil."

"That might be difficult for me to do."

"That's my fee for helping you."

He laughed. "Well, at least let me pay your expenses to walk with us."

"Okay, we can talk about that later. So exactly how do you want me to help you?"

John explained he needed help with the logistics on the Wicklow Way, outlining the daily routine, and setting up the lodging. That would be easy for me, because I'd already walked the Wicklow three times, once leading a group of twelve, the same size as John's group.

John said, "Dr. Stafford, ah, Gil—you know that's going to take a lot of getting used to, but I'll keep working on it. You will forgive me when I revert to old habits? Okay, I take your laughing as a yes. So, the other thing I'm wondering is, I know you've done a lot of work with Carl Jung, and given all your writing and retreats on pilgrimage, could you guide us through some intentional conversations along the way? Maybe in the evenings at a local pub?"

"Sure John. You want me to be kind of a chaplain or spiritual director. The pilgrimage wouldn't necessarily be religious, but it would be spiritual because the people in your group would be working on their inner transformation."

"Gil. . . I'm having to practice. . . that does sound like something that happens on a pilgrimage, doesn't it?"

"It sure does, John. And I think the pilgrimage has already begun in your heart. Now all we need to do is get everybody else ready for the walking. When do you want to go?"

Who Is a Pilgrim?

Who were these like-minded people John was going to invite on his singing pilgrimage? And what would make them pilgrims? The pilgrim is a seeker—one who is searching for inner transformation, what the alchemists called transmutation. The call of pilgrimage continually beckons the pilgrim down the walking road, whether in Ireland, Spain, or some other locale.

My life as a pilgrim began years ago. I was feeling restless. A mentor suggested I sit still with my feelings and listen to my heart. I was hearing the whispering of creation. My heart ached to discover the source of that voice. One day, on a long walk, in the silence of the desert, I felt the call to go on a pilgrimage. I began to feel like the wanderer, the seeker, the Tarot's Fool in search of the Holy Grail. I was becoming a person who would happily give his or her life over to the pilgrimage process in hopes of uncovering the mysteries of life. I began searching for a soul-shaping experience.

For Carl Jung, the pilgrim, while on a physical journey, is also on an interior search, seeking individuation—personal maturity. This, Jung believed, led to an integrated life. A transformational pilgrimage begins with a deep longing of the heart, a yearning to experience life at a slower pace. To see life from a fresh perspective. To hear the sounds of the trail as a symphony. To taste rain as honey. To smell the path with our feet. Pilgrimage shapes the soul like a river smoothing a stone. To go on pilgrimage is to respond to the beckoning sweet whispers of the One who grounds our soul.

The pilgrims I know usually had different motivations for tackling their personal challenges but most felt something was pulling them. Something had put a desire in their heart for pilgrimage. All of them pointed to some urge, an inner voice calling them, an indescribable longing to go on pilgrimage. Sometimes that urge started, like John said, with a crazy idea.

Deciding to walk across Ireland or to walk the Camino or to go on any destination journey does not make a person a pilgrim. Psychologist and author

M. Scott Peck (1936–2005) wrote in his book *In Search of Stones: A Pilgrimage of Faith, Reason, and Discovery* that life is a pilgrimage, a road less traveled in the Age of Reason; for while "mystics of all ages and cultures have seen life as a pilgrimage, until recently they have been a tiny minority."[18] My purpose in walking this road less traveled, the pilgrim's path of inner transmutation, is to create more wisdom in my soul.

Peck had written throughout his career about the challenges and rewards of taking "the road less traveled" and wrote a book by that title. The road less traveled is rarely taken because, indeed, it is the painful way to becoming an authentic person. It is a risky road because it typically goes against the grain of culture, peers, and group identity. To be true to one's self is to risk being real, not the person someone else wants you to be. My authentic road has taken me from a career as a professional baseball player, to a high school teacher, to a college baseball coach, then the president of a Southern Baptist college, and now an Episcopal priest. Such were the careers along the road. But the soul transformation along the path was my own pilgrimage. From being an orthodox conservative Southern Baptist whose life was dictated by religious rules and "correct" answers—to now living comfortably in the ambiguity of questions. Still, I have not arrived at the destination of being transmuted, or fully individuated. Instead, I am a pilgrim on the road of always becoming who I authentically am—a lifetime of traveling the road less traveled.

The Journey Ahead Is a Crazy Idea

When I answered the phone at five o'clock in the morning, the voice on the other end of the line asked, "Did I rouse you out of bed? I apologize if I disturbed your sleep."

"No worries," I said. "I've been up for about fifteen minutes." Then the young man apologized profusely in his lovely Irish brogue for not realizing I lived on the West Coast of the United States and not the East Coast. He was calling to confirm my booking for our first two nights in Dublin. He asked if I needed any further reservations while in Ireland. I told him I didn't.

"Kind of a short trip, eh?" he said.

"I'm walking coast-to-coast, from Dublin to Kerry."

"Are you daft?" he laughed and then apologized again. "May I ask you why you would do such a thing?"

"It's a spiritual thing, I guess. Just something I feel I have to do," I said.

He said, "I wish you the best and I honestly hope to meet you."

Having your sanity questioned, being daft, having a crazy idea—these are good signs you have started on the path of an intentional pilgrimage. Everyone must choose how he or she will walk life as a pilgrim. There is no one way. No right way. No best way. Only your way, my way, his way, her way, every pilgrim's way. I've walked alone. I fasted most days. Walking twenty miles. Drinking only water. I've walked with one other person. I've walked with two people. With twelve people. I've walked with professional singers on a singing pilgrimage. Each experience was different. In some cases it was the opposite experience of my previous walk and much different than my expectations. And clearly, my inner journey was different from those I walked with. All my pilgrimages have been life altering in some way or another, major or minor, obvious or subtle.

Walking those roads has led me into some unexpected places with unexpected people. One such place was a tiny two-room apartment in the small village of Kildysart, on the Shannon River in southwestern Ireland. My spiritual director had invited me over to his home to meet another priest, a lifelong friend of his. We sat near the fireplace with one small log flickering, barely enough to heat the apartment. The room was spartan. A worn prayer book and a tattered Bible laid open on a ruggedly crafted table. My director's friend wore a bright green polo shirt that bore the emblem of the local golf club. His black pants had the sheen of too many years and his black shoes were scuffed. When he sat back in the chair, he could have swung his feet like a child's. He rocked his creaky straight-backed chair forward and turned his head slightly toward me, as if he were craning to listen to the final words of a dying man. His gentle brogue softened the tone of having lived an isolated life in the small villages of western Ireland.

"What are you doing here in Ireland, laddie?"

I told him with a bit of unfortunate pride, "I'm on a pilgrimage."

He replied with a wry smile, "You wouldn't be insultin' God by lookin' for him, now would ya?"

Hoping not to insult God, I was walking Ireland, coast-to-coast, from the eastern seaboard of Dublin to Glenbeigh, on the southwestern edge of the island. Counting all the steps I walked when lost, off trail, and having taken the wrong turn, I walked over 353 mountainous miles. Indeed, I was searching. The object of my soul's desire kept evolving. Originally, I thought the journey was about discovering my next purpose in life. Slowly, mile after mile, I began to realize this pilgrimage was about connecting with my inner self. Haunting questions emerged from the darkness within. The pilgrimage became about discovering my authentic self, then nearly sixty years old. Discovering the person I was comfortable living with, no matter what anyone else thought about me.

I have lived with years of feeling misunderstood. I'm constantly being told my ideas are too weird and my theology is not orthodox enough, not even Christian. But I have learned by living as a pilgrim that this is who I am and that I'm okay with me. I can live between the world of the seen and the unseen. It is possible for me to walk, breathe, think, and feel in the mystical world while at the same time staying grounded in my own understanding of reality, my conscious reality. Both are equally real. I can exist on the literal path and at the same time the imagined path.

Through my many miles of walking, I have learned that being on a pilgrimage is about the journey, both the real literal path and the real mystical path. Even when I am on the actual path of the Wicklow Way or the path of doing my job in Arizona, I am a pilgrim, a foreigner in a strange land. My pilgrimage is about negotiating with myself how I am going to live into the life of becoming transformed each day, step by step. Life is different now. Every corner of my being—mind, body, soul, and spirit—is being transmuted. Indeed, anyone who walks hundreds of miles will get in good shape. But will that person gain knowledge and develop a deeper relationship with the divine? Through wisdom walking, I propose, he or she will become acutely aware of the world of the seen and the unseen and discover deep wisdom. This profound awareness shifts the pilgrim's very inner self so she simultaneously sees the past, present, and future. The pilgrim also begins to see herself as she really is. And she opens her true self for others to see. The outward mask is stripped away and the true inner self emerges—the integration of the body, mind, soul, and spirit begins.

To be a pilgrim is to make an intentional decision—first to be a pilgrim and second to go on pilgrimage. To be a pilgrim is to see life as a pilgrimage and to do the hard work necessary to reap all its benefits.

The Possibility of Pilgrimage Is Something Other than the Expected

Several years ago my young friend told me she was going "on pilgrimage."

"Not 'a' pilgrimage?" I asked.

"No," she kindly told her older, not-so-wise friend. "On pilgrimage."

"So, enlighten me."

"'On' is the way. I'm not going to Santiago. I'm going on the way of my life. The way I seek to live. The way I must learn to live. The way I must be."

When she returned from her 500-mile pilgrimage, we washed her tattered feet. We wanted to ritually make a statement that we recognized her way of living would now be different. To be on pilgrimage is to embrace the mission of a personal renaissance, to claim the inner beauty, the haunting, the frightening, the hated, the adored, the soft, the cruel, the humorous, the damaged, the hilarious, the pitiful—every sliver of our conscious and unconscious—and to claim our self as our own, who we are, who we are becoming transformed into. Pilgrimage is also the infusion of the natural world into our spiritual journey, walking with the spirit of creation, becoming one with our surroundings. The work, which is a collaboration of the pilgrim and the spirit, will take days, weeks, years, and countless miles. The experience is like the shaman's inner world vision quest, which is often an interior struggle experienced on a dangerous external journey.

A major task of the pilgrimage is gaining the wisdom to navigate the distance between our outer reality and our inner world. Sometimes these worlds are at the opposite ends of our understanding. I may want to walk the Camino because I'd like to explore Spain. But somewhere along the way I discover that I am also dealing with my inner world. The interior work may have been beyond my original intention. This pilgrimage will take us into new places of sensing, thinking, feeling, and imagination.

Radical ideas are always a good place to start when you're planning a pilgrimage. John started out by telling me he had a crazy idea. His idea of finding a place where the music and the pilgrim's way converge into a spiritual reality was a great framework for a pilgrimage. Both music and pilgrimage, by their very nature, are agents of changing the soul. Both share characteristics that will bring about a recognizable shift in our lives. In addition, each has its own unique subtleties that can aid the process. To walk the slow pace of miles on end allows us to observe the world and see what otherwise goes unnoticed. The music, no matter how familiar, will reveal new dimensions of life through listening. I would discover that to bathe in the majesty of the forest is akin to being awash in the choir's polyphonic mystery—as if for the first time and the last time. To go on pilgrimage is the willingness to engage our crazy idea in the hopes of experiencing a soul-shaping transmutation. But your pilgrimage may not be about music and walking. Your journey must take its own shape.

A soul-shaping pilgrimage might include traveling to a foreign land. The faraway territory may indeed be Ireland or Spain. I've walked Ireland, journeyed to Rome, and traveled to Chimayo, New Mexico, on spiritual pilgrimages. Then again, the road less traveled could be a local path right out your back door. As I made my way across Ireland on foot, the locals would tell me how "brilliant" it was that I was walking coast-to-coast. They reveled in the thought of doing such a thing themselves one day. I wondered why they didn't just put on a pack and walk out their back door. Pilgrimage, though, is more about the process than the trail on which we walk. It is more than just a matter of convenience and money. The wisdom way of walking necessitates that we open the front door of our ordinary life and walk into another reality. At first, the dream is to walk. Then the walking becomes the dream. And then another dream emerges in the walking.

Sometimes, though, those dreams feel like nightmares. These are the journeys in our lives that feel interminably long—paths we may not have chosen to walk. A pilgrimage can be any journey—physical, emotional, psychic, spiritual —that has the potential to shape our soul and change the way we sense, think, feel, and imagine our life. The trails we walk could be many—a new job, a new town, or the challenge to lose weight. The pilgrimage could take us on a journey through depression, disease, divorce, loss of a job, or aging. New discoveries, vocations, personal challenges, and life's trials are all alien lands, whether we choose to visit them or find ourselves transported there. We walk many pilgrimages in our life. The question is, how will we walk the unfamiliar miles we encounter?

Pilgrimage is about finding our own way. Walking Ireland coast-to-coast, I started my day by planning the route. Then, to make sure my plan was a good one, I would ask a local for advice. Usually I got a question in response to my question. "And how would you be walking today?" They wanted to know if I'd done my homework. I told them what I thought. Then I would hear, "Oh. Who told you that? No, no, here is the way." In the end, given their well-meaning advice, I was left to sort out my own path. I was the one doing the walking.

My trek alone across Ireland took me south from Dublin along the Wicklow Way. Then I turned southwest to walk the South Leinster Way, the Munster Way, and the Blackwater Way. I finished by walking towards the western coast on the Kerry Way. Each route took me down forest roads, over mountains, farm lanes, boreens, muddy single footpaths, waist-high grass, river banks, mossy bogs, sheep trails, rock stacks with running water, and slick grass hills. Each way was marked with a yellow arrow and the symbol of a person hiking.

Some trails were better marked than others. A few markers were misleading and, at a point or two, incorrect. To rely totally on the way markers would have been a mistake, taking me miles out of my way. I carried good maps. Still, even with a compass, the trail could be confusing. My other constant companion was Paddy Dillon's *The Irish Coast-to-Coast Walk*,[19] the Irish walking bible. Of course, reading the bible literally can lead to walking down the wrong road as well. Still, I am an Episcopalian who relies on the five-hundred-year-old Anglican convention of the three-legged stool of scripture, reason, and tradition for theological support. That said, I felt my best chance of being in the right place when the sun began to set was to listen to the local lore (tradition), carry a map and the book (holy text), and use reason (at the end of the day I was responsible for my own choice). The truth was somewhere in the middle of it all, and some of the best lessons I have learned were while I was walking on what seemed to be the wrong path, but turned out to be the right one for me. It was my pilgrimage, the good and bad of it all.

My hope is that in reading this book, you will be able to discover your own pilgrimage path, your own reason for going on pilgrimage. I also hope that through the process of pilgrimage you will have a transformational experience, what I will describe through this book as an "alchemical pilgrimage" that leads to transmutation of the mind, body, soul, and spirit.

Okay. It's time to get ready. Where's my pack? Is my passport up to date? Ah, I may need new boots. I need to lose five pounds. Do I have to go through all of this again? Indeed. Pilgrimage, like life, is a spiral that will lead us back to the chaotic beginning, always.

:

The Pilgrimage Begins before the Walking Starts

*In order to acquire the "golden
understanding" one must keep the eyes
of the mind and the soul well open, observing
and contemplating by means of that
inner light which God has lit in nature and
in our hearts from the beginning.*

—Carl Jung,
Psychology and Alchemy[20]

John Wiles, the leader of the musical pilgrimage, sent me an email. It seemed he was in one of those moments of existential crisis about the preparations for his singing pilgrimage.

> I have started and stopped this email no less than seven times
> in the past five minutes. I have a personal concern about the
> trip and would appreciate your thoughts. I've been struggling

with a nagging intuition that once I speak aloud my own purpose and goals for the [singing pilgrimage] trip, those very goals
will become inherently unreachable. Today I was reading Merton
and came across this: "I, for one, realize that now I need more.
Not simply to be quiet, somewhat productive, to pray, to read,
to cultivate leisure—*otium sanctum*! There is a need of effort,
deepening, change and transformation. Not that I must under-
take a special project of self-transformation or that I must 'work
on myself.' In that regard, it would be better to forget it. Just to
go for walks, live in peace, let change come quietly and invisibly
on the inside. But I do have a past to break with, an accumula-
tion of inertia, waste, wrong, foolishness, rot, junk, a great need
of clarification of mindfulness, or rather of no mind—a return to
genuine practice, right effort, need to push on to the great doubt.
Need for the Spirit. Hang on to the clear light!"

John continued, "I suppose my question, then, is how have you formulated
your thoughts/expectations/goals/mindset for pilgrimages past?"

John's email plunged me into thinking about going on pilgrimage. I had
to sit and ponder for a while how to answer him. His question stirred in me
both the excitement of going to Ireland for another pilgrimage and the trepidation of entering into yet another personal alchemical process. Consciously
or unconsciously, John was asking me to sort through my pilgrimage shadow
work, those places of deep transformational work. How could I answer his
question in a few paragraphs? I finally responded.

When I walked across Ireland, those first days, I thought I was
looking for the divine. Eventually that turned into what I thought
was seeking my life purpose. Then my thoughts evolved into realizing I was looking for my inner Self. My Self, I discovered, would
be found in what the Irish call the thin place—the world between
the seen and the unseen. I realized I was beginning a process, not
concluding one. I imagine this work will last a lifetime—my life
as a pilgrim, one who is on a continual pilgrimage.

John, your pilgrimage has already begun. You are in the first
phase of the alchemical process, known as the cauldron of chaos,
the moment of an existential crisis. There are three more phases
and they spiral, all to be repeated at some time, many times
during the pilgrimage and in life. During this place of beginning

focus on what your senses perceive, focus on your experience. Don't let your feet get ahead of your soul.

Some pilgrims need an intention to walk with, a question. Others just want to wait and see what will emerge. I think a pilgrimage is like drawing a mandala. By deciding to go on pilgrimage, you've drawn the sacred circle of the mandala. Now sit with it and see what happens. In the end, because you are paying attention, you won't be disappointed. I have learned many things from your dad. One is to hold things lightly. All will be well. Thomas Merton wrote, "The geographical pilgrimage is the symbolic acting out of an inner journey. The inner journey is the interpolation of the meanings and signs of the outer pilgrimage. One can have one without the other. It is best to have both."[21]

There are many layers, cycles, and phases to a pilgrimage. Both the outer experience and the inner interpretation of that experience need space and time. Go slow. Breathe. Take your time. And let the pilgrimage emerge on its own pace.

Shortly after our email exchange John's group began to form. He was recruiting twelve professional singers. They had to be accomplished musicians, able to perform complex medieval music a cappella. Each person had to be willing to pay his or her own expenses. And they had to hike the strenuous Wicklow Way. He had a group ready to walk within a few weeks (although the composition of the group would change slightly over the next few months). All the while he was contemplating a name for the project. I hadn't named any of my pilgrimage walks, but I was intrigued by the possibility. When he invited me to a private Facebook group he set up for the pilgrims, I was surprised and moved by the name he had chosen—"Vox Peregrini." Years ago I had stumbled across the Gaelic word *peregrini*, the pilgrim—a word that has great meaning for me.

Peregrini—the Pilgrim

In 2004, the year before I was ordained as a priest in the Episcopal Church, I traveled with twelve folks to Ireland for a pilgrimage retreat experience at Glendalough, the glen of two lakes, fifty miles south of Dublin. Glendalough is the ancient monastic community of Saint Kevin (d. 618), an ascetic who modeled his life after the Desert Fathers, especially Anthony of Egypt (251–356). During my monthlong stay in Ireland I had begun to discover the many ways that pilgrimage is a metaphor for life. One theme of pilgrimage is discernment

—to carry a question while walking. At the time, I was pondering my eventual ordination. Was I hearing a call from God? Or was the fact that I didn't have a job driving my desire to be ordained? Was I really called to be a pastor of a parish? Or should I pursue life once again in higher education? Did I really want to take a vow to obey my bishop? I was at a loss for answers and it was a heavy weight to lug around Ireland. Yet, being on that journey, with a safe community of fellow pilgrims, in the ancient holy site of Glendalough, was the perfect environment for me to make some significant decisions about my future.

Then, in 2005, I was ordained. My first job was to be chaplain in charge of the Episcopal Campus Ministry at Arizona State University (ECMASU), in Tempe. Serving ECMASU was a natural fit. I had graduated from ASU thirty years earlier with a bachelor's degree, and a few years after that with a master's. While the campus, and definitely the students, had changed, I could at least find the Memorial Union and the campus chapel. My bishop thought I could handle the ministry even though some might have thought that, at fifty-two, I was a bit old for the job. I had just finished a twenty-four-year career in higher education at Grand Canyon University in Phoenix, Arizona. I had been the head baseball coach, held various administrative positions, and eventually became the university's president.

When I started my campus ministry work at ASU, the language and stories of pilgrimage felt like a natural way for me to connect with college students. They are on a journey, making many of life's serious decisions. I asked my spiritual director, who is an Irish priest, what the Gaelic word for pilgrim is. *Peregrini*, he told me. And that became the name for our student gathering.

After a few months of hard work, a spattering of students attended our Wednesday afternoon mass. One day, late in the fall semester, a professor showed up at the service. After worship I introduced myself. He promptly told me he was a linguistic professor and that the word *peregrini* was not Gaelic, but Latin. Further, the word did not mean pilgrim but rather was a demeaning term for foreigners. In his professorial tone, he suggested I immediately change the name of our group to something more fitting—a name that would not proclaim to the university my apparent lack of education. As an Episcopalian, he was embarrassed.

Well, of course the professor was right. Not about the uneducated part, though, I will readily admit I never studied Latin, which at that moment I deeply regretted. I am pretty sure the professor took pleasure in schooling a former university president.

The word *peregrini* is indeed derived from the Latin word *perigrinus*, which is a "stateless person," or "exile," or "alien." The Romans used the derisive term in their reference to the fifth-century Irish Christian monks who were wandering through Europe as missionaries.[22] The Irish monks began referring to themselves as *peregrinus pro Christo*, "pilgrims for Christ."[23] *Peregrini* made its way into the Gaelic language when the monks returned to Ireland. My spiritual director, fluent in Gaelic, was sharing a common Christian usage of the word. Despite the professor's insistence, I kept the name for our college group. After all, many of us, including college students, feel like aliens in a foreign land looking for answers to spiritual questions.

This little episode was a mini-pilgrimage all on its own. A linguistics professor, proficient in Latin, showed up at an Episcopal mass on a college campus in the middle of the desert attended by a half-dozen students, simply to correct a stubborn novice priest, who in turn researched the word to prove the validity of his Irish Catholic, Gaelic-speaking mentor, and who, though discovering the professor was partially correct, changed nothing but his resolve. Long sentence. Long walk. The way of the pilgrim and living life as a pilgrimage is neither simple nor clear. Like an Irish conversation, the pilgrim's path is erudite, poetic, lyrical, colorful, intimate, intense, messy, and hard to pin down, which often leads to more questions than answers. So, too, is the life of a pilgrim. I should have invited the professor to the local pub for a lively discussion over a Guinness. There, I imagine, the conversation would have been filled with personal stories, which would have added color and hue to the meaning behind our words. Over a pint of Guinness, or two, maybe a relationship could have begun.

John's choice of "Vox Peregrini" as the name for his singing pilgrimage made me feel I had arrived at a new place in my own understanding of pilgrimage —the past connecting to the future. The spiral of pilgrimage was moving upward for me. I was preparing for yet another journey. Joining John's group would take me on more than just another geographical pilgrimage. It would indeed lead me on another journey into my inner world—cycling through the phases of alchemy once again. Taking yet another wisdom walk.

Preparing for the Geographical Pilgrimage

It was the summer of 2012. "Why are you walking alone across Ireland?" asked the server, who set my second Guinness of the evening in front of me. "Are you doing it to raise money for a charity?"

"Ah, no." I said. "It's a soul thing, I guess."

"Did you hear a voice or something?" she chuckled.

"No, I just feel like it's something I gotta do."

My 2012 pilgrimage across Ireland had begun years before. In 1996 my wife and I celebrated our twenty-fifth wedding anniversary. I was the head baseball coach at Grand Canyon University (GCU) with no idea that one day I would be its president. Our son was a freshman in college and our daughter a junior in high school. Given the age of our children, we planned the "last family vacation," settling on two weeks in the UK. Part of the trip included three days in Ireland, where we spent a few hours on a Glendalough tour. I told my wife as the tour ended that something was drawing me back to that holy monastery. I didn't know what it was or why, but I had to return.

By the end of 2003, I had left my job at GCU after twenty-four years, capped by a disastrous four years as president. The first six months of 2004 I was unemployed, severely depressed, and discerning a call into the Episcopal priesthood. That probably wasn't the best of circumstances for effectively discerning my future. But that was my reality. The priest of our church invited me and eleven other people to join her on an eight-day monastic experience in Glendalough. My wife thought it would be a good chance for me to get away, an opportunity to heal. Indeed, the experience was therapeutic. While in Glendalough, I met some folks who were walking the Wicklow Way. When I returned home I told my wife something was calling me to go back and walk the Way. By 2006, I was in Ireland again. My son and I walked the first half of the Wicklow Way to Glendalough and then turned west along Saint Kevin's Way, where we walked four days towards Kildare, the home of Saint Brigid. Before I returned home from Ireland I was already planning to walk the country coast-to-coast. Circumstances and life would cause me to wait another six years.

A year before I left on my solitary pilgrimage across Ireland, I started my preparations. Nearly sixty years old, my body needed daily attention. I'd stayed in reasonably good condition over the years. Having previously walked one hundred miles from Dublin to Kildare, I thought I knew what it would take to walk another 250-plus miles. Actually, while walking 353 miles across Ireland, I came to realize I had had little idea what the trek would demand from my body. Without my conditioning regimen, I could never have finished the journey. I also knew I needed to tend my soul and emotional well-being. I couldn't have prepared for or known, however, that my mother would die three months before I left for Ireland.

My grief triggered the realization that life itself is a pilgrimage in process. We are on a pilgrimage no matter where we are walking: at home, at the hospital, or in Ireland. Oftentimes, even when we think we are fully prepared, the burdens and questions we take with us on pilgrimage can weigh heavier than our backpack. None of us can know what tomorrow will bring. We might be presented with an opportunity, or a disappointment that will change our life forever. We may be preparing for a journey we will never take. Yet we can accept the journey of everyday life and prepare each day as if tomorrow is the day we will begin a pilgrimage, even an unintended one. We carry our past, while being present to the footsteps of today, and at the same time imagining the possibility of what is to come; the three are held together in one timeless moment. We can work the body, tend the soul, stretch the mind, recognize the unconscious, and surrender to the alchemical process that is working in our soul. To do so, we must be present to the ground we are walking on.

Everyone's pilgrimage is unique. We'll experience the path through our own senses. Each journey will be interpreted differently because of how we think about it. We might walk with someone a hundred miles, see the same sights and share similar experiences. But it's still our own pilgrimage, like our own dreams. We all dream. We may encounter animals, birds, parents, and even enemies, familiar places, buildings, a body of water, forests, and deserts in our dreams. While respecting the similarities in our dreams, we interpret them depending on the context of our life, our feelings. So it is with the geography of a pilgrimage.

But much of our processing of the pilgrimage is done out of the sight of our fellow pilgrims, in our imagination—the place where the art of the interior pilgrimage takes place.

Preparing for the Inner Pilgrimage

In October 2013, more than a year after my first coast-to-coast walk across Ireland, my wife, Cathy, asked me what I wanted for my sixtieth birthday. I told her what I really wanted was to the walk the Wicklow Way with my family. Cathy had been my support team on my solitary walk across Ireland. This time she wanted to walk the Wicklow Way with me. She contacted our two adult children and their spouses. Our daughter and her husband were in. Our son and his wife soon discovered she was pregnant and they decided they needed to stay home. We began planning the trip for the summer of 2014.

Later in October, our young adult group at church, called Saint Brigid's Community, surprised me with a birthday party. Someone asked if I was going to do anything special during my sixtieth year. I told them about our family plan to walk the Wicklow Way. Before long, some in the group asked me if they could walk with us. All the stories I'd told this group about pilgrimage must have created a desire for them to walk as well. Within a few weeks, we had a group of thirteen who planned to walk the Wicklow Way with us. Saint Brigid's was going on pilgrimage.

I spent a lot of time encouraging them to prepare for the geographical pilgrimage, get in shape, buy good boots, get a comfortable backpack, acquire some rain gear. "You do have a passport, right?" I asked.

When I'd been preparing for my other pilgrimages, people had told me they wanted to go along. I always invited them and helped them plan. But I've learned that until someone buys an airline ticket, they aren't truly committed. By March, all thirteen of us had tickets to Ireland. Our Saint Brigid's group included me, Cathy (a retired school superintendent), our daughter and son-in-law (both business executives), a lawyer, a hospice chaplain, a speech therapist who owns her business, a naturopathic doctor, two neuroscientists, two teachers, and a businessman who travels extensively. Three of us were in the sixty club, three in their early forties, and the other seven were under thirty. The group was set. Now it was time to begin making some preparations for the inner journey. Cathy and I invited the group to our home several evenings for dinner, conversation, and Guinness. Because this group had been a regular part of our weekly church gatherings, I felt that I had the freedom to dive in deep with my thoughts and ideas about pilgrimage.

I opened our gatherings with a reading from Carl Jung's *The Red Book*. His words were offered as a prayer for our inner pilgrimage.

> You, my soul, I found again . . . where I least expected you. You
> climbed out of a dark shaft. You announced yourself to me in
> advance in dreams. They burned in my heart and drove me to
> all the boldest acts of daring, and forced me to rise above myself.
> You let me see truths of which I had no previous inkling. You let
> me undertake journeys, whose endless length would have scared
> me, if the knowledge of them had not been secure in you.[24]

I followed the reading with some reflections I'd prepared about our undertaking. A pilgrimage is often an encounter with the unknown. We're going to walk across Ireland, a place you've never experienced. You're going to see, hear, taste, touch, and smell new things almost every day. Your senses will come to life like never before. At the same time, you are going to take a journey into your interior world. As you sense this new world, you're going to have a lot of time to think about what you're experiencing. And the longer you walk, the more your hidden feelings and emotions are going to make their way to the surface. To make a pilgrimage requires the courage to be open to both what you can see and what you cannot. We must hold lightly to what might come our way on this journey. We cannot force, or control, or cajole the experience to happen. Like a dream, the mystery of the pilgrimage will emerge in the walking, on its own account.

Traveling unfamiliar territories, whether the seen or the unseen, demands that you, as a pilgrim, activate your imagination. Through Jung's journeys to foreign lands, his encounters with shamans, his work with the symbols of ancient cultures, mandalas, stone, and alchemy, his dreams and imaginative visions, he was able to experience his personal unconscious, and the collective unconscious, which were working to communicate with his consciousness.

His conscious connecting to the unconscious allowed him to see both sides of his personality. He already knew the side he liked, the side he wanted to see. But he was now also able to recognize the shadow side of his personality— the side we are less familiar with, are often unwilling to acknowledge, and may not like about ourselves. Through his pilgrimage, Jung was able to move towards what he called individuation—the integration of both sides of his personality, the light and shadow. Individuation allows the Self, that which we were created to be, to emerge. This is our work as modern-day pilgrims.

Candace, one of the younger members of the group and a neuroscientist, spoke first. "Nice, Gil. So what you are saying is, we're all going to have a mystical experience, and that will lead us to become more mature?" The question was laced with twenty-something sarcasm and her well-trained skepticism.

"I don't know if you'll have a mystical experience or not. You might see faeries." I laughed. "But you probably won't experience what you're intended to experience if you're not open to all the possibilities."

"My faeries or your faeries?" she said.

"The faeries might resent being called yours and mine. I think most of you are going to be in Ireland a few days before the walk. Maybe the best way to start the trip would be to visit Newgrange. It's a five-thousand-year-old burial mound. It's a place known for provoking the mystical—and for seeing faeries as well.

"The first time I visited Newgrange, I had just finished walking a hundred miles. I had started in Dublin, walking the first three days of the Wicklow Way to Glendalough, the same trail we're walking. Then I went west to Kildare, the home of Saint Brigid. After a few days in Kildare, I took the train back to Dublin, then north to Newgrange, just like every other tourist. I went there because a friend had told me I should visit the site."

"You got some pictures? I'm a visual person," the young businessman said.

I popped open my laptop and scrolled through a few pictures of Newgrange. Before arriving in Ireland, I had been too busy to read any literature about the ancient burial mound. I simply stepped off the bus and was suddenly faced with an enormous Stone Age temple. My emotions started to swell. I had no idea why I was so touched by this place. Yet there I was, unexpectedly moved by the beauty of what the ancients Celts named in Gaelic Brú na Bóinne, the Palace of the Boyne. After several visits to Newgrange and many pilgrimages later, I am still working through my experiences of encountering the tomb— the womb of the pilgrimage between this world and the next.

"That's all cool, Gil. But it doesn't sound like we're going to see this place walking the Wicklow, right?"

"That's right, we won't. But I think I can give you some ancient history of Ireland that will help your walking experience as well as explore your own imagination."

Newgrange sits on a hill above the Boyne River, just a few miles outside the port town of Drogheda, forty-five minutes by train north of Dublin. Legend says the Tuatha Dé Danann, the people of the goddess Danu, built the colossal burial mound as a temple for their gods. The burial mound looms from atop a ridge, peering over a rolling green valley. The façade of quartz across the face of the tomb glimmers, even on a cloudy day. The imagination of the people who constructed this holy site must have been brilliant.

The tomb is a tribute to the ingenuity of those who designed and constructed the marvel. The Brú na Bóinne was built six hundred years before the Egyptian Giza Pyramids and a thousand years before Stonehenge, around 3,200 BCE. It was constructed without the use of metal tools or mortar to hold the stones together or keep the inner sanctum dry. Yet the interior has never suffered any water leaks. Two hundred thousand tons of earth, 44,000 square feet of dirt, was used to construct the temple tomb. The mound's diameter is 320 feet, approximately 50 feet high at its center. There are 97 kerbstones, 8 feet long and 4 feet high, that each weigh as much as 2 tons. These stones are situated around the circumference and support the mound. The kerbstones contain some of the oldest Neolithic spiral etching in the world. Most likely these stones were floated down the Boyne River and then rolled up the hill about five miles to the construction site. The wall of quartz covering the front of the tomb, where the entrance passage is located, was most likely brought from sites south of Newgrange, as far as a hundred miles away in the Wicklow Mountains, where our group was going to walk. This feat of construction took thirty to fifty years to complete.

For me, the most intense experience of visiting Newgrange is traveling down the 97-foot-long passage into the interior of the tomb. I had to crouch low to make my way down the path. The center is 21 by 17 feet wide and 20 feet high. The complete interior shape resembles an egg. Hence the term "the womb of pilgrimage," the place where this world meets the otherworld. There are three ritual recesses in the inner sanctuary, where evidence of two bodies and three cremains were found in the mid-nineteenth century. A few hundred years of looting removed valuable artifacts and remains prior to the work of archaeologists in the 1970s.

The light box above the entrance passage makes Newgrange unique among Ireland's many burial mounds. The box provides a perfect stream of light for seventeen minutes at sunrise on the winter solstice. A guide who has been in the center space of the tomb at the winter solstice described the experience with misty eyes. He said the light travels up the floor of the burial mound like hot molten lava. Reaching the pitch-black center, the light bursts alive with a climactic crescendo, illuminating the stones with an iridescent glow. Then, as the sun moves, the light retreats down the tomb's floor, as if to carry the souls of the dead, who were resting in the tomb's center, out into the otherworld.

The Palace at Newgrange was built to be what the Irish call a thin place. This is where Dagda and the other gods of the peoples of Danu retreated to begin their pilgrimage to the otherworld. Through the solstice light they would find paradise waiting for them on the mystic "Island of Women." Then, from time to time, the gods and goddesses would reappear as faeries in the world we see. The faerie people could be helpful to pilgrims on their own journey. Or they might show up as tricksters—for those who needed some reminders about how to be good human beings.

Candace broke in. "So you have seen the faeries!"

"Well, all I can say is, maybe. Who knows what they are really seeing with the third eye?"

"The night before or after your hangover?" Candace asked.

"Depends on what I had been drinking." I said.

She said, "So, it's either the Gaelic cult Kool-Aid or the Matrix red pill. Which is it?"

"I'll admit, I swallowed the red pill—Jung's *Red Book*—the one filled with his mandala drawings."

I can imagine Jung describing Newgrange as a three-dimensional mandala. He explored his imagination using the mandalas as images of how he envisioned his soul. The vastness of the soul makes for a limitless number of drawings. For Jung, the mandala is a sacred circle of imagination where we can get a glimpse of the soul. At Newgrange, I can imagine seeing the ancient faeries dancing in a mandala of an Irish shaman. There, the Brú na Bóinne would represent the collective soul of the people, the "Womb of the Soul," revealed in the bright light of a full moon. The temple of Newgrange was a place that would stir the universal archetypes—of gods and goddesses, chieftains and druids, warriors and shamans—found in the collective unconscious of the ancient people. Today, eons after Newgrange was built, the sacred circle of the tomb is still telling the story of the Celtic people, life and death, as pilgrimage.

Throughout the history of humankind, a fear of the dead combined with a fascination with the afterlife has played a part in the rituals of all peoples working out their psychic pilgrimage in the final stage of life. Newgrange is a reminder of humanity's preoccupation with the cult of the grave,[25] which is a mirror of the penultimate pilgrimage.

My sixty-year-old colleague, a hospice chaplain, said, "So we're going on a death march?"

I said, "Going on pilgrimage is kind of like facing the death of the things in our life that we know need to die—like our illusion of control. Those things that cause us to frustrate ourselves."

"And others," my wife added.

I smiled. "Yes, indeed, others as well. Pilgrimage exposes those points of frustration to the day-to-day 'heat' of walking. The pilgrimage becomes the alchemist's container of transformation. Jung was convinced that certain ancient alchemists held some of the secrets to the process of integration of opposites, what he called individuation."

"I thought alchemists were trying to make gold out of lead?" the lawyer said.

"For sure, some were misguided. Some were charlatans. Some were scientists doing experiments. But Jung's work led him to discover that a few alchemists were after something much more important. He suggested those alchemists envisioned their work as a metaphor for the process of psychological maturation.[26] Their work, Jung said, was something akin to alchemy of the soul. The alchemist's work was primarily concerned with unity: the unity of the four elements (air, earth, water, and fire); the unity of opposites in our life, light-dark, birth-death, love-hate; the unity of the conscious and the unconscious, that which brings wholeness and integration into our life. The pilgrimage of the unification of opposites was a common theme among many of the alchemist writers. German alchemist and philosopher Michael Maier (1568–1622) wrote of the symbolic peregrination, leaving one's homeland in order to engage the divine at the four corners of the world.[27] The four corners represent the four phases of alchemy, the four directions, and the four elements —unified in a pilgrimage of the soul."

One of the teachers in our group said, "Gil, we don't have a lifetime to make a pilgrimage. We have eight days. We're only walking a hundred miles. We're not walking to the four corners of the earth. Is it possible for us to experience any sense of this unity you're talking about while we're on our pilgrimage?"

"My experience is that, yes, we can. It will, though, be difficult. Jung said, 'The practice of the art [of alchemy] is a hard road and the longest road.'[28] You each have already begun your pilgrimage. When the idea first entered your mind, you started the process of being on pilgrimage. Now you've really made a commitment. You've bought a ticket. You've purchased boots and backpacks. You've been hiking and working out, getting in shape. You have been preparing for your outer pilgrimage. You've also begun working on your interior pilgrimage. The real difference, however, between the exterior and the interior pilgrimage, is that when you stop walking, the geographical pilgrimage will change locations. You'll leave Ireland and return home. No matter your geographical location, the process of the alchemy continues. The interior work is never finished.

"What can be even more frustrating is that the process isn't linear. Jung said that the path appears to go in spirals.[29] My experience of having been on several pilgrimages is that they build on one another. Instead of them being a series of separate journeys, they swirl on top of one another, making one continual journey—a spiral. While I've walked the Wicklow Way several times and I'm familiar with the path, each journey has been unique. I've used the wisdom gained from each walk to illuminate the psychic trail of the next pilgrimage. As I said before, we sense the environment, the seen and the unseen. Then we think about what we're sensing. Next, we process our feelings. We're constantly repeating the process. Most importantly, these repeated steps are leading us into a more creative imagination, a higher consciousness. Our expanded consciousness guides us into understanding a more integrated picture of our true self."

"This four-step process of sensing, thinking, feeling, and imagining parallels the four phases of alchemy, which is a metaphor for life. The sensing phase is the alchemical cauldron of chaos—seeing, smelling, tasting, touching, and hearing with intensity. Then, thinking—the second phase—causes a crack in the egg of the soul; we focus our attention on the data we've gathered in the sensing phase. Our mental acuity turns up the pilgrimage heat. Next, the feeling phase causes the emergence of the raven with the peacock tail; what we sense and think begins to stir within us what has been relegated to the unconscious. As our feelings rise to the surface, the pilgrimage heat intensifies. In the final step of imagination, we enter the phase of the rising phoenix. Here the full heat of pilgrimage expands our ability to intuit a yet-to-be realized possibility for our Self.

"I've seen this happen so many times in my own life and in others on pilgrimage. As I walk, I find myself delving deeper into the chaos of my interior life, those parts I've avoided dealing with, or denied existed—broken relationships, dashed dreams, unfulfilled potential. With the ever-increasing heat of each step of my life, a better understanding of my Self emerges—the soul gold of wisdom begins to form in the cauldron of walking."

"So what phase are we in now?" someone asked.

"Remember, it's a spiral. While I might be further along the spiral of pilgrimage because this is my fourth trip, we all begin at the beginning. Once we start walking, the process will move at a different pace for each of us. Some of you might linger in the initial phase, taking in the beautiful scenery while simultaneously sensing the heat of a blister on your foot. For you, the thinking, feeling, and imagination may come much later in the pilgrimage, or even after we've stopped walking. Some of you may make your way through each of the four stages in the first day. Then you spiral back through them again and again during the days of the walk—and the days, weeks, and years to follow.

"The first phase is chaotic, like a storm rapidly approaching. By being so keenly aware of your senses, a clash of your unconscious with your conscious may occur. You'll probably have dreams about trying to get ready. You might dream about some fear you have, being late to the plane, flying, heights, dark places, getting lost. The dreams appear because you are placing the psychic elements of your life under the influence of the moist, brooding heat, like that of a hen. In this phase you are using your senses to the extreme in preparation for the trip. For Jung, we are pouring the very elements of our ego into the alchemical egg, as the ancient Celts did at Newgrange. We take a risk to do this in order that our pilgrimage will aid our process of individuation, the integration of our opposites, the hatching of a new imagination."

"Okay then, walking on the pilgrimage is going to help us become an integrated person. So tell me again where the Self fits in?" my wife asked.

"The best way I can explain the Self and the ego is to use this metaphor I read by a Jungian analyst named Irene Gad. She used the example of a symphony. The Self is the conductor and the musicians working together to create beautiful music. The ego is the orchestra's manager who makes the decisions about bookings, tickets, hotels, transportation, and meals. The manager is obviously not the music. You can't confuse the manager's role with that of the conductor. But without the manager's services, the orchestra doesn't play.[30] That's how a healthy ego and the integrated Self function together in the individuated person."

"Okay, how did I miss all this in Psychology 101?" Candace said.

"Well, I missed it and I took a ton of psychology classes," Blair, the other neuroscientist, said.

"I'm not a psychologist," I said. "But I am a pilgrim. And Jung's work is the only thing I've found that has helped me process all the stuff that comes up in my soul while I'm walking. His work has also given me a language to deal with what happens when I stop walking—that weird feeling of being somewhere between an afterglow and a hangover."

"I knew that's where the faeries and the Guinness came in," Candace said.

"Yep," I laughed.

"The best I can do is to share with you what has arisen in me while I walk. My sister has Prader-Willi Syndrome (PWS). More than seventy percent of couples with PWS children divorce. Somehow my parents beat those odds. They had been married sixty-four years when my mom died. Typically, many members of families with PWS children suffer from chronic depression. That's been true in our family, myself included.

"Because I was the 'normal child,' lots of unconscious expectations were projected on me. Those projected expectations continued as an adult. I was a professional athlete, college baseball coach, university president, and an Episcopal priest—all of that almost ate me alive. But that's my own human complexity of dark and light. That's what I have to work through. Each of us has our own stuff and the awful crap others project onto us whether they mean to or not. We have to find some way to work through it so that none of that unprocessed grief, anger, pain, whatever it was or is, consumes us, constricts us, owns us, or eventually destroys us. Our goal is to live into our Self—who we were created to be, that fully integrated, individuated, wise human being.

"Unfortunately, what happens over time is that these outside expectations can force us into becoming someone we were never meant to be. These unwanted projections need to be separated out, some burned off, and some re-integrated. That's what happens during an alchemical pilgrimage. We can recognize what's not ours, what others have projected onto us. The projections, the expectations, things we never imagined could exist in our shadow, come out into the light of our consciousness. There we must battle our own lack of self-awareness and absence of interior work. But once we identify the projections, accept their presence, and do our work, then they can be burned off in the alchemist's vessel from the heat produced on the long days of walking."

"So, the only way to process all this sh. . . stuff is to go on a pilgrimage?" one of the teachers said.

"In a way, yes. I've discovered that life is a series of pilgrimages—some walking, some metaphoric, and some we never intended to walk. The pilgrimage can happen through the trials and tribulations life forces upon us. The important thing is to process every phase of every pilgrimage. We must be willing to struggle through what is preventing us from becoming our true integrated Self. Someone who has been driven into a pilgrimage through illness, loss of a loved one, unemployment, or some other difficult strain in life can recognize some of the unwanted projections and expectations that are being slowly cooked away. The difficulty they will encounter is to separate out the necessary and healthy experience of the grief, or anger, or frustration, or loss from the intentional process of working through what they've buried or avoided in their life—those things that have stifled their imagination of an integrated life. Then the healthy aspects of pain will need to be acknowledged and re-integrated; the dark and the light held in simultaneous tension.

"We, however, are deliberately planning to go on a walking pilgrimage. At first, if we're not paying attention, we might not fully explore our senses. The process of preparing for a pilgrimage has already cost us personal time, resources, and energy. That sacrifice brings heat to the process. And we've just gotten started. We must go through each phase even though we haven't begun to walk yet.

"Already though, our hidden expectations are beginning to rise to the surface. Our friends and family might question why we would want to 'waste' our vacation time walking a hundred miles when we could be seeing the sights in Ireland. I know some of us have been asked if we're physically capable of walking the rugged Wicklow Way. When other people question our motives and capabilities we might be getting a sense of what they are projecting onto us. They can't imagine walking through the forest of Ireland when instead you could take a tour bus to all the sites. Of course, we need realistic answers to honest questions. But often our answers will not be understood or accepted by the person who is projecting his or her expectations onto us. Others want us to live life the way they do. But we are the ones who must deal with what we are sensing, thinking, feeling, and imagining about the questions, projections, and expectations as they are mixed with our excitement about the trip.

"Sometimes, in our exuberance about getting ready to go on a pilgrimage, we don't take the time to completely walk through the reflective process. As a traveler of several pilgrimages, both wanted and unwanted, I have learned I must fully engage each phase, confront my expectations and projections, as well as those of others, as a necessary initiation into the unknown of being on pilgrimage."

The lawyer asked, "Is all this psychic stuff really necessary? I just thought it would be cool to walk through the Irish forest. I'm not sure I want to be confronted by my projections, expectations, and the unconscious."

"I don't know if all this inner work is necessary for your pilgrimage. I'm only sharing my own experience. What I can say is that a lot of the folks I've walked with, and dozens of other people I've talked to about pilgrimage, seem to have experienced a similar kind of psychic process during and after their pilgrimage. If all this Jungian stuff works for you, that's great. If not, just enjoy the landscape of the isle of the forty shades of green. And just for your information, contrary to popular belief, Johnny Cash did not create the term. Like most folklore, it was there long before any modern person thought it or said it. Besides the ancient legends or Jung's ideas, the scenery alone is worth the walk. Everyone's pilgrimage is their own. Okay, I'll see you all in Dublin. The Wicklow Way starts in Marley Park."

"Wait, wait, wait," Candace said. "Do we need to learn any Gaelic?"

"Just one word. *Slainte!* Cheers!"

⋮

Interlude
Boots, Backpacks, Poles, and the Body

Following are some tips about boots, backpacks, and hiking poles, advice for getting in shape to hike, and a list of books to read in preparation for a pilgrimage.

Boots

As the Irish would say, wear "proper boots." Your feet are going to do most of the work. My experience has been if my feet are dry and comfortable, I can tolerate just about anything else. And nothing is more miserable than blisters. Good boots that have been broken in before the hiking starts makes the pilgrimage much more enjoyable. I recommend that you put a hundred miles on your boots before you start hiking a pilgrimage trail.

Inducing misery second only to blisters is wet feet. The odds are very high that somewhere on most pilgrimages you will find yourself walking in the rain and through water. The key is to have boots that will keep your feet dry. GoreTex is great, but my experience has been that mesh boots will not stop the kind of rain and moisture that I've endured in Ireland. I wear leather Zamberlan 996 Vioz GTX boots. (They didn't pay me or give me boots. I bought them after a lot of research.) Zamberlan boots tend to be a bit more expensive but well worth it. I have six hundred miles and counting on the ones I'm still wearing. I have had them resoled once.

SmartWool socks are excellent. I wear one pair and carry another. Most importantly, though, I wear silk sock liners underneath my wool socks (and I pack a second pair). The liners really help prevent blisters. I also rub Aquaphor on my feet before and after I hike. The combination of good boots, sock liners under my wool socks, and rubbing Aquaphor on my feet has saved me from blisters.

The Right Backpack is Important

The journey will carry its own weight. There is no need for you to burden yourself more than necessary. My experience has taught me that my backpack, fully packed, shouldn't weigh more than 10–15 percent of my body weight. Before buying a pack, try it on and make sure it fits correctly. Use all the resources available to you at your local hiking retailer to pack as light as possible. Check before leaving whether the places you'll be staying provide bedding and a towel (of course, if you're camping that's a totally different matter, but still pack light). The same goes for food; carry only what you need. Check ahead regarding what's available on the trail as to accommodations and places to eat. I carry 2.5 liters of water.

When packing, I ask myself, "Do I want to be carrying this on day two after the first fifteen-mile day?" If you don't think you can carry all your gear, on some trails you can find luggage transport. There is a reliable service available on the Wicklow Way website.[31]

Wear the Best Clothing for Hiking

The best clothing for backpacking is moisture wicking and quick drying. Laundry facilities are usually a luxury. Be prepared to wash a few things in the sink. Depending on where you're hiking, raingear is highly recommended. If rain or snow is likely, gaiters can be very helpful in keeping boots and feet dry. Gaiters are worn over the top of your boots and pants; some are ankle high, and others go all the way to the bottom of the knee.

Prepare Your Body

I walk twenty-five miles a week, every week of the year. When preparing for a pilgrimage, beginning four months before going, I'll add five miles a week each month. Two months before the pilgrimage, I start walking every day with my pack loaded with the weight I'll carry on the trip. At the two-month mark, I'll do two ten- to twelve-mile hikes every other week, with elevations similar to what I walk on the trail. The month before I leave, I'll do the longer hikes in back-to-back days. I also do strength training three days a week and yoga twice a week.

Make a Plan

Two of my young pilgrim friends told me, "If you want the trip to differ from a typical vacation, you will have the most success if you make a plan. We made beaded trinkets, one for every day on the trail, to leave at a special place. This became a ritual for us. During the time we were on pilgrimage, we would make a special intention for each day. We also wrote and drew on our trip, packing special journals for the pilgrimage. During downtime it was tempting to go straight to the bar or to bed, but setting an intention ahead of time directed us to fulfilling our goals for the pilgrimage." Good advice from some experienced pilgrims.

Reading

While you're reading about being on pilgrimage, it's very good to learn about the history and lore of the place you'll be walking. Here is a list of books I have found helpful in preparing to take a pilgrimage:

- *The Art of Pilgrimage: The Seeker's Guide to Making Travel Sacred,* by Phil Cousineau; foreword by Huston Smith. Cousineau is an experienced leader of pilgrimages to several sites around the world. The book is a best seller, filled with stories of those who have traveled with him.
- *Backpacking with the Saint: Wilderness Hiking as Spiritual Practice,* by Belden Lane. Lane is a retired professor of theology. He has hiked the mountains of Missouri, Arizona, and the Northwest. His reflections on saints range from Christian monk Thomas Merton to Buddhist monk Thich Nhat Hanh, from Teilhard de Chardin to Rumi.
- *Pilgrimage—The Sacred Art: Journey to the Center of the Heart,* by Sheryl A. Kujawa-Holbrook. The author presents a historical exploration of the interfaith history of pilgrimage. In the second half of the book she explores the "intention" of pilgrimage.
- *Pilgrim Poems,* by David Whyte, who may be one of the best contemporary Irish poets.
- The Poems of R.S. Thomas, especially "Pilgrimages" and "The Moon in Llyen."
- *The Alchemist,* by Paulo Coelho. Any would-be pilgrim should read this classic.

CHAPTER 2

⋮

The Long Days of Walking

The dreamer goes for a walk and finds a blue flower. To go for a long walk is to wander along paths that lead to nowhere in particular; it is both a search and a process.

—*Carl Jung*[32]

I n the summer of 2014, our Saint Brigid's group of thirteen friends set off on my sixtieth birthday pilgrimage. The first day, we began walking along a lovely, flat, tree-lined paved path in Marley Park, just outside Dublin. The first hour of the pilgrimage was filled with exuberant chatter. Our excitement of finally getting started was laced with anxiety about the unknown. Within two miles, we began what would become the daily process of hiking up and down two or three peaks of 1,000 to 1,500 feet. Even climbing that first steep hill up Dublin Mountain, there was lots of conversation among the group. The sky was clear that day and everybody was stopping to catch their breath and to take pictures of Dublin Bay. Gradually, the group strung out in single file and silence set in. Near the end of the day, three of our pilgrims got out ahead of us and missed the turnoff to the hostel where we would spend the night. At some point they decided to wait for us, thinking we were probably only a mile behind them. A few hours later they found their way back to the hostel just in time for dinner.

Within a few days, the trail was already taking its toll on our pilgrims. Packs seemed heavier, boots tighter, the trail rougher. Blisters could not be ignored. Backs were sore, knees creaking under the strain.

"Why do we start every day walking almost straight uphill?" Candace said.

"I guess because we finished the day before walking downhill?" I said.

"Smart ass," she said. "Okay, so how far have we walked today?"

"I don't know. Maybe five or six miles."

"We've walked 8.9 miles," my daughter corrected me. She was wearing a FitBit.

"Okay Gil, do you really have any idea how much further it is to our hostel?"

"I don't know, maybe another five or six miles."

Candace said, "You've walked this before, right?"

"Yeah. Three times."

"So how come you never know how far it is?"

"Maybe because Irish miles are longer than English miles," I said.

"You're so full of shit," Candace laughed. "Well, maybe not totally. The last few years I've listened to all your Irish stories and truthfully, the whole time I thought you were so full of shit. I mean I've hiked all over Alaska and lived in a tent for a month. I figured this pilgrimage stuff couldn't be near as tough as you were making it out to be. But, I'll admit, this is everything you said it was, and more. I guess you're not totally as full of shit as I thought. But still."

"Thanks Candace. That's the nicest thing anyone has said to me in a long time."

Danielle said, "Enough of the love fest. Gil, my blisters have gotten worse, can you work on them some more?"

"Sure, find a place to sit down and take off your boots."

Danielle had bought her boots months before we started the pilgrimage and had put in a lot of miles hiking in the Phoenix area. Her boots had molded well to her feet. But after the first day walking out of Dublin, she had a serious blister on her left heel. By the end of the second day, she had multiple blisters on both heels. I'd been nursing her feet every morning. Now they needed attention twice a day.

I told her, "I don't know how you're still walking. You're one tough cookie, I'll tell you. I don't think I could keep going with all these blisters."

"Have you had any blisters on your walks?" she asked.

"I've been pretty lucky. So far I haven't."

"Do you think it's my boots that's causing my blisters?" she asked.

"I don't know. If we'd been walking in a lot of rain, maybe—but it's been dry. Could be the daily pounding? You probably didn't do much back-to-back hiking at home. That could be it—whatever it is, doesn't matter—you're here now and you're still guttin' it out."

"Are your boots that much better than mine?"

"Mine are leather. They're Zamberlan's, Italian, expensive. But worth it. I've put a lot of miles on them—maybe six hundred. I'm on my second set of soles. It's weird, but my boots and I have become best friends. I don't know what I'm going do when they finally wear out.

"Last year I was at this writing workshop on Whidbey Island, in Seattle. It was one of those things where everybody brought rough drafts and we spent a week critiquing our stuff. It was awesome. Anyway, there was a guy whose writing I really admired. His stuff was relaxed and comfortable, like he was telling the story over a cup of coffee. His first essay was entitled "Boots." It was a story about his annual visit to his daughter who lived in Spain, near the Camino de Santiago. Every time he visited her, he would spend a few days walking the Camino. He'd been wearing the same pair of boots for a few years.

"Every summer he'd pull his boots out of the closet. Clean them up. Get them all ready for his trip to Spain. Then one year, he noticed the boots were showing a lot of wear. At the end of his story, he said his boots were worn out—so he left them at a hostel. He told the owner if someone came along who needed the boots they were welcome to them. I couldn't believe it. I was in shock. Disbelief actually. Who leaves their boots behind? I mean, I guess, if . . . when . . . my boots wear out, I could retire them. But I don't think I could bring myself to leave them here in Ireland, all alone."

"Jesus, Gil, you're not gonna cry are you?" Danielle laughed.

"The thought of my boots wearing out depresses me."

"That doesn't take much for you."

"Nice."

"Sorry."

"Okay, I think I've got your blisters bandaged up. You're good to go."

"Really, I shouldn't have said that about depression."

"No worries. You can buy the first pint tonight."

The rest of the pilgrimage I tended Danielle's blisters, as well as those of others in our group. Feet and knees were getting worse with every step. My own body was suffering a bit from the walk. I'd never had blisters before, but one popped up on my big toe the last day of that pilgrimage. Maybe I was having sympathy pains. Possibly I was experiencing what novelist and Inkling Charles Williams (1886–1945) called the "exchange of love"—through the act of healing we take on the pain of others. Who knows? Pilgrimage walking works the mind, body, soul, and spirit. By the time we had finished that last day, my boots were showing some serious wear. The edge of the boots where the soles and the leather were adhered was separating.

I sent my boots back to the guy who did the first resoling and asked if he could repair them a second time. He told me the leather where the upper part of the boots and the soles were sealed together was getting too soft. That, he said, came from the boots getting wet on the inside and not having a proper chance to dry before continuing to hike in them. I knew exactly the day that happened.

A Long Day Walking and the Beginnings of Letting Go

August 3, 2012. I was nearing the end of my solo 353-mile trek across Ireland. I had left the village of Millstreet that morning in a drizzle. I was within fifty miles of the southwestern coast of Ireland and the seagulls were becoming more prevalent each day. I passed the familiar yellow hiking marker when I left the hostel. But I had a strange feeling I was going in the wrong direction— an ominous beginning for a long day. I stopped and asked a young couple for directions. After a few minutes of looking at my map, they got me back on the right path. I turned around and walked the mile back into the village, past the hostel, and towards the other side of the small town.

As I was walking over the bridge leaving Millstreet, heading towards the Claragh Mountain, a woman stopped her car beside me. She rolled down the window. Told me she was familiar with the hiking trails in the area and asked me if I knew where I was going. I told her I was walking to Shrone and would appreciate her advice. She got out of her car and rummaged through the trunk, looking for some maps. After a bit of searching, she closed the trunk lid.

"Hmm, must have given them all away," she said.

She went on to tell me the hills were filled with multiple loops for walking. She warned me to make sure I was always following the correct markers or else I'd end up right back where I was standing. I thanked her without telling her I had already walked in the wrong direction once that morning.

The trek up the mountain was through a dense forest. I saw four different loop markers within the first mile, each with a different colored arrow. One was the Claragh Loop, another the Blackwater Way, which would lead me to Shrone. The other two arrows were nameless. Before I reached the top of the Claragh Mountain, my route turned onto the northern shoulder of the mountain, which would take me up and out of the forest. The western Irish mountains are filled with forests, pocketed with bald spots covered in brush or bog, sometimes both. By the looks of what I had to step over, the trail was also the path of the local sheep and cattle. The mist turned into rain. The already muddy trail began to flow like a small stream, sometimes ankle deep. I could feel the rain running down my soaked pant legs into my boots.

The trail turned off the shoulder and up toward the top of the mountain. The wind was blowing the rain sideways into my face. Plodding up the narrow path, I met some sheep coming down the trail. When the leader saw me, she stopped, and the six others bunched up behind her. Awkwardly they reversed direction and started up the trail in front of me. In a mile or so the rain got so heavy my woolen friends sought cover under the low brush. I would have followed suit but there wasn't any room for me. I imagined my more intelligent hiking buddies were amused by or (I hoped) sympathetic of my situation. Eventually, I did find some refuge under a low-hanging tree where I squatted against a stone wall. There, I waited for a half hour until the rain let up a bit. The rest of the path took me down the mountain through three fenced pastures. At each field, I had to climb under a hot wire that was used to keep the sheep and cattle in their respective pastures. Now, I was not only soaked but also covered in mud.

I had been walking four hours. Finally, the path dumped me out onto a paved road on the south side of the Claragh Mountain. Once again, I was confronted with four different way markers. This time they were all the same color, all pointing east. My map seemed to indicate that the trail would quickly turn south then west towards Shrone. So I followed what I thought was the correct yellow marker, hoping the trail would turn south and then west.

Three hours later I was standing at the top of a hill amidst twenty-one wind turbines, each 140 meters tall (459 feet). I stood facing a warning sign that read, "Gneeves Wind Farm, Highly Dangerous, Threat of Death from Falling, Drowning, and Electrocution." I'm not the smartest person in the world but I knew I was in the wrong place.

I backtracked down the hill two miles to the last yellow way marker I had seen. The marker was at a T-juncture of two roads in front of a barn. Fortunately two farmers were inside the barn working on some machinery. I'm fairly sure they were speaking Gaelic to each other.

"Excuse me, I need a bit of help."

"Bad day for a hike, hey?" one man said, speaking in a heavy Irish brogue.

I pointed to the way marker in front of their barn. "Are there any other markers up hill?"

They chatted in Gaelic. One answered, "No. Haven't seen any. You shouldn't walk up there. Terribly dangerous, ya know."

"I know. I just walked back from up there. I was following the way markers to Shrone. So where are the markers to Shrone?"

"Shrone?" they chuckled.

"So where does the marker in front of your barn point to?" I asked.

"Nowhere."

"Odd," I said. "So is there a way to Shrone from here?"

"Not up that road," they said. "The junction to Shrone is about eight miles back the other way. Then about another six miles from there."

"I've been walking about eight hours. I don't think I have another fourteen miles in me. Where's the nearest village I can walk to? I think I need to call my wife to pick me up. I just need to be somewhere that she can find on a map."

"The closest village is Millstreet."

"That's where I started this morning," I said, probably looking very pathetic.

"I'll give you a ride," one of them offered.

I wanted to cry, but I knew if they saw any tears, they'd figure I was not so much lost as weird. When he dropped me off near Millstreet, I pulled out my wallet to pay him. He waved me off. I thanked him profusely.

As I crawled out of his truck, he said, "Luck *maith*."

"Thanks, I need some good luck."

I am continually astounded and thankful for that man's hospitality. I think it's simply the Irish way of living, moving, and having their being in this world.

My wife found me easily. When we arrived at the bed and breakfast, the hostess suggested that Cathy fetch me some dry clothes. She didn't want me walking up the stairs of her house in my muddy boots and soaked clothes, carrying my drenched pack. The kind hostess gave me a pile of newspapers to stuff in my boots, which I hoped would soak up the water. She also lent us a hairdryer to help dry out the leather uppers. The next day I thought the boots were dry enough to make the trek. My wife took me back near where she had picked me up the day before and I continued my walk across Ireland.

Now, two years later, my boots were showing the ill effects of having been soaked from the inside out and me not giving them the proper time to dry. Boots are more than a piece of equipment. Boots are companions that care for the most abused body part of the pilgrimage. The feet bear the pilgrim's burden of walking miles on end. The weight of the backpack translates exponentially on the feet. Good boots ease the pressure. Well-made boots will also protect the ankles from twisting in rugged terrain. Excellent boots prevent rocks from cutting into the sole of the foot. The best boots repel rain water. But when you're walking in water, any boot will suffer.

Through all the miles I've walked, I've fallen in love with my boots. The relationship I have with them is like trusting my lover with my heart. I can't imagine leaving by boots alone, in some hostel, by the side of road, for someone else to use. I guess one day they'll simply wear out beyond repair. On that heartbreaking day, I'll have to retire them to the Boots Hall of Fame—that sad day, I'll have to let go of a pair of very good pilgrimage friends.

The Egg Begins to Crack

The heat of a pilgrimage can begin to soften the hard metals of our attachments, making possible the readiness to let go. I must let go of the idea that these boots are the only boots I can or will ever wear. When these special boots, the ones I've walked across Ireland in, wear out, I'm not going to quit walking. I will buy another pair, a new pair. When we are willing to begin letting go of what we thought we never would—ideas, dogmas, and objects—we experience something more profound than transformation; it's what the alchemists called transmutation. The transmutation starts with heating the elements—the idea of letting go of what frightens me for some reason. The heat brings that element to the surface, in this case my attachment to my favorite boots, which is really my romance with Ireland. I extract my memories of past pilgrimages, realizing my hope for new experiences is tied up in my past. I then re-integrate that new bit of realization, and I buy another pair of boots. This process might seem rather silly when it concerns buying a new pair of boots. But, let's say I'm dealing with letting go of a long-held religious idea; or moving on from a community I have long cherished; or letting go of the self-loathing I wear so well (like my old boots). Carrying those thoughts around while I'm walking a pilgrimage could result in the transmutation of my ideas into something that better represents who I am becoming as an integrated person. (I'll deal more with transmutation later in this chapter.)

The physical, emotional, psychic, and spiritual heat created by the daily grind of the pilgrimage begins to heat life's elements: the stuff in life we carry around with us every day. The heat is created by the hours, days, and multiple miles stacked on top of one another. The miles of pilgrimage begin to move us towards a new way of thinking. But we must be patient, slowly letting go of old ideas. Too much too fast, and the process can burst into flames. That's why we need the slow application of heat, which will move us through the many shades of the dark storm in the first phase, where our senses are on keen alert. This phase of chaos will finally take on the many hues of a storm. A dark silver around the edge of the stormy clouds will emerge. It's like looking at a raven's wing in the sun and discovering that the vast shades of darkness include translucence. The heat begins the transmutation of our ego's metals, making possible the second phase of the alchemical pilgrimage, which cracks open the egg of the soul. Here, our thoughts begin processing what our senses have been experiencing.

The heat of this second stage, the cracking of the egg, is like the warmth of smoldering coals, hot enough to roast a marshmallow, but cool enough to touch for just a few seconds. The gentle heat causes the things to rise to the surface that hold us back from individuation—the maturing work of moving into the second half of life. In this phase of life, we begin the process of recognizing the old ways that confine us, the things we've hidden in our shadow. The shadow contains those thoughts and experiences we have repressed, neglected. These are from the negative side of ourselves that we have avoided or have been unwilling to acknowledge in our lives. Things like rage, anxiety, self-loathing, lack of confidence, fear of rejection, selfishness, bigotry, sexism, rigid fundamentalism, and countless other issues we have been unwilling to admit are an unhealthy part of our lives. Whatever is preventing us from our process of individuation needs to be brought to the surface, examined, re-formulated, and then re-integrated into our lives in a healthy form.

You might be wondering why someone would want to re-integrate any-thing negative. Why not just purge it from our lives? The truth is, we can't fully get rid of those things that have become ingrained in our psyche. We must acknowledge these negative characteristics, own them, examine them, re-imagine them, and then re-integrate them in a new form into our life. James Hillman writes about the second phase as being the place where the chaos is transmuted through the varying shades of blue, from midnight, to oceanic, to the sky, which becomes a bluish-silver of the desert air on its way to becoming gold. "Transmutation to silver means cleansing and purifying, which at the same time means becoming more essential and durable."[33] He goes on to say that the issues we struggle with are more than mere inanimate pieces of ore, dead matter, but are instead "vital seeds, embodiments of soul; not objective facts but subjective factors."[34]

Over the years I've often been frustrated by my inability to let go of unre-solved self-directed anger. I have worked on this issue with my therapist and spiritual director. At some points I thought I had a handle on an outburst that would happen at the most unwanted and awkward times. But somewhere along the way, I put the self-loathing anger back in my pack. I felt like I was trapped on a loop trail in my struggle with anger issues, always thinking I was headed towards my destination, only to sadly realize I was back where I had started. I felt like I was never going to be able to fully set down the anger and get rid of the self-hatred.

But my work of alchemically heating the anger in order to bring it to the surface so that I could observe it, acknowledge it, work with it, reform it, and then re-integrate it in a healthy manner has helped me find a way to release the burdens of self-hatred. At the same time, I have been able to maintain a necessary component of appropriate anger. Truly, hours on the trail have burned away much of the self-loathing that has been holding me back in my own individuation process.

The day I got off track on my way to Shrone, I was fuming with self-loathing. I beat myself up—something I'd become really good at over the years. It usually started with, "You stupid shit, why didn't you learn how to read maps like all the good Boy Scouts? Playing sports in school isn't helping you now. You should've been more like Bruce. He was a great Boy Scout. He could read maps. But oh no, not Gil. No, you had to play baseball. What good is that now?"

But standing in front of that sign at the top of Gneeves Wind Farm, warning me about the threat of death, I began to realize that self-anger was not going to help me; in fact it was the real threat at that moment. I needed to be calm so that I could use all my abilities and resources to make good decisions. If my mind was clouded with anger, I could have decided to press on, to prove I knew where I was going. And that need to prove myself worthy and capable could have gotten me killed. But, in a moment of realization, I decided to turn around and walk back to the last marker I saw and ask for help. That's when the elements of my self-loathing were swirling in the cauldron together with my experience of walking Ireland, the experience of having been lost before, the experience of having asked for help many times. I was able to confront the uselessness of self-loathing. My self-hatred began to rise to the surface where it could be burned by the rising heat of psychic alchemy. The self-reproach could be extracted, re-formed, and re-integrated in a healthy manner. Don't get me wrong, not all the sixty-plus years of self-reproach disappeared at that moment, or have since. Slowly, though, it continues to rise to the surface where it is much easier to recognize, confront, extract, re-form, and then re-integrate. Almost every time some inkling of self-reproach appears, I find myself standing in front of that Grieves Farm warning sign making a conscious decision about my next step.

Anger, in the appropriate context, is not a bad element of the human character. Indeed, rage, self-reproach, and violence form the dangerous and destructive side of anger. Those threatening components of anger need to be exposed to the heat, seen for what they are, re-imagined as something valuable, and then re-integrated as anger at injustice, oppression, and the exploitation of other people. This new kind of anger, what the community organizers call cold-anger, can be an asset in life. Herein lies the value of the second phase; this is the place where the egg of the soul can be cracked open, where a sliver of light can shine into our womb of darkness. We cannot live in the egg of the womb forever. Safe as it might feel, we will eventually die in the entrapment of the egg. The light shining in through the crack is what will bring us new life. We must step through the crack into that bit of light because this is where we can begin to do the hard work of recognizing, re-forming, and re-imagining those things that could destroy us. What could have killed me would now be something to use in service for the good of others. Letting go of what holds us back will bring us a liberating new future.

Re-imagining What Was as What Will Be

I've walked the Wicklow Way four times. Twice I've walked with a group of people, Saint Brigid's Community and Vox Peregrini. Each experience was different. But the path remained relatively the same. There aren't any villages along the thirty-three miles of the Wicklow Way from Glendalough to Shillelagh. Walking south out of the Glendalough valley, our Saint Brigid's group started with a steep climb that turns into a relatively comfortable twelve-mile hike south to Glenmalure, the official halfway point of the Wicklow Way. For hundreds of years, this region of rugged and heavy forest had been a famous hideout for Irish rebels and outlaws. Now, the Glenmalure lodge, built in 1801, is host to hikers, fishermen, and outdoor enthusiasts. The next day's walk out of Glenmalure is an eighteen-mile hike to the hamlet of Moyne, which was probably the name of the original settler or landowner of that farmland.

It was a rare sunny day in Ireland when we walked from Glenmalure to Moyne. The heat was stifling, what the Irish call "close." Sticky and tired, we stopped for lunch after about four hours. I had spent twenty minutes after lunch working on Danielle's sore and blistered feet. We had already made our way up and down two major hills of a thousand feet each. And now, we had one more climb ahead of us. Near the end of the day, a few of our pilgrims ran out of water. We were sweaty, thirsty, and exhausted. Finally we were able to drop our packs in front of our B&B, Kyle's Farmhouse.

"So how far do you think we walked today?" my daughter asked.

"I don't know. Maybe fourteen miles."

"Seventeen point eight, to be exact," she said, looking at her FitBit.

"Write that down somewhere, Gil. I know you keep a journal," Candace said.

Our hostess was quick to greet us with pitchers of water, lemonade, and homemade cupcakes. In all my travels across Ireland I have rarely been disappointed by the hospitality. We were staying in the Kyle's home on their working farm. We had walked past the milking barn on our way up the road to their house. Cows were resting in a pasture a hundred yards from the house. Chickens were clucking around the yard. I had stayed at their farmhouse before and had been encouraging our group through the long day by telling them about Mrs. Kyle's amazing meals. That night, dinner exceeded my buildup. She offered three options: fish, chicken, and vegetarian. The bread was freshly baked. The vegetables had been picked from her garden that morning. While there wasn't Guinness on draught, there was plenty of wine. The day had been overwhelming. Now it was time to process the day. Somewhere before the rhubarb pie and coffee were served, Danielle started her story.

The Pain of Pilgrimage Brings Healing

"These last two days, I think I've kind of found my pace. With all my blisters has come an odd rhythm to the walking. It vacillates between, 'Oh dear God take this weight and pain from my body' and 'I don't feel the heaviness of my pack.' It's like I'm getting used to the weight of the walk. It's like I have two sides of my personality and they are trying to make sense of the experience. There's an odd mixture of the pain of walking and the comfort of healing.

"Honestly, guys, my boots were well broken-in before I got here. I'd done a lot of hiking before we started. I truly never expected to have these bad blisters. It's been weird. You know. The second morning, a few of you set up a sort of makeshift triage area outside our hostel. Gil, Becky, and Rhonda prepped, bandaged, and wrapped our blisters, sprains, bruises, and scrapes. This morning I began to realize the routine of dressing my wounds was really a ritual. Hands were washed, supplies were gathered, and a mere glance from Gil signaled he was ready to work on my blisters. Sitting on a bench, outside the hostel, felt sacred, but at the same time, awkward. I focused my attention on the healer's hands: slow, confident, and calming. It became a sort of morning meditation, a prayer for healing and hope for another day of safe walking."

We sat in silence for a few minutes, soaking in Danielle's reflection. Then she continued her story.

"I have worked hard over the last several years to heal from the wounds I've collected through the course of my life." Tears filled her eyes, but she steadied her voice.

"Some of my wounds are deep and they have needed a lot time to heal. Others were more like flesh wounds, superficial yet wide and at times equally as painful as the deep ones. The trouble with these sorts of wounds is that if you don't bandage them correctly they begin to fester. Sooner or later the ignored or mishandled emotional injuries take their toll and a systemic infection sets in. That's the way it's been with me. Years of not tending to my feelings netted a sort of emotional sepsis, leaving me in a cycle of outbursts, anger, and depression.

"At a very low point I reached out for healing. My triage area was set up, healers emerged, sacred space was created, and rituals developed. Just as when my feet were getting tended to, the process of emotional healing was at times uncomfortable, even painful, and almost always awkward, but I tried to stay focused on the slow, confident calmness of the healers.

"While walking, I've realized healing and wholeness have arrived—and perhaps more importantly that I need to accept the healthy me and honor the work I have done to get here. At times the seductive nature of my wounds opens again and I find myself with the temptation to hold on to old hurts or, more damaging, the role of martyr, wallowing in my own brokenness. In so many ways, I can see myself in other people who define themselves by their victimhood. This pilgrimage has caused me to acknowledge that I don't want to get stuck in a cycle of reliving my hurts and reopening my wounds. More significantly, I've realized, it's really okay to let them go."

There were tears in a few eyes. I imagined all of us could connect with Danielle's story on some level. We all have wounds, scars, untended business we've been thinking about on the trail. The weariness of walking brought our emotions to the surface. The exhaustion of the day allowed us to feel comfortable with the silence between the stories. We needed the time to process what we'd experienced and what we'd heard.

Mrs. Kyle quietly cleared the table. I wondered if she had sensed the depth of our conversations. She served more coffee. No one talked—just a few whispers to pass the cream and sugar.

Make Your Own Damn Pilgrimage

Blair is a tall, athletic young woman. She has run a few marathons and spent plenty of time backpacking. She's a neuroscientist, currently doing brain research on autistic adults. She'd left her religiously conservative roots in her Kentucky home when she moved to Tempe to attend Arizona State University five years before. She's rarely the first one to speak in any group conversation. It often takes her a while to open up. But that evening, she had a lot to say.

"I get it about letting go. Weird thing is, what I had to let go of was my expectations about this pilgrimage. I spent quite a bit of time and energy before the trip setting my intentions. I wanted a deeply spiritual pilgrimage. Day two, walking across White Hill, has been the highlight of my spiritual adventure so far. It was that point, where we were walking along that frighteningly narrow path, on the side of that uncomfortably steep hill. That's when those huge billowing clouds rushed over us. I stopped and turned to face the misty air. That's when I threw my arms wide open to welcome the wind and the clouds. Looking straight up at the sky, I felt as though I was fully enveloped by God's top-shelf, best-of-the-line fog machine—a memory I will never forget.

"And that's been it. Not exactly the spiritual journey I was expecting. Here I am with deeply spiritual people, faithful people who wrestle with their theology, and the main topic of conversation always seems to be about Guinness. I mean, we read a quick morning prayer every day before beginning the hike, which is lovely, but that's it, nothing else is planned. I've caught a few cool conversations with some of you, including my priest, who I thought would open the door to some special spiritual revelations. But nothing has come close to rocking my soul to the core that I had hoped. Honestly, Candace and I are both struggling with our expectations. About midway today, seemingly unrelated to our hopes for the pilgrimage, she told me a story. Once on a weekend visit to a friend, a priest noticed that every day, his host bought a jar of peanut butter, a jar of jelly, and a loaf of bread, and made sandwiches for the homeless. The priest thought this was such a wonderful act of kindness that when he got home he wrote a check to his friend with the subject line reading, 'for your sandwiches,' and sent it in the mail. About a week later the check was returned to him with a note that read, 'Make your own damn sandwiches.' I don't remember why she was actually telling me this story but at the moment she finished, something broke inside me. What had I expected on this trip? For my priest and others to walk through the forests of Ireland, channel God, and spoon-feed her to me? I realized I needed to start making my own damn sandwiches. It was a beautiful realization. The rest of the afternoon I had several beautiful moments between me and God."

I've been on enough pilgrimages with groups to expect the stories and the silence that follows. Everyone had walked up the edge of White Hill, along the dangerous, narrow path. Each of us had walked through the clouds at different moments. I wondered if anyone else would tell about their experience in the clouds.

Our imagination can be provoked by someone else's story. But before telling our story, we have to do our own self-reflection on what we sense, think, and feel. When we take the risk to go on pilgrimage we usually are confronted by our expectations somewhere on the walk. That's when we have to face our self—who we really are—and what we actually need. In those places along the walk, those moments of self-reflection, is where the soul-shaping takes place.

Why Isn't Jesus Carrying My Pack?

Erik was the youngest guy on our pilgrimage. He taught Greek, Latin, and classical literature to high school students. He's lean and strong. His long brown hair covers his eyes and his beard hides a slight smile. Erik had rarely spoken a word to the group on the entire trip.

Then out of seemingly nowhere he said, "So Gil, what was that stuff you told me while we were walking up that slick hill today?"

"You mean that slick spot where I slipped and nose planted myself in the mud?"

"Yeah. That spot. After you fell, you didn't finish what you were saying."

"Okay, so give me a clue what I was talking about?"

"Re-integration."

"Right, okay. Well, my experience of being on pilgrimage is that our long days of walking will create a spiritual heat in our souls. The longer I walk, the hotter it gets, and the more my stuff comes to the surface. There, I can examine it for what it is and then what I imagine it can be. It's exactly what Blair was describing. She had a certain expectation. Then she examined that expectation in light of her experience of actually walking this pilgrimage. She re-imagined the expectation and then re-integrated it. She moved from the point where someone else was going to channel God for her, to a place of engaging her own work of the spiritual pilgrimage.

"I think the difference between letting go and what I'm describing, which is the alchemical process of cracking open the egg, is more than semantics. Letting go means that I probably will take back up whatever I originally tried to set down—nothing has changed. There are things that I thought I had let go of, but they never seem to really disappear. In the second phase, though, as the heat from my pilgrimage rises, the things I want to let go of become hot enough to float on the surface so that I can see them. I can scoop them up. Look at them. Re-mold them and then re-integrate this newly imagined part of my Self as something very useful in my life. Danielle has been re-imagining her felt need to keep reliving her pain. She will never really be able to let go of those past experiences as if they never happened. But if she keeps working with those past experiences, she will be able to re-imagine the pain, then, as a source of strength instead. Once she can do that work of re-integration, she will be set free from the old cycle of reliving the pain."

Danielle said, "If that's what's happening, then all the money and blisters might be worth it."

Erik began to tell his story. The words came out as if he had replayed them a thousand times in his head. It was as if he had written this secret story and now, during the pilgrimage, he was free to tell us about his painful experience.

"Less than a year ago, the wisest person I have ever met—a bright but humble and utterly selfless young woman with whom I believed I was going to spend the rest of my life—passed away in her sleep. Unfortunately, I was on vacation on what I had anticipated would be my last journey without her.

"It's odd, I haven't wrestled as much with the question of how a loving God could allow this to happen. Instead, I have thought a lot about what vengeance would be sufficient to unleash upon the callous God that allows people to spout clichés about God's supposed plan.

"I've struggled with whether my own life still holds any meaning. I learned slowly and painfully over the course of several months which people are really my friends and which ones only pretend to be. My seemingly immature and sometimes rowdy high school students proved to be in the former column and my boss in the latter.

"I felt like I had lost everything. My grief overwhelmed me. My boss thought that I shouldn't bring my pain to work and that I should have been able to move on. That's when I lost my job.

"I had just bought a home that I could only afford on the salary of the teaching job I'd just lost—the job that was the only reason I came to live in Arizona in the first place. And then, of course, there is my family. Why, they asked, was I about to throw away my entire savings, and even borrow money, for what they thought was a privileged vacation? They thought I should have been hanging onto every dollar just to keep my house. But I needed to go on this pilgrimage. Even though it was a crazy idea—actually because it was a crazy idea, I knew it would work.

"Since I was going to burn through my savings, I decided to come to Ireland early. The iconic moment that helped me understand what pilgrimage is all about came two weeks before we started the Wicklow Way. I climbed Ireland's highest peak, the Carrauntoohil, 3,400 feet. It's on the western slope of Ireland in Kerry National Park. It was supposed to be an easy shuttle bus ride to the trailhead, a six-hour leisurely climb up and down, and an evening recovering at the pub watching the World Cup. Instead, the shuttle bus turned out never to have existed. Needless to say, the day ended much later than I had antici- pated. At last, though, I stood atop the mountain, fittingly before the large iron cross that is the highest object on the island. I looked to the east, across seven mountains that I could barely believe were passable to anything less sure-footed than sheep, and I realized something: Every single one of them had been my test, and I had passed. There is truly no feeling more incredible than knowing you have walked every single bit of that trail.

"I realized then that my pilgrimage really began when I decided to move to Arizona. I have learned that my guide has not been the fake Jesus of the Christianity I used to follow, the one who swoops in and picks up his followers whenever the trail gets rough. If my guide is Christ, it's the one who works in inexplicable and frustrating ways, who shows up in the form of people whom the world doesn't recognize as Christians—like my late beloved. He is Christ who has trained us. Now we have to walk. I imagine that he derives far more satisfaction from sitting atop the cliff, watching his protégés pick their way across rocky trails without an ounce of help from him. He said we have to carry our own cross. I wouldn't have Him, or Her, any other way."

We sat in silence for a long time, sipping wine and coffee. Words spoken would have sounded like a wine glass dropped on the tile floor. But we were all exhausted, and someone had to give us permission to find our way to bed. Tomorrow would come too early.

"Good night," was all I could muster.

I went back to my room, desperately needing some sleep. But I couldn't stop thinking about the stories I'd heard that night. I know the things Danielle, Blair, and Erik talked about, the letting go, the pain, the re-imagining, the re- integration—seemed to be just about each of them individually. But I couldn't stop wondering if what I was really hearing was that they were beginning to discover what spirituality and community might look like after their walking was over.

We were walking as individuals but we were walking together. We were alone but we were in community. Our spirituality, what we call our relation- ship to the divine, was being shaped by the experience of being on pilgrimage with one another. I had walked a pilgrimage alone, in solitude with my thoughts and feelings. Then, at night, I would tell my wife what I had experi- enced that day on the walk. But we had not shared those experiences together on the trail. I was telling her something for which she had no context. Now that my wife has walked the Wicklow Way, we hear our stories of our individual experiences from a re-imagined perspective. Walking with Danielle, Blair, Erik, and the others gave us a common narrative. We were characters in the same story. We could understand each other's personal experiences at a deeper level because we were bound together by the context of the pilgrimage. Our personal spirituality was taking shape within a community.

The concepts and practices of spirituality and community do have life cycles. They are born, go through adolescence, become adults, grow old, and then die. And both can experience evolving levels of maturity, what Jung calls individuation. When our personal spirituality and our communities go through the process of the alchemical stages, they both must endure the heat of pilgrimage in order to be transmuted (heated, extracted, re-formed, re-integrated). My spirituality, my relationship with the divine, has gone through the phases of alchemy several times during my life. But I wondered what that process might look like for a community.

My Spirituality in the Alchemical Brew

When I woke up the next morning, my head was spinning with questions. Is there such a thing as a group spirituality—in other words, does a group have a collective connection with the divine? If so, can a group evolve in its spirituality? And if a group can evolve in its spirituality, can it collectively progress through the alchemical stages? I felt like a spiritual anthropologist. I thought maybe the best place to start answering my questions about a group spiritual evolution was to explore my own evolution. I thought if I could delve into my past personal journey that might lead to some ideas about the dynamic of the group maturation process. Walking sixteen miles a day, I had a lot of time to think.

I was born into a Christian family. My parents faithfully took my sister and me to a Southern Baptist church near where we lived in Phoenix, Arizona. I would consider my parents to have been on the progressive side of the Southern Baptist Convention (SBC), but in general they were still theologically conservative. My wife and I got married when we were eighteen. We kept attending the same church because of my parent's strong encouragement. And besides, Cathy played the organ and we had friends our own age at the church. After we finished college, we moved to another town and joined the local Southern Baptist church there. I had my fits and restarts with Southern

Baptist theology and its way of life, but we stayed in the church. In a few years, when I was twenty-seven, we moved back to Phoenix where I took a job at Grand Canyon University. GCU was a Southern Baptist college at that time. By the time I was forty, though, SBC theology and life had become too narrow. I began to deconstruct my religious beliefs. I broke down my faith to its basic elements, trying to eliminate any stifling dogma. Once I got to the ground floor, I took on the question of the existence of God. My deconstruction left me with what I valued most, my experience of the divine. My experiences of God felt real and worth holding on to, while the teachings and orthodoxy of the church seemed unnecessary. We stayed, however, in the Southern Baptist church, mostly because of the university's requirement that I be a member of the SBC. But it wasn't long before I started the deconstruction phase again. I felt like religion and the church were obscuring my spiritual experience and hindering my ability to reflect upon a relationship with the divine.

Finally, I changed Christian denominations. I thought some new scenery might help. I left the Southern Baptist church in my mid-forties to become an Episcopalian—a very liberal Episcopalian. Fifteen-plus years later, I now find the Episcopal Church, and the universal Christian church, as well as the Christian religion in general, lacking, incomplete. For me, Christianity does not contain the entire possibility of my experience. I am sensing a deep hunger; but not for another cycle of deconstruction and reconstruction. This time I'm looking for a re-imagination of what a life of faith might look like for me in the last few chapters of my life.

A friend told me that being born into a religion is like belonging to a tribe—hard to leave and even if we do find an exit point, the markings of the tribe are indelible. I wear the tattoos of the Christian tribe, but I am beyond the fringe of the fringe. It is there, just beyond the outer ring of Christianity, where I hope to re-imagine what an evolved Christianity might look like, what Dietrich Bonhoeffer called "religionless Christianity" in a "world come of age." Bonhoeffer and Jung were contemporaries. Both imagined that the Christian story, while still life changing, would look different in the next eon, the one in which we now live. I have been searching for what that re-imagined story might be.

I guess you might ask why I don't just laser off the markings of Christianity, create a new palette for another story? For one, I doubt any religion has the capacity to contain all expressions of the human experience in relationship with the divine and that includes Christianity. John Shelby Spong, a retired bishop in the Episcopal Church, wrote in his book, *The Fourth Gospel: Tales of a Jewish Mystic*, "God cannot be limited to one mediator."[35] However (and this is my second reason for not totally leaving Christianity), I am very familiar with the Christian and Hebrew myth—and honestly, I'm not finished exploring the depths of those stories. My intimate knowledge of the narrative gives me something to build upon, and reflect against, while I'm considering stories of other faith traditions. I don't use the Christian story as a barometer, but instead as a framework on which to construct other rooms. Jung wrote, "The advocates of Christianity squander their energies on the mere presentation of what has come down to them, with no thought of building their house and making it roomier. Stagnation in this matter is threatened in the long run with a lethal end."[36] I continue to wear the markings of the Christian tribe while I'm working on ways to integrate some of the myths and practices from other more ancient traditions—a way of making my mind, body, soul, and spirit a roomier place to live.

A spiritual pilgrimage is an experience of raw presence, like walking naked in the forest without fear or trepidation. When I am truly vulnerable before the holy soul of creation, I begin to see the divine. I see with the third eye, my intuition, my imagination. In those moments, I get a brief glimpse of the holy. I see and engage with God with all my Self: mind, body, soul, and spirit. Franciscan monk and priest Richard Rohr writes in *The Naked Now*, "God becomes more a verb than a noun, more a process than a conclusion, more an experience than a dogma, more a personal relationship than an idea. There is Someone dancing with you, and you are not afraid of making mistakes."[37] I've had those momentary experiences of dancing with the divine while on a walking pilgrimage. Those instances of wisdom rolling over my soul like a cool, misty Irish cloud continue to sustain me now while I live my life in the desert of Arizona. I want to live life in a constant state of being present to my surroundings, other people, my Self, and the divine. I need a religious container with an expansive vision that includes the language and rituals that nurture life with the divine—through the mundane, exotic, and tragic times of my life. Such a possibility exists within my Christian tradition, but only in the mystical realms. I imagine the same could be said of most religions.

The process of spiritual evolution is never over because there is so much to learn. Like many others, I have had to peel back the layers of my religion that has been handed to me as indisputable fact. That religion had little room for doubt, question, ambiguity, and mystery. I started my re-imagination phase of Christianity by asking questions about Jesus and Judaism.

The Jewish people had suffered captivity and exile under the hands of onerous foreign rulers. Their story had been somewhat influenced by the religions of their captors, as well as those like Zoroaster with ideas about angels and the afterlife. The Jewish religion was an amalgam of thoughts and ideas that splintered into varying sects. By the time Jesus appeared on the scene, there was not a unified way to interpret Hebrew scripture. In fact, Jesus would interpret the Jewish scriptures through an array of lenses, from literal, to allegorical, metaphorical, and the mystical.

Jesus was a mystic, living his life in a swirling dance with the divine. Jesus was a wisdom teacher, mystic, healer, shaman, who called himself the Son of Man in the tradition of the ecstatic mystic Ezekiel. He lived in the cultural crossroads of travelers who exposed him not only to the pagan Roman religion but also to Greek philosophy and Eastern traditions. These outside ideas also contributed to Jesus's and other Jewish thinkers' ways of seeing the world. Jesus became an evolved master in the wisdom tradition. He established his way of living as a model for his followers who wanted that same experience with God. He was not the designer of a new religion; that came at the hands of others after Jesus was killed.

During the first three centuries after Jesus's death, his followers came to be known as Christians. Some Christians identified Jesus as the expected Messiah of Judaism, the anointed one or savior. There were, however, during those first three centuries, various other interpretations of Jesus, many of which were obliterated by the establishment of the Nicene Creed in 381 CE. Even so, the conversation of who Jesus really was, what he said, and what he meant, continues still today. Modern writers like Karen Armstrong, Dietrich Bonhoeffer, Marcus Borg, Cynthia Bourgeault, Matthew Fox, Amy-Jill Levine, Elaine Pagels, Richard Rohr, and John Shelby Spong, just to mention a few, have written about how to approach the divine with the same imagination as Jesus. Like countless others, I am trying to follow the version of the mystical path Jesus created. I trust in his faith and his experience with the divine—not in my belief in Jesus.[38] I have come to understand that Jesus's way of living and his teachings were not about the afterlife, but instead the now life, living life in the present moment. Richard Rohr said in *Immortal Diamond*, "Jesus did not come to change the mind of God about humanity, but to change the mind of humanity about God."[39] Jesus was pointing his followers to living life like they a wisdom pilgrimage. His followers are walking toward God, while at the same time with God—not trapped in a dogma, which lacks a mystical third eye.

The world of the unseen, the mystical, the world we see with the third eye, is a significant part of Jesus's story, but is often left out of the conversation because it seems too non-rational for the enlightened mind. In my opinion, that is unfortunate. The God that Jesus experienced cannot be seen. Jesus was living in what philosopher Ken Wilbur calls in his book, *Integral Spirituality*, "a nondual state of mysticism."[40] Jesus was in union with everything. Why, then, do we ignore someone today who might experience the unseen world? Many Christians have encounters and conversations with the realm of angels. They hear messages from the communion of saints, the dead. The Hebrew story is full of accounts of people's encounters with the world of the unseen, as well as nature's stones, birds, and animals.

Celtic spirituality predates the story of Abraham and has a keen focus on the Creator and its relationship to the Earth and all that is a part of creation. The Celtic pagan story has been woven tightly into the fabric of Irish Christianity. I have already written earlier in this book about the ancient Celtic tradition and its influence on Christianity. Mother Earth, the feminine, Sophia (wisdom), and nature are critical to Celtic spirituality, but for the most part have been sadly cut out of the modern Christian context in the West. The feminine divine has been integral in the creation of all. Are She and Her creation no longer capable of speaking to us? Or are we unwilling to listen? My experience has been that when I open myself to hear from Her and Her creation, the birds, animals, trees, even the stones will cry out and I will hear the voice of the Creator and all Her attributes. "Ask the animals and they will teach you; the birds of the air, and they will teach you, ask the plants of the earth, and they will teach you; and the fish of the sea will declare to you. Who among all these does not know that the hand of the Lord has done this?" (Job 12:7–8). A mystical relationship with the divine through creation lies just outside our door. All we must do is step outside and commune with God's world. This viewpoint has long been a part of the Jewish mystical tradition found in the Kabbalah.

The Kabbalah arose in the mid-thirteenth century. This mystical strand of Judaism has much to offer us about how to encounter the unknowable divine. The Kabbalah's symbolic Tree of Life, the *Sefirot*, provides mystical imagery for the attributes of God. "Spiritual and psychological wholeness is achieved by meditating on the (ten) qualities of the Sefirot, by imitating and integrating the attributes of God."[41] The *Zohar* provides a lyrical canon for the Kabbalah, with its liberating interpretation of the Torah—a basis for Jewish mysticism. While the Kabbalah is cryptic and can be difficult to navigate, the basics do begin to open a window to the masculine and feminine sides of YHWH, as well as the dark side of the divine, much like alchemy. Many alchemists studied the Kabbala. And Jung's writings also reflect that he was extremely familiar with the Jewish mysticism of the Kabbalah. And I have found it to be an endless resource from which to activate the imagination needed to live life as a pilgrim and a follower of Jesus who lives at the edge of the religious world.

The more I study, the more I am confronted with the human condition and our struggle to connect with the divine—the God who exists in the world of the unseen. In working through my own wrestling with the Holy One, and with encouragement from my therapist, I began to study Carl Jung. His work has opened my eyes to the language of archetypes, the world of the alchemists, and the Kabbalah. The symbolism and mystery of ancient myths, pagan spirits, Celtic spirituality, Judaism, and the medieval alchemists' understanding of Christianity has begun to make more sense to me living in the post-Christian era. The ancient is informing the present and shedding light on the future, creating an ancient/future faith. What is emerging from my work and conversation with others, I hope, is a new language about the archetype of the "Cosmic Christ"[42] for a new age. I'm over sixty years old and still exploring the endless realm of the divine; there I'm discovering my own sense of spirituality. I continue to search, research, try on new ideas, and let go, burn away, re-imagine, and re-integrate. I have more questions and very few answers. But the imagination is taking over. For that I am extremely excited.

The point of telling you the story of my personal journey is not to convert anyone to my way of thinking. I tell it to encourage you to explore your own faith journey and to ask yourself why you might be seeking a relationship with the divine. Jung wrote that

> hysterical deceivers, and ordinary ones too, have at all times
> understood the art of misusing everything so as to avoid the
> demands and duties of life, and above all to shirk the duty of con-
> fronting themselves. They pretend to be seekers after God in order

not to have to face the truth that they are ordinary egoists. In such cases it is well worth asking: why are you seeking the divine water?[43]

Don't be afraid to seek the divine, ask questions, and voice doubts. Trust what your heart and mind desire to learn. Ask for spiritual guides to appear in your life. We are curious by nature. Trust that the divine is urging you, calling you, fetching you to enter into a deeper relationship. The pilgrimage of searching is a means of connecting with our deeper self and a way to re-imagine our spirituality.

We are usually reticent to let go of those parts of our lives into which we have invested a lot of time, energy, and resources. Often, though, it is the pilgrimage of life, the unwanted challenges, that turn up the heat enough for transmutation to take place. When our spirituality is put to the test we are often pushed to consider moving beyond our positions of safety and comfort. Then we start looking for words, metaphors, myths, and rituals that will help us tell our family and friends what we've newly discovered about ourselves and the divine. It means we will have to work hard at developing a new language to explain what the pilgrimage is cooking up in our lives. We will need a new way of telling our old communities that we have had a life-changing experience —and they may not understand us or be willing to accept how we are now different.

Re-imagining Community as My Favorite Boots

For many of us, we've had to search what seems like the ends of the earth to find a community worth investing our lives in. A sports team was my community as a young person. Being on a team gave me a sense of purpose and identity. I searched for community in other ways as well. Church was also a source of community, even in times when I felt God didn't exist. In fact, I've found that some of my friends go to church primarily for the sake of being in a community. Several folks who attend the church I once pastored are, by their own declaration, agnostic. Yet, they told me they went to church because of the relationships they built. They felt like they belonged. They felt that other people cared about them.

Being in community sustains our sense of well-being. Belonging gives us a feeling of identity. We experience others' care for us. It matters to them when we show up at gatherings. They miss us when we're absent. Many of us are also looking for a community where we can share ideas, test new thoughts, and question the divine. And we hope we can voice our doubts without condemnation or judgment. In community we can ask others to hold us accountable for our behavior. We learn from others how to play well together and forgive. Community is the cauldron for learning how to live life as an integrated human being.

Integrated living embraces the opposites in life—the good and the bad, the dark and the light, the joy and the pain. Living as part of a community exposes us to a vast number of the pairs of opposites. Others experience circumstances in their lives we have yet to encounter or situations we will never face. We learn from their stories. They in turn learn from us. To live an integrated life is to acknowledge all parts of life. We learn how to live with all that we are—not just the way we want our life to be. Life happens in the darkness of night just as much as the light of day. Being in a community can help us see how to live life the best possible way in both the light and the dark.

My dear young friend Jillian walked the El Camino de Santiago while she was still an undergraduate. I remember very well when I heard Jillian was going to walk by herself. Frankly, my parental self kicked in and I was worried about her. I spent a lot of time praying for her while she was on pilgrimage. When she returned, I could see she had gone through something unique, something powerful—what I now know as transmutation. I've listened to her stories of pilgrimage over the past ten years, and every time she talks about her walk it seems as if her mind, body, soul, and spirit immediately return to Spain. She talks with the pace of carrying a pack up the mountain. She pauses to catch her breath. She steadies her tired body against the edge of the table. She leans back in her chair and smiles with the satisfaction of having completed another day. From that space, years ago, she can share her experience. Walking a pilgrimage with other people is a microcosm of living in community. She wrote to me:

> [My pilgrimage] began as a dare—an uncalculated risk that I
> assumed I would be taking alone. Although I was physically alone
> for much of the walk across northern Spain, I realize these many
> years later that I was never truly alone. And by that, I don't mean
> a sentimental reference to God. I mean I was constantly aware
> of my interdependence with other humans who were also alone.
> Somehow in our mutual solitariness, we became linked together

in ways that weave in and out of my life still. It is the best dare I ever accepted.

It was in those thirty-two days of varying levels of loneliness that I came to understand community and my own self. My pilgrimage started long before I was dared by a friend, and has continued long since reaching Santiago. My pilgrimage community began with the people at home who walked while I walked. It continued throughout my travel to reach my designated starting point, and as I walked, and walked, and walked. Some days were light footsteps and some days were heavy with pain. Yet community was always present.

Sometimes the community was broken. One group of people I walked with who were from South America preferred to judge other pilgrims, rather than focus on the elephant-sized dysfunction that existed within the controlling nature of the group. There is one thing I am certain of—a pilgrimage cannot be controlled. I learned deeply about myself when I chose to leave that group of people and walk on. Days later when I was in physical pain, it was that community who passed me by on the side of the road. Ironically, it was the very "heathens" they judged who stopped to help me.

Other communities consisted of people who were broken but were open to the healing nature of pilgrimage. They openly shared their pain in vulnerable but non-oppressive ways that included laughter, tears, and profound silence. In this community it was acceptable to let my own brokenness surface. I let the elements of nature have their way with the brokenness in order to erode some of that pain. The constant physicality of this type of pilgrimage is already heavy enough. I didn't need to continue to carry all my pain with me as well. It was in the community of vulnerable brokenness that I learned we are all broken, walking a road of healing, if we are open to it.

There was also the community I carried with me. Sometimes while walking for days alone, I would sing entire albums to the wind. Each song brought the presence of a loved one, someone I had wronged, someone who had wronged me, or people I barely knew. All those saints were intensely present throughout the pilgrimage. With their help, I became more centered. In a paradoxical way, the more deeply I grew within, the more I thought of others. I grew to understand the power of words, boundaries, brokenness, healing, forgiving self, forgiving others, and the need to let go. I learned to be a part of a community. I learned to not just give, but to accept help when it was needed.

When I returned home, a community met me. I recall feeling internally disheveled. How would I share what had happened? I felt as if I had lived an entire life and was returning to a world where mere seconds had passed. Words seemed nonexistent and woefully inadequate. Instead of talking, this community washed my tired and beat-up feet. There would be plenty of time for words later. I watched intently as this community embraced me, for who I was and who I am. I dared myself never to forget that pilgrimage has no beginning and no end. I dared myself to live this as a promise to myself and be a part of the community of pilgrims.

Jillian had learned about walking alone, walking in loneliness, walking with others, the disappointment of community, and the joy of being cared for in community. For Jillian, life is a pilgrimage that has no beginning and no end. For in walking a pilgrimage, we are blessed with the reality that every day we begin again. She also came away from her pilgrimage with the idea that our communities may not only be the small group of people gathered around us at any moment in time. Instead, our community is those sisters and brothers, other pilgrims, who share our way of life.

Walking for eight hours in silence is wonderful and at the same time daunting. Sometimes it's good to have another person to talk to, especially to share thoughts about the magnificent scenery, the tough walking, the unexpected surfacing of emotions. I'm an introvert, so walking alone is easy. But making pilgrimage with a group has touched my soul in ways being alone might not have.

I found it very helpful to have other eyes looking for the way markers, "the yellow hiking man," particularly those times when the marker was hiding in the overgrowth. Having someone else looking at the map with me assured me that we were, indeed, going in the right direction.

At the end of the day I loved listening to others process the walk. In the state of exhaustion and when our emotions were raw, sharing with others shed new light on my own experience. I learned from each person's unique perspective. They saw things I didn't. And the things we shared reflected our varied angles or viewpoints. My story is incomplete without their story.

Being on a pilgrimage creates natural moments of community. As Danielle mentioned, each morning we gathered to tape up sore knees and bandage blistered feet. Fortunately, we had a nurse and a former athletic coach along to help me tend to injuries. Caring for the walking wounded can build a bond between pilgrims like few other experiences. Simply walking through rough terrain can bind a group together. The previous two times I had walked the Wicklow Way over White Hill, the highest point in western Ireland, we had walked in dense fog and driving rain. We could barely see the path. The experience built the camaraderie of shared misery and mystery. But with Saint Brigid's group, as Blair said, our band of twelve (one member of our group had been forced to stop walking due to blisters) had walked across White Hill on a perfect day. The sky was spotted with billowy clouds of white, blue, and gray. There was a light breeze, comfortable temperatures for a steep climb. The view was spectacular. On one side of the hill we could see far into the ocean; on the other, far below, was Guinness Lake. The previous two times I had walked over the hill I could barely see my hand in front of my face. I was so happy, this time, to be able to share the experience, fresh and new, with fellow travelers. I wouldn't have realized that my joy was so obvious except several of them kept referring to the big smile on my face.

But the thing that brought the most laughter to my heart while walking with Saint Brigid's group was listening to two couples sing their own lyrics to familiar tunes as we walked the Wicklow Way. Singing and laughing feels good when you've got three more hours of grueling hike ahead. Watching them holding hands as they walked ahead of me reminded me that love is a divine power. Holding hands, singing songs—it sounds so simple and childlike. I like it. And I plan on doing it more myself with my lover.

Walking with Danielle, Candace, Blair, Erik, and the others was the first time that I reached the end of the pilgrimage with a group. I had my own sense of completion, yes. Yet my personal feelings were nothing compared to the immense satisfaction I enjoyed in watching them accomplish a goal many of them thought was impossible. Their experiences enriched my walk, touched my soul, made me laugh, brought tears to my eyes, taught me much about life and myself, and stirred within me the continued desire to keep living life as a pilgrimage. In witnessing those folks realize their achievement, I felt a glow in my soul that I also saw on their faces. I want to hold that moment in my mind's eye for the remainder of my life; it feels that good.

We shared an experience. We walked together. At the same time, we walked alone. We had to carry our own pack. There were times, though, we needed help. Those times, we needed others to step forward and do more than just feel sorry for us. We needed someone to carry a part of our load for a short distance. We needed others to care that we were hurting. We needed them to do something—bandage our wounds and check in with us to the point of being annoyed by the question, "You okay?" When one person ran out of water or food, we counted on someone else to share. When we wanted to be left alone, we were relieved that others would be sensitive to those moments. When we needed to complain, we were grateful someone would listen to our grumbling.

Walking a hundred miles through the Wicklow Mountains in eight days is an intense experience of living in community. Cosmetics are left behind, clean clothes are a privilege, a well-placed tree is enough when you need a toilet. Amenities are what you carry on your back. A pilgrimage community sees each other at their best and their worst, at their most vulnerable moments and their moments of strength. A healthy community that can live well with people within that tension can touch and change our lives. We love those communities, we remember them, and we cherish them for a lifetime. Letting go of them can be one of the hardest challenges we must face. And pilgrimage communities, like all communities, are a part of the cycles of life. All things come full circle.

At the end of the walk we celebrated our accomplishment with a pint of Guinness. We took one last group picture. And within a few hours we began to go our separate ways. Some went home to Phoenix, others to Seattle. My wife and I stayed in Ireland for another two weeks. The walking pilgrimage community came to an end, but each pilgrim will live with the profound memories and continue to carry what we learned, cherish what we experienced, and be better people for having been together. Now new opportunities for community will emerge. Those new communities will be seasoned with the spicy lessons we learned while being a part of the Saint Brigid's pilgrimage community.

Pilgrimage communities, good communities, healthy communities, are like well-worn comfortable boots. Of course, our favorite boots, like our favorite community, didn't come off the rack broken in and ready to walk a hundred miles in rugged terrain. We had to take the time of going through the process of getting those boots to be one with our feet. Once those boots become our best friends, we wouldn't walk a mile without them. But then our best boots, the communities we love, simply wear out and must be retired to the Walking Hall of Fame. Communities don't come to an end or die because they were necessarily bad. Every community must go through the cycle of life—birth, maturity, death, and resurrection (new life). If we continue to wear our boots past the point of their usefulness, we can run into some serious problems on the trail. The same can be said for all communities. Man, I hate letting go of my old boots and good communities. But when the time comes, it is the best thing to do.

How Do I Tell You This Weird Story?

Only in the last year have I been able to talk and write coherently, honestly, authentically about my pilgrimage experiences. My normal is not normal anymore. I feel like a raven with a peacock tail. I don't know whether to be proud or embarrassed. I think I should be able to fly, but I'm pretty sure I can't. When I look in the mirror, I think I'm looking at myself, but then again, I'm not all that sure. Everything has changed, but nothing has changed. I'm still a happy husband, father, grandfather, enthusiastic writer, and employed priest. All seems well—just very. . . well, odd, weird at times. How do I tell you how I feel? That's what I'm doing in this book.

Our pilgrimages are opportunities to walk ancient paths while being consciously aware of our senses, thoughts, feelings, and imaginations. Every step of awareness has the potential to carry us through the alchemical phases of chaos, cracking of the egg, raven with the peacock tail, and the rising of the phoenix from the ashes. The combination of these two ideas of wisdom walking and alchemical pilgrimage will move us higher on our spiral journey of consciousness as well as into the process of individuation.

The spiral of alchemy is not a story whose point is "something good will always come out of a chaotic situation." Honestly, such a notion is either bad theology or wishful thinking. That kind of thinking is an attempt at a mental bait and switch; something difficult has happened and now we try to make ourselves or someone else feel better, when deep down we know our words will never be enough. The second phase of alchemy, the cracking of the egg, acknowledges the pain of life's fire. The purpose is to experience a different level of consciousness, where the reality of life is neither ignored nor denied, but instead integrated into our story as an individuated person. The maturity gained from this phase can be hard to achieve, at times a more difficult way to live. Carl Jung and Richard Rohr both say that not everyone will move from the first half of life into the second half—a place where we will experience a growing maturity and become more comfortable with ambiguity, while living with more questions than answers. Not everyone will mature or develop a higher level of consciousness. Not everyone will individuate—everyone could, it's just that some will not choose to walk the road less traveled. This is the road that leads to the third phase of alchemy where the raven with a peacock tail emerges from the cauldron.

Interlude
Ahmad's Mecca Pilgrimage

$\mathbb{S}$ince September 11, 2001, spiritual safety has been a priority conversation among interfaith groups, especially when Christians and Muslims are in the same meeting. In March of 2010, I was invited with Ahmad, imam at the Islamic Cultural Center in Tempe, Arizona, to attend an interreligious conference at Virginia Theological Seminary (VTS). The conference organizers, funded by a grant from the Henry Luce Foundation, invited twenty Anglican (Episcopal) and twenty Muslim global leaders to discuss a peaceful response for the tenth anniversary of 9/11. Ahmad and I were invited because we had been leaders of a gathering on September 11, 2009, in Tempe—a program held in response to the threatened burning of the Holy Quran by Terry Jones, pastor of the Dove World Outreach Center in Gainesville, Florida.

The VTS conference consisted of three twelve-hour days, each packed with listening to intense stories like Ahmad's. On November 20, 2006, he and five other imams had been escorted off a US Airways flight bound for Phoenix out of the Minneapolis–St. Paul International Airport. They were alleged to have said prayers and made comments to each other in Arabic, apparently making some passengers on the flight uncomfortable. Ahmad told the conference that one imam was blind. All six were handcuffed, escorted off the plane, forced to walk unassisted down a ramp, placed in separate police cars, and taken to a detention center for interrogation. After hours of questioning, a federal agent determined the arrest was unwarranted and the six were returned to the airport. US Airways refused to issue them new tickets or let them board another flight. The imams had to purchase new tickets from another airline. A year later, US Airways reached an out-of-court settlement with the six imams.

Ahmad and I had already been friends and the VTS conference brought us closer together. During lunch one day he told me about his pilgrimage to Mecca, and he has given me permission to share a part of his story with you.

> My first pilgrimage to Mecca was in 1989. I was twenty-five and living in Jordan. I made my second pilgrimage to Mecca in 2008. I was forty-four and living in the United States. Each trip takes about fifteen days, but only five of them are for the religious rituals. The rest are for the travel time and for touring other places.
>
> All Muslims are required to make one pilgrimage to Mecca in their lifetime. There are exceptions, however, for those who are physically or financially unable. The holy journey is called the *hajj*, which is commanded in the Quran. "And the pilgrimage to the House is a duty unto God for mankind, for him who can find the way thither." (3:97)
>
> The hajj commemorates the journeys and lives of Abraham, Hagar, and Ishmael. The pilgrimage begins six miles from the Ka'ba, at the outskirts of Mecca. Pilgrims, both men and women, enter a state of purity (*ihram*), which they remain in throughout the pilgrimage. During the ihram, pilgrims may not cut their nails or hair, engage in sexual relations, argue, fight, or hunt. The men dress in two white sheets and sandals. The women's requirements are less stringent but most wear white, covering all but their face and hands. The simple white clothes represent the equality and unity of the pilgrims.
>
> When the pilgrim enters Mecca, they walk around the Ka'ba seven times while reciting the *talbiya* (prayers), then kiss the black stone, saying two prayers towards the Station of Abraham, and then make six trips (running if possible) between the mountains of Sarfa and Marwa. There are other rituals we practice, but require much more detailed explanation. My second trip, which is not required, was as a volunteer to guide a group of people from my community.
>
> The Pilgrimage to Mecca is the experience of a lifetime. Pilgrims will have the opportunity to meet people from all parts of the world. More than two million people attend the hajj every

year. The pilgrimage has to be during the eight to twelve days of the twelfth month of the lunar calendar, which is eleven days shorter than the solar calendar. The hajj experience was a factor in changing the life of Malcolm X and many other Americans. Imagine yourself interacting with people from all cultures, colors, and ethnicities of the world, calling each other brothers and sisters. All these diverse people came to the same place, at the same time, walking the same route, repeating the same prayer, dressing the same, having the same goal, which is to seek God's forgiveness.

The walk is a season of flashing memories going back to Prophet Abraham and his family. I've had many spiritual experiences on my pilgrimage. But it's difficult for me to put these experiences into words.

CHAPTER 3

. . .

The Unexpected Experiences of Walking

Wisdom is never violent:
where wisdom reigns there is no conflict
between thinking and feeling.

—*Carl Jung*[44]

I n the 1980s, my dad built a cabin in the Bradshaw Mountains just outside of Prescott, Arizona, about ninety miles north of Phoenix. I find the history of the area fascinating because I think the past has affected the region's unconscious. Understanding the psychological history of a place, including the effect that manifests in the psyche of the inhabitants, the landscape, the animals, and the plants, will significantly help the pilgrim understand their pilgrimage. Jungian psychologist Craig Chalquist, author of *Terrapsychology: Re-engaging the Soul of Place*, insists that when a particular place, like the Bradshaw Mountains, suffers or witnesses injustice, the region needs, as much as a human would need, to be listened to with therapeutic ears.[45]

In the Bradshaws, the white man used brutal force to drive the native people off the land. And the landscape is still scarred today from mining, which subsequently damaged the aquifer. The wildlife has only recently returned from being overhunted. And while the ravens are still present, I fear no one is listening to their message. These mountains need a terrapsychologist.

Historically, the Yavapai peoples had populated the Bradshaw Mountains at least since 1000 CE and probably millennia before. The Wipuhk'a'bah, as the tribe is named in its own language, lived peacefully in the pine forests that provided plenty of water and wildlife. They coexisted with at least the Dil'zhe'e, one of the five subgroups of the Apache Nation, from about the fourteenth century. By the beginning of the nineteenth century, the Yavapai and Apache Nations together probably numbered no more than two thousand people living in small family bands in the Bradshaw Mountains. Life would dramatically change with the arrival of the white man.

By the early 1800s, a small number of trappers, miners, and settlers began to arrive in the Bradshaws. Fort Whipple was established in the area in 1863. That same year Joseph Walker and his party of miners ventured into the Bradshaw Mountains (near where my dad built his cabin a hundred years later). Jack Swilling, a former Confederate soldier who became most noted in Arizona for establishing an important canal system, was their guide. Late in 1863, Walker discovered gold in Lynx Creek. Soon after Walker made his discovery, an estimated three thousand miners roamed the mountains, searching for gold. Quickly, the town of Walker was established.

Both the Yavapai and Apache Nations responded to the intrusion of the white man into the region. They defended their rights to the land and the wildlife that supported their livelihood. Soldiers from Fort Whipple carried out retaliatory attacks on the two native tribes, killing more than eighty natives on two separate occasions. At one massacre, carried out west of Prescott, the soldiers left the dead Yavapai unburied. That area was subsequently named Skull Valley, and the name remains today. By 1865 both the Yavapai and Apache Nations had been decimated and were moved onto reservation lands. On the 150-mile march from the Bradshaws south to the reservation, one hundred women, children, and elderly Yavapai people died from starvation and exposure.

The traditions of the Yavapai and Apache people still hang in the mountain air around our cabin like what Jung called "the lament of the dead."[46] The communication between humanity and nature was lost when the Yavapai and Apache people were taken off their land. Greed and violence broke the flow of the relationship between humans and creation. The dead were crying out in defense of the earth, the land, and its creatures. They knew a relationship with humanity had to be re-established in order to preserve creation.

The Yavapai shamans gathered agave plants and made mescal for their rituals that would create the thin place in the flow of relationships that assisted in establishing the flow of relationship between humans, the earth, and its creatures. The Yavapai had a belief that supernatural little people protected their nation. The Apache believed that coyotes, insects, and birds had previously been human beings. Both groups of natives placed significance on the presence of ravens. While native peoples have different beliefs about ravens, in general, the birds are considered to be messengers from the spirit world that signal when danger has passed and good times are ahead. The spirit of the ravens has been passed on through the eons by what Rupert Sheldrake calls morphic resonance, fields of patterns that move across time and generations of all creation.[47] In other words, for centuries, humans—the Yavapai and the Apache—had listened to the ravens. The last one hundred years, however, the peoples that inhabit these mountains have not revered the message of the raven. Still, the ravens have passed along the message from generation to generation, ready for people who would listen to them. I believe I have experienced Sheldrake's phenomena in the Bradshaw Mountains among the ravens. I have heard the ravens speak.[48] Those experiences began while walking the woods near our cabin in the Bradshaw Mountains.

Over the past thirty years our family has enjoyed this little oasis my dad created for us. I've spent countless days exploring the abandoned mines and hiking the woods that are home to white-tailed deer, javelina . . . and ravens. In 2012, when I was preparing for my solo walk across Ireland, I spent a lot of time hiking the familiar mountains. The terrain, the elevation climbs and descents, and the altitude made the Bradshaws a perfect place to get ready for my trek.

At dawn one day, I stepped out the front door of our cabin and was surprised to be greeted by four large ravens foraging the ground for breakfast. When they saw me, the birds flew about twenty yards beyond the house, landed on the ground, and continued their search for worms. I eased toward them and was amazed that I got within ten feet of their circle. For five minutes, they kept an eye on me while they picked the ground. Finally, the largest bird let out a very loud *prawck*, which startled me. My sudden movement caused the ravens to fly up into a nearby tree. I stood still. They watched me for a bit and then flew off.

The experience was exhilarating. Questions swirled in my head. Why would they let me get so close? Were they trying to tell me something? I hoped they would show up the next day and felt sad when they didn't.

A few months later, however, I was at the cabin again and started a hike just before sunup. Heading down the hill toward one of my favorite walks, about a mile from the cabin, I spotted four ravens searching the ground for something to eat. Surely they were the same ravens. As I got closer to the little group, they *prawcked*, almost like they were laughing at me. I got within thirty feet before they flew off, low to the ground, through the trees. A few hundred yards down the road they were resting in the trees. I stopped and stood under the tree where the largest raven was sitting. A little in jest, I told the bird that in all the years I had walked through the area, they had never left me a feather. He *prawcked*. Who was I to ask for such a thing?

I had walked another three miles down the mountain road when one of the ravens flew just ahead of me, crossed my path, and landed in a tree next to the road. When I got to where he was perched, to my pleasant surprise, there was a large black feather on the ground. Amazed and humbled, I bowed to the raven and thanked the bird for the gift. Admiring the feather, I walked another few dozen steps.

Then the raven swooped in front of me again and landed in a tree on the other side of the road. The bird was squawking what seemed to be a warning alarm. I felt like he was calling me to his side of the road. For some reason, though, I didn't heed my intuition and started to walk away. The raven changed his tone to what sounded like someone screaming. That rattled me enough that I walked across the road toward him. By then the raven had moved to the back side of the tree, away from the road. I moved around to his side of the tree and stood there, staring up at him.

Suddenly, there came a truck barreling down the road. I turned in time to see the small pickup clip the rocks on the blind, narrow side of the road— exactly where I would have been standing. The driver would have never seen me in time to swerve away.

My heart dropped. My stomach rose. My soul smelled eternity. I leaned against the tree. I thought I was going to pass out. I knew I was going to throw up. What had happened? Could that raven have knowingly saved my life? Maybe it was synchronicity? Possibly my intuition had been working in my best interest? I know, someone reading this is saying, "God saved you." Could be. I don't know. Raven, synchronicity, intuition, the divine, each of them unexpected experiences—I'm glad one, some, or all of them stepped in. I'm glad to be alive.

When Matter and Spirit Collide

Carl Jung wrote in *Man and His Symbols* that intuition is an irrational involuntary event, a hunch.[49] Then he offered a clear and concise explanation of the four interior functions of sensing, intuition, thinking, and feeling: "Sensation tells you that something exists; thinking tells you what it is; feeling tells you whether it is agreeable or not; and intuition tells you whence it comes and where it is going."[50] The experience with the raven was so unexpected that I spent a lot of time reflecting on the shocking event. I've spent so much time studying Jung that it was natural for me to use the four interior functions as a way of reflecting on what had happened. My senses had been in tune with the raven. I was seeing and hearing him while I was touching the feather. "Who asks a bird for a feather?" I thought. Was that a random event—or maybe not? I had thought about walking past the bird while he was squawking at me. Do birds give warnings to humans about impending traffic accidents? I don't know, but fortunately, I was curious, and my thinking drew me across the road toward the bird. My feelings were also involved. I was grateful for the feather and I was feeling affectionate toward this bird. Honestly, though, I don't remember having any inclination, or intuition, that a truck was coming down that road. I guess I could have heard it, but I was focused on the bird, and besides, he was yelling, screaming, so loudly. My experience that day defies rational thought. But I believe that at that moment, the wisdom of nature was flowing into my soul.

I've always enjoyed being outdoors, in nature. I have admired wild birds, their beauty and flight patterns. But I never imagined I would have such an encounter with four ravens. Since my experience on the mountain road, I've spent a lot of time researching ravens, watching them, listening to them, wondering about them. That momentous day brought about a revelation—an epiphany—rooted in the ancients' wisdom. I have become convinced from my experience that all of creation—trees, stones, animals, birds, every blade of grass, everything—has a soul, and we are all connected. I am also quite certain that some of those souls, for instance, ravens, communicate with my soul. Soul to soul—the raven is my guide. The raven is not my god. But the Creator, God, created the raven, the trees, the stones, and me. We—humans, animals, birds, stones, and trees—are all a part of creation, all connected, and we can all communicate with one another.

This understanding is not new. It's not something I discovered. The native Yavapai and Apache peoples hold these beliefs. Pre-Christian Celtic people understood their connection to the world in this way. Christians wrote about the intertwined relationship of all of God's creation. For example, Pelagius (354–420 CE) said, "There is no creature (or plant) on earth in whom God is absent."[51] Therefore, if God is present in all of creation, humans can be one with God by being one with creation.

Modernity fought against this idea, however. Dualism, the idea that matter and spirit are separated into opposite realms, has been a part of philosophical thinking at least since the Greeks. The advent, however, of the Enlightenment and the church's subsequent theological rejection of the materiality of a living science drove a wedge between the material and the spirit. Johns Hopkins University chemist and historian Lawrence Principe wrote in his book *The Secrets of Alchemy*:

> Pre-moderns tended to conceive of and visualize the world in multivalent terms, where each individual thing was connected to many others by webs of analogy and metaphor. This view stands in contrast to the modern tendency to compartmentalize and isolate things and ideas into separate disciplines. This crucial feature holds a key to understanding European alchemy more deeply.[52]

The alchemists lived in premodernity as modernity emerged. Their goal was to create a language that revealed the union of matter and spirit. They used language like the "mystical marriage of the sun and the moon," the light and the dark, the day and the night. They found their inspiration in the Lord's Prayer—"Thy Kingdom come, thy will be done, on earth as it is in heaven." In other words, in the tradition of Hermes Trismegistus, they worked to bring about the unity of that which is "above (spirit) and that which is below (nature),"[53] or in Jungian terms, the synthesis of spirit and matter, the dark and the light, the unconscious and the conscious.[54] The alchemist's work, according to Principe, had been lost for centuries—until science's recent discovery of unified and integrated theories. All things are interrelated, argues Principe, including that which is unseen (spirit) and that which we perceive with our senses (matter).

The breach between science and faith might be repairable. However, undoing the damage done to nature might be a formidable, even impossible, task. Humanity's seeing itself as different from the bird, the tree, the stone has led to the false conclusion that humanity is more important than creation. Because dualistic thinking has dominated the post-Enlightenment era, we find ourselves living on a planet where we might soon be the endangered species —most likely due to the damage we have inflicted upon our island home. Viewing life as a pilgrimage, though, might bring us to some much-needed moments of transmutation, creating a systemic change that will lead us to act like we depend upon, and are intertwined with, everything on this planet—the sun, moon, the stars, and beyond. Maybe if enough of us open our hearts to the soul of the world, we can do something before it's too late. Oddly though, our final hope for this world might be in our absence. Even if it is too late to change our fate, Mother Earth still might heal herself as she has done before, long after humans might become extinct.

I would like to be more optimistic about the fate of humanity. There is evidence among us that the human desire to enjoy and care for the magnificent beauty of the natural world does exist—the deep yearning not to destroy the earth. I want to believe that the global community will care enough about the earth to take the actions necessary to halt or maybe even reverse the damage we have done. I prefer not to give in to the cloud of apocalyptic threat because my experience continues to guide me into a deeper relationship with the creatures of the earth. Therein lies my hope—a hope that everyone could have an empathetic connection with all of creation. I do pray that wisdom will prevail. And I do believe that the wisdom needed to care for the earth and all its inhabitants can be found by wandering in the glory of creation herself. For in the unexpected experiences of pilgrimage we can fall into a childlike love of nature. When we bring wisdom and love together in the synthesis of matter and spirit, our lives and the world we live in can be transformed.

Wisdom from the Unexpected

August 2, 2012, on my solitary pilgrimage across Ireland, I walked from the Nadd Pub to the village of Millstreet in County Cork, Ireland. Nadd, *nead an lolair* in Gaelic, means "the nest of the eagle." The "Nest of the Eagle" Pub originally served the men who, during World War II, cut, stacked, and hauled the Irish bog that would become the fuel replacement for oil. Now the pub is a quaint tourist attraction and a place the old timers hang out to tell their stories of ages past. That stretch of the Blackwater Way covers about sixteen miles of logging roads and rugged bog trails across the Boggeragh Mountain range. I started that morning walking up a mountain on a narrow, muddy trail. Within the first hundred yards, I stepped over a severed raven's foot that was lying in the center of the path. I couldn't help but wonder what kind of omen that might be for my day, one of the few times I walked Ireland when I thought trekking alone might not have been the best idea. My physical stamina would be tested for sure.

While in the forest, I had to hunch over as my pack brushed against the low-hanging branches of giant pines. Once out in the open, though, the wind howled and the rain blew sideways as I slogged through knee-deep grass. I crossed a few deep gorges, hidden gullies cut by years of rain. I slipped and fell twice, once at the edge of a perilous ravine. I had to walk over hard clumps of sharp grasses growing between mossy swells of water and black mud. I used my walking stick to test each clump of grass to see if it would hold my weight. Every step was measured. Finally, the ridge dropped down onto an abandoned road where (I later learned) workmen from the World War II period had left slices of bog stacked in small pyramids. I was glad to leave that part of the route behind.

The unused rutty path turned into a graveled road used by loggers and electrical workers. I followed the road up a mountain to several enormous wind turbines, each 140 meters (459 feet) tall and topped by a trinity of wings. They made a swooshing sound, like a flying dragon sucking the air out of an angel. Thankfully, but not fast enough, the trail sloped down the mountain, away from the turbines and into another long patch of forest.

Weary from walking in the wind and rain, I dropped my pack and sat on a stone to regroup. I felt good about making it through what I thought was the riskiest part of the day. Evidently, at that moment, my intuition was not working too well.

The narrow road meandered down through the close forest until I came to a clearing where the path had been cut out by bog workers, slowly dropping the road about ten feet below the forest floor. The walls of the path were black bog. It was an odd feeling. I was walking downhill, below the forest floor. I could, therefore, see a long way in front of me, but very little directly above my head. In about half a mile, I saw a very unexpected sight. There, about a hundred yards down the road, I thought I saw a giant head. As I got closer, I realized it was a wild ram as big as a full-grown bull you would see at a rodeo. Over four feet tall, he had a long, mottled gray coat and a swirl of thick horns. I thought that if I somehow upset him, he would charge me, leaving me helpless against his speed and power. Fortunately, he stood motionless. I tried to walk lightly, tiptoeing down the trail. I must have looked ridiculous. Instinctively, or stupidly, I slid my phone out of my pants pocket to take a picture. What was I thinking? But I clicked my camera twice. The ram turned his head to look at me. I obviously had failed to be invisible. He was the ruler over his kingdom, and I was a simpleton serf. He must have thought I was a tiny curiosity, a jester providing a moment of amusement. Slinking down the road, I looked back. He still hadn't moved as he stood guard over his domain. I felt he had given me something. But I wasn't sure what it might have been. My life? Maybe he let me live because he sensed I'm a vegetarian. Silly? I don't know. But I did feel he gave me the courage to continue walking deeper into the wild, to keep searching for more wisdom. Being in the Irish forest, alone, face-to-face with the realization that I was not in control and that my life was at risk, while at the same time being in awe of nature's power, was a spiritual moment, a portion of the transmutational experience. That unexpected experience turned my thinking upside down. Being close to the wind turbines reminded me of man's unquenchable desire for power; it made me want to run away and hide. But standing within a few feet of the ram, creation's power, I found myself longing to abide there in the pristine bliss of that holy instant of timelessness. I keep the picture of the ram above my writing desk as an icon, reminding me of the liberation I still experience from not feeling the need to be in control of my life any longer. While I fearfully respect nature's strength, I am willing to place my trust in her wisdom.

The next few miles, I hiked a switchback down the mountain and then up the other side of the Boggeraugh Mountains, known as the Mushera. The long, sweeping ridge across the bald mountain was exposed to the whipping wind and rushing clouds of the rain. The perilous trail was along the northern edge of the ridge. I trudged through a mile and a half of mud, rough tall grasses, slippery rocks, and water-filled sheep trails.

Two miles after slogging off the Mushera ridge, the rain let up, and the road entered a scraggly forest, peppered with wide, sweeping, grassy hills that were littered with sheep, and then to a small field where the Knocknakilla Stone Circle stood. The prehistoric worship site had probably been erected two thousand years before Jesus. With all the reverence I could muster, I stood in the middle of the circle. There, I sensed the haunting of ancient voices. As I touched the tallest stone, one that had been standing against the winds of times, I felt the prayers of four millennia of people and dared to add my own humble words—thanksgiving for the raven, awe of the ram, and the blessed safe care given me by the divine. Indeed, the ancient and the modern were woven together in that moment. There, I unexpectedly experienced a sense of divine timelessness—I was transported into an awareness of being aware.

Mystical Transmutation

I've reflected a lot on my walk from Nadd to Millstreet. Stepping over the severed raven's foot was an omen of the paradox that lay ahead—the most perilous and, at the same time, the most rewarding day of my walk across Ireland. For the Celts, the raven at your doorstep meant death was imminent; for the Navajo people he is a trickster; for the Yavapai people he is a symbol that something good is about to happen. The raven is a symbol of paradox, the container of the pair of opposites.

My walk from Nadd to Millstreet was a fascinating journey, but what did it have to do with transmutation? How has it affected my life? I got more from that day than simply a great story to tell. Indeed, my life was changed, transmuted, altered in such a way that my default system had been altered, shifted, remade into something altogether different, yet the same person. Who I am— my authentic self—is still me, with the same genetic makeup, same personality type, same scratchy-sounding voice; the matter of what makes me *me* is the same. Yet at the same time, the spirit of me, the part of me that is intertwined with the divine, the metaphysical me, the mystical me, has been transmuted; what is above (spirit) is below (matter) and what is below is above.

Gavin Ashenden, one of the Queen of England's thirty-five chaplains and lecturer in the Psychology of Religion at the University of Sussex, is an Anglican priest and pilgrim. He wrote in his book, *Charles Williams: Alchemy and Integration*, "The metaphysical authenticity of a life is dependent on the existence of a capacity for change; and those who do not change are faced with the prospect of ultimate decay."[55] Pilgrimage creates a space for change, a capacity for transmutation. Metaphysical authenticity in one's life is the expression of one's inner desires, ideals, and beliefs that in turn outwardly express who one really is. In other words, the outward expression reveals the inner identity, what Jung calls your "Self." He or she embraces the fullest spectrum of their sensing, thinking, feeling, and imagination to generate their inner and outer transmutation, to become someone they thought not possible. In psychological terms, this effort brings about change, the evidence of maturation.

Ashenden is defining the value of alchemy in a person's process of individuation. My inner world (where my soul and my spirit intersect with the divine) is being changed, which then changes my outer world (my material reality). The alchemist was exposing his inner life to the transmutational work of the divine in relationship to his spirit. His inner world was made evident in the cauldron of his outer material existence. The alchemists' third phase revealed the transparent membrane, what the Celts call the "thin space," between the inner, spiritual and the outer, material world. For me, wisdom walking is an agent of change in the pilgrim's life, which creates a transparency in the way we live. Pilgrimage experiences will transmute the essence of one's being, one's thoughts, and one's actions, so much so that his or her inner light will shine onto their outer world. Through pilgrimage, I have experienced the work of the raven with the peacock's tail—transmutation that turns a leaden life into something dark, yet diffusely translucent.

The Raven with a Peacock Tail

This phase of the alchemical pilgrimage increases the heat of our inner and outer life, allowing us to move into a high level of creativity. On this level of the spiral, the beginning of translucence, we are walking in the thin space between thinking and feeling. For Jung, *thinking* and *feeling* are a pair of opposites. Thinking is the rational side of the pair. Jung called feeling the "irrational" side, meaning that it is not held captive by culture's logic; feeling is willing to operate outside the box. Here, in this place between thinking and feeling, the imagination is birthed. Here in this thin space, it's as if we are walking awake in a dream—where our way of seeing life is turned upside down, transmuted.

I dreamed I met the gatekeeper, a ceramist who lived in Ireland. At the summer solstice, he stood at the eastern gate of the druid stone circle. He protected the ceremony, held at the sun's rising, from unwanted spirits. The gatekeeper knew which spirits were allowed into the ceremony and which were not. In the dream, he gave me a bowl, big enough that I had to hold it with both hands. It was deep enough to contain my journal. The bowl's exterior was a reddened brown. The interior was an explosion of red, turquoise, and gold that radiated from a small black center shaped like the kidney bean of a month-old fetus. The gatekeeper told me to take my bowl and stand in the center of the stone circle. I was to stand perfectly still, holding the bowl, waiting for the dawn of the solstice sun.

At first light, I could see the mist of my breath in the heavy Irish air. The sun's rays began to stream across the horizon, filling my bowl with light. The bowl began to vibrate, to dance, to burn with a brilliant fire. The earth shook. A wind swept chaos across the land. My clothes were ripped from my body. The Great Raven began to rise out of the bowl. I could see that she had a peacock's tail. The black raven with the peacock tail flew toward the sun, on the way to transmutation into the phoenix. I could see myself standing there, naked, with the scene tattooed on my back. When I woke from my dream I knew I was changed by it, that I would be living life in this dream.

My dream contained the four elements of alchemy: chaos, cracking of the egg, the raven with a peacock tail, and the phoenix. In the phase discussed in this chapter, the raven with the peacock tail is an image used by the alchemist Gerhard Dorn (c. 1530–84). He wrote about this vision as the strange juxtaposition of thinking and feeling.[56] The brain tells me that I rationally shouldn't be able to fly but my body feels that it can. The integration, then, of mind, body, soul, and spirit is the work of creating the quantum amount of internal and external dis-ease necessary for transmutation to occur.

In this third phase of alchemy, the heat creates a multi-coloring of the elements in the cauldron (like the many translucent colors of the peacock tail). As the heat rises it creates within the cauldron the instant between the expectation of tremendous change and the actual transmutation into gold. The changing of colors happens in the space between when the divine breathes air into the clay and the next instant when life emerges from the earth. These are the fragile seconds between when the baby leaves the womb in silence and when he screams for air. Herein lies the anxious seconds between when the potter cracks open the kiln and the second she sees for the first time what the fire has born into her art. This is the angst-filled moment before hearing the answer to the question—when both yes and no are possible. This is the time when the past has scrolled forward into the present and the future does not yet exist. These experiences are the moments of timelessness. There is a tremendous tension and yet peace within timelessness. We can't let go, but we might be ripped apart if we hold on for one second longer. This is the moment between death and rebirth, when the unstable ingredients could explode in our face. This phase is painful, dangerous, risky. Yet we must hold on to the bowl of fire, so the raven with the peacock tail can be born, knowing she will fly into the sun to become the phoenix.

Wisdom is born out of those precious moments when we experience the thin space between thinking and feeling. When our unconscious dream experience is integrated with our conscious pilgrimage, then our imagination can explode into the present now. In that moment, all of creation will sing us a new song.

Vox Peregrini

"Listen to the wind. Match your voice to the rhythm of the trees," John told his choir. John Wiles is the founder and creative genius of Vox Peregrini: A Pilgrimage Choir. He is also an enigma. He can exhort, beguile, and woo others into the creative imagination of the music in his head, yet to be performed. He is an artist, a musician, a pilgrim. His expectations for artistry are exacting yet liberating. His laugh is as brilliant as the sun and as beguiling as Beethoven's "Ode to Joy." John can cajole his singers to match their voices to the wind in the trees and somehow they make it happen.

Not yet thirty-five years old himself, John envisioned gathering twelve other young professional singers who would walk the hundred miles of Ireland's Wicklow Way and sing Tudor Cathedral music set against James Taylor and U2. He said he was tired of performing for audiences. He wanted to be reminded of why he fell in love with singing. He wanted to sing for the sake of the sound his voice discovered among other musicians, unencumbered by the expectations of those who simply bought tickets.

June 23, 2015, Vox Peregrini gathered at Most Holy Trinity Catholic Church in Bunclody, Ireland, one hundred miles south of Dublin. From this place, we would begin our pilgrimage walking north to Dublin. John Wiles, twelve singers, Cathy, and I sat in a circle in the choir room of the church. We introduced ourselves. All of them knew John. Few of them knew each other. John had sent his singers the sheet music before they left for Ireland. They had, however, never sung as a group before that evening.

Then John took out a tiny tuning fork, struck it to his head, and placed it behind his right ear. We heard nothing. He heard a note. He sang the first note. And they sang "Ave Verum Corpus," a piece written by William Byrd in 1610. No piano. No reading through the music. They just opened their mouths, and a glorious sound reverberated through the room and my soul. I have never been privileged to be present at the generative moment of such art. To my amateur ear, they sounded as if they had been companions for years. We had not taken one step, and these thirteen people had already implanted their spirits in my heart.

One of the sopranos said that night, "John, your taste in music is my emotion." With every piece they sang, I felt my suppressed emotions clawing their way out of my darkness into the light of beautiful music. Individually and collectively, Vox Peregrini, as well as Cathy and I, would experience a full range of emotions throughout the eight-day walk and two subsequent days of concerts.

The group rehearsed eleven pieces that evening. John decided that they should quickly memorize "That Lonesome Road," a song by James Taylor. John told them that people would want them to perform along the way simply because they were a choir. There's a line in the song that says, "And only stop to rest yourself when the silver moon is shining high above the trees." Little did John know there would be a full moon the night we would finish our walk in Dublin. Vox Peregrini would sing "The Lonesome Road" every day at least once. They sang to people from Australia, Germany, New Zealand, France, Spain, England, America, and of course, they sang to the Irish. They sang before we started hiking each day. They sang at lunch. They would stop along the trail and sing. They walked and sang eight to ten hours a day. Then every night, they rehearsed before hitting the pubs to sing for those tilting a pint.

Even when I didn't understand the Latin lyrics or connect to the composers or understand what it's like to sing as a trained professional, I could sense a transformation was happening among the group members, something like they had not experienced before this pilgrimage. That first night John had made an off-the-cuff comment that has stuck with me. "Just because the audience shows up doesn't mean they get to understand everything." I wondered if that was going to happen to Vox Peregrini as well. Just because they showed up to walk did not ensure they would understand everything that was going to happen to them on the pilgrimage.

After that first night of rehearsal, I had what was (for me) an unusual dream. Before that night, I can't remember having had a dream about flying. I have dreamed of falling, but never flying through the air—unaided, untethered, self-directed flying. That night, however, I had a dream I was flying twenty feet above the ground. I was enjoying the freedom of traveling where I wanted and seeing far below in all directions. It was a joyous dream. When I woke up that the first morning of our walk, I felt like I was ready for the unexpected that would happen on every pilgrimage.

I had walked with groups before. In many ways, Vox Peregrini was no different. My flying dream did not foretell a problem-free pilgrimage where everything would unfold without a bump. It fact, the walk did not go that way at all. The walk was more difficult than many had expected, and most of Vox Peregrini came unprepared. Morgan H. had to drop out from walking after the first day because the blisters on her heel turned into a wound larger than a silver dollar. She would spend the remainder of the journey traveling by car with Cathy. Several packs were too heavy, and the second morning their owners offloaded some of the weight into bags that were then transferred by car to the next hostel each day. All thirteen pilgrims suffered blisters. An unusual number experienced multiple blisters on both feet—on their toes and heels, on the tops and the soles of their feet. By the third morning I was spending an hour before we started walking tending their battered feet. Three had knee problems, one a bad ankle. Fortunately, we had enough knee and ankle braces to go around. It seemed that every time someone needed a brace, another person would produce one they had been carrying "just in case" they needed it. I thought I had brought plenty of bandages, gauze, and tape, but we had to restock three times. We spent over $300 on Band-Aids, Second Skin blister pads, gauze, and tape. I had brought along naturopathic remedies that I distributed freely for sore muscles and aching joints, as well as one sore throat. Cathy also packed essential oils, and we used them quite extensively as aids in healing.

While I tended their feet, I prayed for healing, relying on Inkling member Charles Williams's (1886–1945) theology of substitution and the exchange of love.[57] Williams suggested that the healer make an exchange with the one who suffered, offering the love of healing and also carrying the burden of the suffering. I had begun working with Williams's ideas on the previous pilgrimage with Saint Brigid's Community. However, with Vox Peregrini, every pilgrim had physical problems, some serious. To pray prayers for healing and to be willing to take on some of their burden would mean putting myself at personal risk. One, I didn't know if I could be the conduit of healing. And two, what physical or emotional problems might I encounter in dealing with their issues? Could I get blisters simply because I was bandaging other people's feet? Was their grief transferrable to me? I wasn't sure, but I opened myself up to the possibility. I used essential oils extensively on my hands as a way of aiding their healing while preventing the transfer of their blisters and sore joint issues to my own body. I was willing to carry their pain, but only they could walk with their wounds.

My load felt heavier each day. My knees ached more than I had experienced on other walks. My feet were sore, although I didn't develop any blisters. On the next-to-last morning, before I started to bandage the first pilgrim at the triage, she told me she thought her feet were getting better. My experience was that blistered feet don't get better until after you stop walking. Upon careful examination, though, it appeared her feet were healing. The next person told me the same thing, as did others that morning. The day after we stopped walking, almost every one of those who had serious blisters told me their feet were nearly completely healed. I have no explanation. But the sheer number of people, the amount of injury, and the pain suffered from that pilgrimage had given me a glimpse of the possibility of being fully present for healing in others. Since the pilgrimage with Vox Peregrini, I have continued to work with Williams's ideas of substitution and exchange as well as healing prayers and healing touch.

In retrospect, I think most of their problems were due to their choice of boots and not enough hill climbing before we started. Hill climbing is difficult in Ireland, not to be taken lightly. I wondered along the way if they had read the blog posts I had written and sent months in advance of our walk. The information was intended to assist in their preparations. Most said they had, but still, a walking pilgrimage is one of those things you have to experience in order to believe, like the beauty of the Irish landscape.

Over the more than ten years I've been hiking Ireland, I've noticed more and more people walking the Wicklow Way. There has been an international increase in walking pilgrimages, probably due to the movie *The Way*, about walking El Camino de Santiago in Spain. The Wicklow Way is attractive. The scenery is spectacular. It's only a hundred miles long. So far, it's not overcrowded. And I've met some fascinating people from several countries along the way, like Marc and Roz from Australia, whom we met on the walk from Glendalough to Roundwood.

Vox Peregrini had stopped at a three-sided hut for lunch. We had been at the shelter about twenty minutes when a man and woman who looked to be my age (early sixties) walked up. The couple had stopped for a moment, when someone in Vox asked them their names.

"Marc and Roz," the woman said.

"Where are you from?"

"Australia. Are you all together?" Roz asked.

"We're a choir. Do you want to hear us sing?" John asked her.

I think Marc and Roz were taken aback, but Roz sat down on the bench. Yes, she said, that would be lovely. Marc had a smile of skepticism.

The group gathered in a tight semicircle—shoulder-to-shoulder like the inside of a crescent moon. John struck his head with the tuning fork. He gave a note and out came "The Lonesome Road." When they finished the song, the trees applauded; Marc, Roz, and I remained silent.

"Would you like to hear another one?" John asked.

Roz said yes. Marc was silent. I saw him rub his eyes. After the second song, Marc told the group he had walked around the world and never experienced anything like that. He seemed moved by this group of young adults singing to them in the middle of Ireland.

The next day, walking across the infamous White Hill, we saw Marc and Roz again at our lunch break. We had stopped at the highest point in eastern Ireland, a bald spot exposed to the cold wind and the cloudless sky. From our vantage point, I could see for miles into the sea that separates Ireland from Britain. It was too windy for the group to sing, so I took advantage of the moment and chatted with Marc about his journeys. He was a retired teacher and coach who still was an active basketball referee. He told me he enjoyed being around young people and had taken his sons hiking several times. Roz and he were enjoying their retirement by hiking as many places in Europe as possible. But in all his years, he had never had an experience like the day before.

That night we would stay at the same hostel as Marc and Roz. Knockree Hostel has a conference room with concrete walls. Because of the acoustics, concert groups from Dublin often rent the room for rehearsal. Marc, Roz, and several other guests and some employees of the hostel joined to listen to Vox Peregrini's final rehearsal before arriving in Dublin. I sat next to Marc, and he told me how surprised he was by what this group was doing to him.

"Something spiritual," he said. "But I can't put words to it."

I told him, "For me, their voices put sound to what happens inside me when I'm walking a pilgrimage. It's the sound of how I see the world differently."

He nodded in agreement.

On pilgrimage, seeing can have more to do with the third eye than the two we're accustomed to using. I think that last night of their rehearsal, sitting next to Marc, was when I began to understand what my flying dream might have meant. Vox Peregrini's music and their spirit opened my soul a bit further than I could have imagined. As I pulled back the hidden layers of my shadow, the salve of their musical spirits applied the balm of a new imagination to my being, which would bring healing to my wounded soul. I had been invited into their sacred crescent moon, and the width and depth of my soul had been expanded as I walked and listened to them sing. My soul felt like a spacious mandala that was filled with the colors of the sky, the sea, and the forest. My soul reached behind, above, below me—looking, seeking, searching, discovering, finding new elements to pour into my alchemical cauldron, which I had prayed over in hopes of bringing forth the translucent soul gold. My psychic imagination, the imagination of my Self, becoming integrated, was working on a new possibility for me.

My imagination along the pilgrimage trail brought the faeries of light out to play. The gods and goddesses of the ancient world, who in the darkness of death had traveled to the other side through the passageway of the great burial mounds like Newgrange, were present as faeries of light, little people, for pilgrims in need—much like the fantasy images of a raven with a peacock tail. The raven can fly high while the multicolored peacock is relatively confined to the ground. The faeries and odd ravens appeared as part of what Jung calls the active imagination. The alchemist used strange images like the raven, the faeries, and the mystical marriage of Sol and Luna (the sun and the moon) to express the union of light and dark. The images of the opposites appear in our dreams and in our waking imagination as vehicles for our unconscious to expose our shadow to the light of our consciousness.

The energy needed for this transmutation is created when we have the courage to hold together the tension created by the confrontation of the opposites in our life. This energy creates space for our interior growth and the possible making of soul gold. The tension experienced by holding the opposites in my life cracked open a new place deep within my inner world, where light had not flickered before. What does it all mean? The answers come slowly after days, months, years of self-reflection.

Each pilgrimage is connected to my previous experiences of walking. My consciousness spirals higher in the spirit above while at the same time my soul spirals deeper into the unconscious, where I confront the opposites of light/dark, birth/death, god/goddess, raven/peacock. As the hermetical alchemist of ancient past said, "What is above is below and what is below is above." The alchemical pilgrim's goal is to unify what is above with what is below, to integrate the conscious and the unconscious. In pilgrimage, we seek the psychic wholeness found in the paradoxes of life—the choices that cause us sleepless nights, the what-ifs that nag us, and the unanswerable questions that haunt us. The work of alchemical pilgrimage is complex and filled with strange images and contradictions, because the pilgrims are being confronted with images of who they really are. "Who am I?" The question cycles through every stage of our life. Jung said, "Self-knowledge is one of the most difficult and exacting of the arts."[58]

The alchemists believed that they were experimenting on themselves. Their work, getting their hands dirty and using risky, volatile chemicals, was done in the laboratory. Jung also saw in the alchemists' labors a complicated psychic work. They were immersed in the world of bizarre images, esoteric knowledge, and a secret magic that they hoped would birth their renewed soul.

The alchemical pilgrim's effort is similar, though his laboratory is life. This personal psychological work is so challenging that, unfortunately, few today are willing to take it on. But for those who do, liberation can create a new translucent beauty in their life. I think that's what Marc was experiencing unexpectedly as he listened, watched, and walked alongside Vox Peregrini. I know that was my experience.

I Can't Breathe

Melissa came late to the Vox Peregrini group. She contacted me shortly after she accepted the invitation to walk, barely two months before we left for Ireland. She was in a mild panic. "What have I have gotten myself into?" Melissa had never done anything "outdoorsy or athletic," she told me. She didn't have any equipment; she had never imagined walking a hundred miles in Ireland, or anywhere else for that matter. But she was willing to take the risk.

The first day of the pilgrimage, an hour into the walk, partway up the first steep incline—she stopped. "I . . . can't. . . breathe," she wheezed. "I . . . ."

"Take off your pack." I helped her drop the weight.

She took an inhaler out of her pack and took a puff.

I whispered. "Look at me. Match my breathing." By looking at me, she had to stand up straight, lift her head up, hands on hips. The air returned. The panic subsided.

"I'm okay." She started to reach for her pack.

"Let's just stand here. You're not ready yet," I said. "We're in no hurry. This isn't a race. The objective is to reach the end. In one piece, alive."

The look in her eyes said that fear was like a black bag being thrust over her head. Air, air, everywhere, and she couldn't breathe. The sun was shining, and the lights were going out. She was suffocating inside a bag of air. She was walking uphill carrying a twenty-pound pack. How far had we walked? Three miles?

"I can't do this."

I said, "Look at me. You can do this."

Melissa put her pack on. We started up the next hill. I walked in front of her. I could hear her breathing. I tried to match my breathing to hers, working on Williams's theology of substitution. She kept pushing. Fighting. She stopped. I stopped. After her third stop, I dropped back to walk alongside her. As she started to gasp, before she struggled for her inhaler, I said, "Let's stop." She looked at me.

"I'm sorry."

"Don't apologize. Ask for what you need."

"What?"

"This is your pilgrimage. Ask for what you need. Don't apologize."

"I . . ."

"Be in rhythm with your breathing. Trust your body. Stop before you're out of breath. It's too hard on your body to recover from not having any oxygen. Find your pace. Find your rhythm. Before you start gasping, stop. It's counter-intuitive. That's why you do it." The truth lies in the ambiguity of the paradox.

A few days later in one of the local pubs, Melissa told me, "I can't believe that after all these years of singing, rehearsing, taking lessons, learning how to breathe, that I had to come on this pilgrimage to learn how to really breathe. To be in touch with my body."

I said, "I don't know anything about singing, other than I love to listen to you guys. You're all really amazing. For me, it's all about listening. Listening to the birds, the wind, the trees, your breathing."

Melissa said, "My earliest teachers told me that in order to sing, I can't listen to my own voice. They would tell me that I would never hear the music or find my place unless I listened to what's going on around me. So finding my place in the singing feels easy. Finding myself on this pilgrimage is hard. But you've been telling me from day one to listen to my own breathing."

I told her that we can listen to our breathing by being in rhythm with our breathing. At first, the listening is intentional. Then it becomes intuitive. To know when to go, when to slow down, when to stop—in order to allow our body to be in sync with our breath. We have to learn to pay attention without paying attention.

Melissa was learning how to become in tune with her mind, body, and soul, through her spiritual experience. Finding her rhythm had been frightening, because it was opening her up to a mystical experience of repeated little births and deaths in her life. She had to let go, to unlearn, and then re-imagine a new possibility. She was beginning to understand that life is an alchemical pilgrimage. Those tiny birth experiences come about because we have gone through the fire of the mini-death trials we have endured, like every hill she climbed in Ireland. Each death brings a new birth, a new realization. With every hill she climbed, she gained confidence, not only in her ability to walk the Wicklow Way but also in her capacity to face daily life from a new, transmuted perspective.

Melissa was giving birth to a mystical experience in her life, one found in that thin space between life and death. She was at risk. She felt like she couldn't breathe. If she couldn't breathe, she would die. In order to breathe, she had to find a place where her mind, her body, her soul, and her spirit could be in rhythm with each other. She had to be in tune with all aspects of herself—her sensing, thinking, feeling, and imagination. Could she move past the immediacy of sensing and the subsequent thinking about what her body was sensing? She was probably feeling fear. Would it be fair to ask her to do any imagining at the moment when she couldn't breathe? No. That would have to wait until later, in the pub, in a quiet, safe moment when she could reflect and then imagine a new level of consciousness. The alchemical process was in the early phases of producing gold in her life.

Melissa carried her own pack all one hundred miles. She suffered multiple blisters, including a large blister on the sole of each foot. And she sang beautifully every step of the way. In the first few days, Melissa was afraid she couldn't finish, that she was holding the group back. By the end, even though she was still bringing up the rear, she had become an encouragement to others. And I believe she had discovered something unexpected, something new about herself. She told me she realized that she didn't need to be in the front to lead. Indeed, the transparency of the multicolored peacock was emerging in Melissa.

TV or Girlfriend?

Vox Peregrini finished the one hundred miles of the Wicklow Way on July 2, 2015. They walked the final fourteen miles from Knockree to Dublin in what felt like group melancholy. Almost to a person, they privately told me they didn't want the experience to end. At the top of the final hill, overlooking the Bay of Dublin, most of them sat down to take it all in, as if stopping would hold back the inevitable.

The next morning we assembled at Christ Church Cathedral in downtown Dublin. Vox Peregrini would perform the noonday concert. Few people came to listen to the concert. Most of those hanging around the edges of the performance were tourists. Without notice and to our surprise, Marc and Roz showed up. They had delayed their train reservations for Northern Ireland so they could come to the concert.

As I have said, I'm not a musician. But listening to the group, I could sense something wasn't quite right during that first concert. They sounded good but not as pristine as their rehearsal the night before at the Knockree hostel. From that first ravishing moment in Bunclody to the divine rehearsal in Knockree—every time they sang, it was exquisite. There in Christ Church, I felt that something was different, a bit off. I didn't say anything. I couldn't say anything. How could I?

After the concert we went to the pub at the hotel where the group was staying. Cathy and I sat down, ordered a Guinness, and waited for the group, who had gone to their rooms to change out of their performance clothes. John came down first, ordered a drink, and sat down with us.

"That was beautiful, John," Cathy said.

"You want another Guinness, Gil?" John got up and went to the bar without responding to Cathy.

One by one, the members of Vox Peregrini came down through the pub and excused themselves to go explore Dublin. John came back with the Guinness. He set the pint on the table and, without finishing his drink, apologized and went out the door. Cathy and I were left alone in the pub.

The next day, Vox Peregrini was going to sing at Saint Patrick's Cathedral in Dublin. Cathy and I got there a few minutes before the noonday concert. I noticed as the group stood at the front of the church prepared to sing that they were standing much closer together than they had the day before. And the lead soprano had moved from the end of the semicircle to near the center. The first song was brilliant. The concert was otherworldly, divine. That day, even the tourists stood still, stopped, and listened. After the concert, I asked John how he compared the previous day's concert with the one they had just finished.

John said, "Yesterday was like watching TV. Today was like making out with your girlfriend." Then he turned and walked away.

On the way to the pub after the concert, I asked some of the singers how they compared the two concerts. One told me she thought it would have been better if they had waited twenty-four hours before singing the day before, because they were, she thought, still on pilgrimage. Another member felt that the first day they had tried to revert to "performance mode," and that had failed. "Today," he said, "we just sang for ourselves. Like we did in the woods. Without an audience."

Richard, who had walked in the lead most days, told me that at the second concert, he intentionally looked at the other singers, not the audience. He looked past the performance clothes, the makeup, the clean hair, and remembered the way they looked on the walk—sweaty, tired, and in pain. The pilgrimage, he said, had made a difference in how he imagined he would perform in the future.

I asked one of the singers what John said to them before the concert. "He said to match our voices to the rhythm of the trees. That's all he said. That was enough. It changed everything."

My most profound memories of walking with Vox Peregrini are filled with laughter, amazement, and tears. I remember Morgan K.'s incredibly positive attitude in spite of the fact that his bag hadn't arrived that first night and he had to borrow boots, pants, a shirt, a pack, and a stick from fellow pilgrims for the first day's hike. He breathed into the group a spirit of "all will be well." His attitude shined a light on the path for his fellow pilgrims the remainder of the trip. In the face of countless opportunities to complain, I never heard one second of grumbling.

Morgan H.'s courage to stop walking after the first day reminded me that we are all on our own pilgrimage, whether we walk or not. Jonathan's deep bass *ohm* rattled my imagination free on Glendalough's mountainside. Ian's ability to be everywhere to take the best "money-shot" pictures widened my eyes. Samantha's innocent curiosity about faeries and her deep desire to see one caused me to giggle with glee, and I prayed she would see one, too. Allie's steady pace as she quipped, "We're a herd of turtles," made me slow down to her wisdom. Richard's Eagle Scout confidence steadied my own insecurities in map reading. Michael's open heart and his theology that was more spiritual than intellectual buoyed my hope for Christianity's future. Briar's fierce questions reminded me daily that the value of the question far outweighs the necessity of any answer. Arlie's servanthood presence reminded me of one of leadership's core values. Melissa's bold courage to confront her fears and overcome them filled my eyes with the fresh tears of the spirit when she crossed the finish line—encouraging me to take up yet another pilgrimage, another day, to walk with another fellow pilgrim. Pastor Amy's blessing, given to her by her mentor, which she offered midway through a most difficult day, poured healing grace on my wounded spirit.

> May the Lord bless you and keep you.
> May the Lord's face shine upon you and give you grace.
> Grace not to sell yourself short,
> But grace to risk something big for something good.
> Grace enough to see that the world is now too dangerous for
>   anything but truth and too small for anything but love.
> So may God take your minds and think through them.
> May God take your words and speak through them.
> May God take your hands and work through them.
> And may God take your hearts and set them on fire.

John Wiles opened my inner ear. Sitting in a pub after the second concert, he let me listen to the silent tuning fork he used. I tapped it to my head, held it behind my ear, and heard the perfect note. It sounded like John whispering to his choir, "Listen to the wind. Match your voice to the rhythm of the trees." He had opened the inner ear of my soul. John walked with hope and fear, with anticipation and dread, with courage and timidity. I believe that John held the tension of the opposites in the group while he worked on his own alchemical individuation process. John gained wisdom as he walked his pilgrimage, and his insight came with boldness. As we walked up the final hill on our way into Dublin he told me with wry laughter, "Gil, the Episcopal Church ordained you because they believe God couldn't trust you as a lay person. I hope your bishop has a strong chain attached to your collar." Too radical. Too weird. Too far outside the circle. I'll take that as a compliment.

W. B. Yeats (1865–1938), poet and the first Irishman to win the Nobel Prize in literature, wrote:

> Have not poetry and music arisen out of the sounds the
> enchanters made to help their imagination, to enchant, to charm,
> to bind with a spell themselves and the passers by? . . . And just

as the musician or the poet enchants and charms and binds with
a spell his own mind when he would enchant the mind of others,
so did the enchanter create or reveal for himself as well as for
others the supernatural artist or genius.[59]

Pilgrimage is an art; it is the integration of poetry, music, painting, sculpture, pottery, the artistry of every medium. Everyone who has the courage to embrace life as a pilgrimage can experience the mystery, knowledge, and magic of the supernatural found in the art of pilgrimage.

Indeed, as John told us that first night, "Just because the patrons show up to the concert and buy a ticket doesn't mean they get to understand everything." His words were a prophecy for Vox Peregrini. Such is the hidden wisdom of pilgrimage. Such is the power gained by walking your own pilgrimage. There is a great paradox found within the journey. Just because you walk doesn't mean you will always find the wisdom. You have to take a risk, so the mystery, knowledge, and magic will be revealed to you.

Unexpected Experiences

More than a few alchemists died or were seriously injured while working their magic in the lab. These early chemists were experimenting with nature's fragile elements under constant heat with very primitive equipment—a program for a violent catastrophe. Yet the dangerous work proved to be of great value for those who followed in their footsteps. According to Lawrence Principe, "Alchemy forms a part of not only the history of science, medicine, and technology but also the history of art, literature, theology, philosophy, religion, and more."[60] Alchemy has indeed produced some truly unexpected results and experiences along the way.

The pilgrim's quest for the philosopher's stone of gold is what produces wisdom. The continued walking creates the alchemical heat. That flame rests under the pilgrim's sacred vessel, which contains the elements of our lives— the attachment of our egoic identity to our career, titles, and family history; the projections of others that bend our will; and our religious ideals that contradict our way of living. The pilgrimage exposes these elements to the imagination (the heat) of the journey. The heat of the imagination, created by the unexpected, begins the transmutation of our elements into something new— our true Self—the integration of mind, body, soul, and spirit.

I did not walk to have a unique encounter with ravens. Melissa did not walk to uncover her power to lead from the edge. John did not walk to realize he could match his voice to the rhythm of the trees. We did, though unexpectedly, discover these beautiful peacock feathers along the way. And still, despite these unique treasures that each of us now holds, we realize we must continue walking. The pilgrimage is not over. We each will face more difficult journeys. But because of the pilgrimage work done on our inner Self, we each are better prepared to endure the tension that comes our way in life and in death. We will need this newfound strength, because there will be days ahead when we feel that we can't finish the walk.

$\vdots$

Interlude
Crystal's Annapurna Circuit
Pilgrimage in Nepal

Crystal was a high school friend of my wife, Cathy, and she sang at our wedding. They had lost touch over the years, but when Cathy began posting pictures of our trip in Ireland, Crystal reached out to Cathy about her own pilgrimage. Here is her story.

I was on a family vacation in British Columbia with my son, Tim, and his wife, Cathie. Somewhere on our vacation she announced they were going to trek the Annapurna Circuit in Nepal the next summer. I had no idea what that was, or anything about it, but I heard myself say, "I wanna go." I don't even remember if I was invited. I just knew I couldn't pass up such an adventure.

Thus began my inner war with "What-if Kid." I had been an educator for thirty years and I am familiar with the what-if kids. As soon as a teacher makes any definitive statement such as: "This project is due on Friday," the what-if kids begin with, "What if I'm sick on Friday? What if my grandma dies? What if my house burns down and my project is in there?" They aren't being contrary, or trying to waste time, and they don't really think those things will happen. All they want is assurance that those bad things won't happen. I understand the what-if kids because I am one.

For a year, as I prepared for this trek through the Himalayas, the adventurer and the worrier battled it out. "What if I am too old and too out of shape to do this?" I worried about altitude sickness, slowing down the group, freezing to death, not having the right equipment, and especially spoiling everyone else's trip of a lifetime. Sometimes I wanted to call the whole thing off. How many times did I ask my long-suffering husband, "Do you think I can do this? No really—do you think I can do this?"

His answer was always the same. "Of course you can. You've trained every day to do this. You're strong. You can do it." I hoped that as I boarded the plane to Kathmandu and there was no turning back my doubts would quiet down. For a while they did.

After a harrowing six-hour bus ride from Kathmandu to Besisahar, we began our twenty-day trek. We were supposed to stay in Besisahar and start trekking the next day, but our guide, Santosh, had other ideas. He wanted to get to higher ground where there were fewer mosquitoes and he was anxious to get started. We hiked along the Marshyangoli River for five hours that first day, getting our first views of Manaslu and Himal Chul.

That evening after dinner, our guide began what was to be a daily ritual of telling us what was to come the next day. That first night Santosh told us some things that I will never forget. He told us the Nepali people think of the tourists as gods because the tourism brings prosperity. Because of you, he said, we have schools and bridges and an economy. He also told us that first night to stop worrying about altitude sickness and not to take the medicine for it we had so carefully packed. Don't think about it, he said, and it won't happen.

I wasn't convinced. I asked him, "Do you think I can do this trek?"

His answer was, "I will be with you every step of the way. I won't let you fail." Case closed. I believed him! So began our days of trekking.

The Nepali people don't measure distance in miles or meters, only in how long it will take. I didn't know until later by looking on the internet that the Annapurna Circuit is 130 miles long. On the road we experienced what my son called trail time. Have we been hiking fifteen minutes or an hour? How many days have we been walking? We didn't really know or care. What mattered was the here and now. We passed Nepali walking on the roads who always greeted us with a cheery Namaste as we passed. School children in neatly pressed uniforms, teams of small, hardy horses carrying necessities to the villages, water buffalo rolling in the mud, sacred cows grazing by the roadside, shaggy yaks, and herds of goats became our daily companions. Sometimes we talked— deep conversations, or silly stuff. Most of the time passed in silence. Each of us together, but alone with our thoughts. During those quiet times my doubts would sometimes awaken. My son and daughter-in-law are major athletes, frequently winning Olympic distance triathlons. I am a sixty-two-year-old retiree. What if they think I'm too slow? What if I'm holding them back? Am I spoiling their vacation? When I expressed these concerns to my son, he was shocked I would even think it.

"What difference does it make how fast we go?" he answered.

It was then I realized the only way I would spoil their trip was to keep asking that question. Case closed. I believed him.

We passed through lush green valleys and fascinating villages that offered impressive views of the snow-capped Himalayas. We hiked through important Hindu and Buddhist pilgrimage sites, and passed through a variety of different landscapes, from lush sub-tropical rainforest, deep valleys, and cultivated fields to wooded alpine and high deserts. We enjoyed frequent spectacular views of massive Himalayan peaks, including the Annapurnas and Manaslu. I felt like I was breathing in the beauty of this country and exhaling the cares of the world.

While the landscape in Nepal is impressive, equally impressive are the Nepali people. Each night was spent in guesthouses in the villages. Besides feeling that we had the country to ourselves, one of the advantages of trekking here in the off-season was being able to see the villagers going about their business of daily living. In the high season, much of the villagers' time is taken with seeing to the needs of the tourists. We were treated to a view of the unhurried village life. We saw flooded fields being plowed by oxen in handmade wooden yokes. Women in carefully tucked skirts, following behind the plough, planting the young rice plants. Everywhere gardens were tended. New guesthouses and streets were being built with hand tools from the available materials. Lower in the pine forests guesthouses were being built from lumber. High above the timberline rock structures served as shelter. We joked often about Nepali CrossFit. It seems there is nothing the Nepali people can't put in a basket and carry with a strap on their foreheads. We saw people carrying rocks, food, rebar, sacks of cement, children. The strength and industry of the Nepali is truly amazing.

As we climbed higher and the air became thinner, occasionally I would think, "what if I can't continue?" But by now, I had an answer for those nagging self-doubts. It was a mantra of questions. "Are you moving now? Can you keep moving at this speed?" If the answer was no, then I slowed a bit. If the answer was yes, then case closed. I realized I was learning how to control those nagging self-doubts. When I thought, "this is hard," I could answer with, "of course, it's hard. If it were easy everyone would be here."

Of course it's hard when you're walking uphill at high altitude. That would be hard for anyone, but I was doing it. I developed an answer for every negative thought. By the time we reached Manang at 11,600 feet, I was beginning to feel empowered. The days ahead were supposed to be the hardest part of the trek, but I felt like the hardest battles, the ones in my head, had been won. I was a trekker and I was going to trek. Every day I felt stronger, both physically and emotionally. I was going over that pass. I felt like nothing could stop me.

After spending two nights in Manang to acclimatize, we began the trek first to Yak Kharka (13,100 ft) and then to Thorong Phedi (14,600 ft). Some people start the trip over the pass from here, but we made the decision to only go as far as the High Camp (16,076 ft) and spend one more night at high altitude.

At the High Camp we made friends with a young girl from Germany named Sarah. Sarah asked to go over the pass with us. I could tell Sarah had her own What-if Kid. She had many doubts about her ability to make it over the pass. I told her I was with her every step of the way and I wouldn't let her fail. Case closed. She believed me.

We left High Camp at four in the morning, lighting the trail with only our headlamps. It was cold, it was dark, it was steep, and the air was thin, but it was thrilling! This was the day we had been dreaming about for a year. We huffed and puffed our way toward the pass. After many false summits we finally saw the colorful prayer flags that marked the Thorong La Pass. At 17,770 feet, Thorong La Pass is one of the highest places you can get to by trekking. It was a challenging ascent but we were rewarded with the sight of the most magnificent mountain scenery in the world. I made it. It might have been the altitude, but I felt euphoric. As we looked out toward the pass we could see the clouds below us. We were walking above the clouds.

As I added my prayer flags to the pass, I thought about all the internal battles it took to get me here. I thought about how I almost didn't come because of them. All the doubts now seemed like a waste of time and energy. As I watched my flags wave in the breeze, I realized my prayer was never to let those feelings of doubt and inadequacy overtake me again. What-if Kid will always be with me, but I now feel I can recognize her for who she is and tell her I'll be with her every step of the way. I won't let her fail. Case closed. She believes me.

CHAPTER 4

:
:

When You Think You Can't Finish

At first the process of integration is a
fiery conflict, but gradually it leads over
to the melting or synthesis of opposites.

—*Carl Jung*[61]

What do you call a bad joke that's told poorly, but still makes your four-year-old grandson laugh so hard he pees his pants? I don't know. But right now I feel like I've been told the worst joke about male urination, except I can't pee. As I write this, six months ago my doctor said I had a node on my prostate. He said, though, that my Prostate Specific Antigen (PSA) was in the safe range. He wanted to check me in six months. Then, two weeks before Christmas, I went in for another exam. The doctor told me my PSA had gone up one point. Too much, too fast. He didn't even do the usual digital physical exam (to my relief). He did, however, want to do a biopsy. Because of the holidays, I would have to wait another week before the biopsy, then two weeks before the results. Between the time the doctor told me he wanted to do a biopsy and the time I found out the results, I could have walked across Ireland, which would have been a whole lot better to do than circle the airport of what-if scenarios. This was a bad joke told poorly, and I had to be careful not to pee my pants.

My wife thought I should tell our two adult children. Our daughter lives in Seattle, and she would be with us for a few days during the Christmas holidays. Our daughter always tells us she wants to know what's going on in our lives, including the bad stuff. While we are still our children's parents, we have developed wonderful adult friendships with both of them. I decided not to tell our son and daughter. Why ruin their Christmas? "There's nothing to tell," I thought. "I'll save them from doing all the internet research on prostate cancer and possible treatments that I've done." I understand that need to know what's happening to your loved ones. Having been a priest and worked as a chaplain in a hospital, I've sat with lots of people waiting to hear the results of the latest test. I've walked that journey with my mother as she made the pilgrimage through breast cancer and then leukemia. She died during the chemotherapy, in the hospital. Her body couldn't take it anymore. Too much, too fast.

I'm writing this in the dark of the morning, long before I normally get up. Typically, I don't sleep that well. Lately, I don't sleep at all. I wake up at the witching hour, 2:39 a.m. Lie awake. Trying to think about something else. Anything else. I'm tired of the what-if scenarios. Now I just want to know. What I want to know is that I don't have cancer. So, I'm writing this. Do I treat you like my children? Do I tell you if the test results come back negative? If the test does, I'll breathe a sigh of relief. Will you? What if I do have cancer? Will I feel well enough to write? I've known men who've gone through prostate cancer treatment. They seem okay. Except for those who've died because it spread to some other part of their body. But surely that's not my situation. I don't feel physically bad. Surely, we've caught this early enough. I've gone to my doctor regularly over the years. He seemed very positive when I left his office two weeks ago. No one knows except my wife. Now I'm writing this because this is how I deal with my thoughts and feelings. I write them to get the words out of my head so I can confront my experience. I look at the words. I tell myself that writing keeps me from obsessing. My writing, however, does reflect a bit of the madness in my soul. James Hillman says that soul-making is illuminated lunacy.[62]

Ironically, the day I write this, I was reading the final chapter in Carl Jung's opus *Mysterium Coniunctionis: An Inquiry in the Separation and Synthesis of Psychic Opposites in Alchemy.*[63] It's one of those books that everyone who's an expert on Jung tells you not to read. The title of book is usually enough to scare away even the most curious. Too dense, too complex. Of course, I had to read it. In the final chapter of the 556-page volume on the intricacies of the ancient history and practice of alchemy, as it applies to the process of individuation, Jung finally gets to the point. The work of discovering who you are, really are, is worthwhile and the most difficult thing you'll ever do.

What is his key to individuation? What nugget did I mine from reading this massive tome? What little tincture of gold did I distill from the alchemy of this obscure cauldron? Jung says the most important thing that I can do in order to deal with my shadow, the parts of me I don't want to know about myself, is— drumroll now—to write about my feelings. That's right. By writing about it, I have evidence that this is how I am feeling, what I don't want to feel, what I could shove back into my shadow and deny that I feel. Jung says, "Only in this painful way is it possible to gain a positive insight into the complex nature of one's own personality."[64]

My temptation right now is to tell you that I know things are going to be all right. The odds are in my favor. I just need to think positive thoughts, and in a few weeks, all will be well. Then I'll probably delete what I've written here and find another way to open the chapter. Or maybe not? I could say right now that things could be worse. That's true. But saying such a thing trivializes what I'm experiencing. I would never say that to someone else. Because my shit is my shit, no matter how trivial it is—and your shit is your shit. Your pain is your pain. Your "dark night of the soul" is yours, just as you experience it, and so is mine. And I'm pretty sure my editor won't let that line about my shit and your shit get into this book. But, it's the best truth I've probably ever thought, said, and written.

If this little personal anxiety attack is making you nervous and you just want me to move on—or you wish my editor had told me not to include this, or if you want to flip to the end of the chapter to find out that I'm actually okay, or not, and the results of the biopsy were negative, or positive—then you are feeling the heat of the alchemist's pilgrimage. Reading the rest of this chapter will probably make you feel worse before it makes you feel better. Because this chapter is about people who, at one point, felt like they couldn't finish their pilgrimage. They had expected the bright morning sun to rise, but instead, the eclipsed sun of the dark night of the soul appeared. Those darks moments of feeling alone and abandoned had enveloped their lives. Life had gotten too difficult. Too much, too fast. But in spite of, or because of, the dark night experience, they were willing to keep walking, to gain wisdom, and to become healing alchemists of the pilgrim's way.

Learning How to Create the Healing Stone

The stories you're going to read in this chapter are about the pilgrimage of my friends who have learned the painful craft of healing. In *The Red Book*, Jung confronts us with the paradoxical truth about the art of healing. He reminds us that Christ, the healer, also brings us the "beauty of suffering."[65] Once again we must work with the paradox of the opposites. The grotesqueness of suffering is also the agent of healing. The symbol of healing is the evil serpent. In John 3:14–15, Jesus equates himself to the serpent. He says that just as Moses lifted up a serpent on a pole, so the stricken Israelites could look at it and be healed of venomous snake bites (Num. 21:8–9), so he, too, must be lifted up on the cross of suffering in order for the world to be healed. The ugliness that inflicts our pain heals us of our pain. Like heals like. Repeatedly, Jesus tells his followers that suffering is a central tenant of his teachings about the way to higher consciousness, a way that Jesus imagined his followers had to experience as he did.

Jesus told his followers, "Blessed are you when people revile you and persecute you and utter all kinds of evil against you falsely on my account" (Matt. 4:11). Then Jesus told his disciples, "If any want to become my followers, let them deny themselves and take up their cross and follow me" (Matt. 16:24). He keeps up the mantra. "Very truly I tell you, unless a grain of wheat dies, it remains just a single grain, but if it dies, it bears much fruit. Those who love their life lose it, and those who hate their life in this world will keep it for eternal life" (John 12:24–25). "If the world hates you, be aware that it hated me before it hated you" (John 15:18).

These are among the hard teachings of Jesus. They also mirror the words Carl Jung imagined the Christ telling him in *The Red Book*. The Christ came to teach us about the beauty of suffering. And what exactly is such a thing? We do not suffer for the sake of suffering. We see our suffering for what it is—painful. Neither Jesus nor Jung suggested that the way of discovering the Self, or the God within (our spirit), is through masochism. The words of Jesus and Jung, though, are not intended to provide us with a way to avoid the suffering with platitudes like "it's God's will." God forbid. Suffering finds us plenty often enough as we walk the human trail. Jesus and Jung are not expecting us to find some secret hidden purpose, or payoff, from our suffering. Can we find the art of healing by contemplating the serpent on the pole? Can we see the sublime in the crucified Christ? Can we admire the gash of our pain for what it is without attaching any sadistic meaning to the wound? Jesus and Jung are asking us to look at the beauty of suffering as the agent that creates the alchemist's healing tincture. The hope is that after time and reflection we will be able to acknowledge that our suffering can become a healing agent for another person.

Alchemists were trying to find means of healing for both the body and the soul. Thus, they were doctors of the soul, as well as chemists and pharmacists. They needed fire to do their healing work, and suffering ignited the fire that enabled healing of the soul. The fire's spark created the heat of transmutation. Out of the melding of the soul's elements came the stone of gold, the healing agency of the tincture.

A pilgrimage might be a personal journey. But a pilgrim walks for the sake of others. Without the heat, without the beauty of suffering, our soul gold will elude us and then we will have little to offer others in their time of need. The wisdom we have gained on our pilgrimage will become the serpent that is lifted high for the sake of our own healing and others as well.

Walking in Pain

I've told you the story of the genesis of the pilgrimage of Saint Brigid's Community. That pilgrimage began prior to my turning sixty. Cathy asked what I wanted for my birthday and I told her, without thinking, that I wanted to walk the Wicklow Way again. I told her I wanted our kids and their spouses to go with us. Cathy had been my support team when I walked across Ireland. At that time, she couldn't have imagined doing the walk herself. But when I told her what I wanted for my birthday, she asked me if I thought she could make the hundred-mile walk. I told her she could do anything she put her mind to, but that meant her pilgrimage would begin immediately. For nearly a year she made significant lifestyle changes. She lost thirty pounds, exercised every day, and began to do the necessary spiritual preparation. But obstacles got thrown in her way. Two months before we were to leave for Ireland, she was diagnosed with diverticulitis, a painful and unpredictable ailment. Undeterred, she drastically changed her diet once again. Then a month before we left, she broke her toe. She had to wear one of those boot-cast things to stabilize her foot. She couldn't walk to exercise, so she started riding a stationary bike. She would not throw in the towel. Four weeks later, through sheer self-determination, she started to walk the Wicklow Way.

She was doing fine the first six days. Then, the next-to-last day, midway through the walk she started to really slow down. Her limp made me wince with every step. Cathy wrote on her blog:

> My right knee began screaming pain with every step I took. It was excruciating pain encircling my right knee joint as I placed my foot down for the step. Each step caused me to catch my breath. Because I couldn't bear the pain, I had this fear my knee would buckle and I would fall. The Wicklow Mountains can be dangerous, and the fear of falling was frightening. There came this odd rhythm walking with the pain for seven miles—left step, no pain, right step, agonizing pain. I tried to embrace the pain knowing the next step was free of the torment.

That evening at the B&B, our stay was filled with anxiety, exhaustion, pain, and raw emotions. Cathy started crying. I worried that I wasn't helping the situation. She wrote in her blog:

> I broke down in grief-stricken tears. Tears filled with an abundance of raw emotions—real physical pain, grieving the possible loss of completing an unimaginable feat, disappointing my family, remorse, anger, being inadequate. Gil said that crying wasn't going to help. He told me to breathe, calm down, and try to rest. Nothing had to be decided until the morning. During the night the grief continued its wave over me like a torrential river. I just knew the other pilgrims would think I was a loser. I felt like I was ruining everyone's pilgrimage. Okay, I told myself, breathe, be still, let go and embrace the pain. Then the peace came. It's okay if I can't walk. All will be well.

I lay in bed, worrying, imagining the worst. How severely had she injured herself? Should I take her to a hospital? There's no urgent care in Ireland. The next morning she could barely get out of bed. She wrote:

> When I tried to get out of bed and take the first step, my knee hurt so bad that I screamed out. Shit! I had naively thought my knee might heal overnight. Instead, it felt a hundred times worse.

> It was like I had three strands of barbed wire wrapped tightly
> around the inside of my knee, wire to bone, bone to wire.

I told her she didn't have to finish. She told me she wasn't going to walk. Cathy said she didn't want to cause drama on the walk. I told her she could take a taxi from where we were staying to the final village where the group would finish.

Our daughter, Alicia, and our son-in-law, Phil, came to our room. They told Cathy that she had already accomplished a great feat. She didn't need to walk the final fourteen miles to be successful. But both Alicia and Phil are athletes. They told her, "It's okay to not go. I totally understand. But, if you want to, you can do this! It's just one more day. You know what the pain is like, so now you can adjust to it. Besides, when you finish, it will be a ticket you'll never have to punch again. You've done it!" Phil was speaking from personal experience, having suffered severe knee pain while on the Iron Man, limping for hours to the finish just ahead of the twenty-four-hour time limit.

I really didn't think it was possible for her to walk in that condition. If she did decide to walk, all I could imagine was that somewhere along the way, miles from a road, we'd have to call mountain rescue to come get her. As I fretted about Cathy's condition, I felt that my own anxiety and fears were not helping the situation. Cathy later wrote:

> Something inside me warmed to the idea of finishing. I knew
> I needed to embrace my feelings of being alone while at the
> same time I needed to accept the love and encouragement of my
> family. They believed I could do it. But they also gave me the
> permission to stop walking. The toughest mountain to climb
> would be the first one. I had 30,000 steps ahead of me. The most
> challenging would be the decision to take the first one. I wanted
> to punch that ticket.

Fighting her fears, her tears, her doubts, her pain, she decided to finish what she started. Her hard work and the intention of walking the path had been her motivation and inspiration when she had faced other roadblocks. She decided the knee pain was not going to stop her. She wanted to walk the Wicklow Way with her family, and she was determined to finish what she had begun. Fourteen miles and seven hours later, she achieved her goal of walking one hundred miles in eight days.

We wouldn't return home for two weeks. Cathy was in a lot of pain during that time, practically immobile. The day after we got home, she went to the doctor. When she told her doctor how she hurt herself, the doctor was shocked she finished the trail. It took Cathy a month to fully recover. Still, a year later, her knee reminds her of the decision to finish the way.

The following year, she would see our wise lady of the Wicklow Mountains again when she joined me in supporting Vox Peregrini on their pilgrimage. She had planned on walking a few of her favorite days of the Wicklow, especially the day over White Hill, but not every day. But that was not to be. After the first day, one of the members of the choir group had to drop out. The blisters on the back of her left heel were nearly to the bone. Morgan spent the next seven days traveling with Cathy in the car. Cathy wrote about her feelings:

> Every evening when the Vox Peregrini walkers gather at dinner someone, or two, or three graciously ask me about my day. My Perfect Judge screams guilty words in my head. "Nothing compared to the grueling hiking you've done. I just drove here and hung out. Whoopee." But I take a breath and say, "I had a lovely day of writing, reading, and traveling." Why do I feel guilty about that? I did make all the arrangements and assure everything was ready at their arrival. It left me wondering if my Loyal Soldier was working overtime to keep my Wild Child in check. I wonder if I'm learning how to integrate both my inner Mary and Martha? Am I making peace with my Perfect Judge? So, I stay on my own pilgrimage.

Without Cathy's ministry of presence and her experience of having suffered while she walked, the group's ability to continue would have been at risk. Her pain, her suffering, her healing, and her continued personal work of integrating the pain of her pilgrimage into her life made her the healing stone that Morgan needed to help her see the beauty of her suffering. Cathy knew how to ask the questions that allowed Morgan to process what she was sensing, thinking, and feeling. Cathy was able to support Morgan and help her imagine a new kind of pilgrimage in her life. Like heals like.

Cathy was able to finish both of those pilgrimages. They were different. But the second depended on the first. Neither ended like she had planned. But she punched both tickets.

Making Friends with Enemies

The very nature of a pilgrimage is that they rarely end like we had intended. This is especially the case when we are surprised as we walk an unexpected pilgrimage. Being a priest, I've sat with people who were dealing with tragedy and heartache in their lives. Sometimes they wanted to talk. I would listen. I didn't have any answers to offer. I usually encouraged people to journal their thoughts and feelings. As Jung said, sometimes writing can help us find our own answers.

I met Sally in the cancer ward while I was working as a hospital chaplain. She told me her story, which started with the question, "Why is this happening to me?" Somewhere in her story she told me that once she got her head around the idea that this was the journey she had to travel, she seemed to be able to face it much more easily. She made friends with her disease. She gave it a name: Sissy. When Sally was tired she would tell her husband, "Sissy needs to take a nap now." Or when she had to go for a treatment she would tell her friends, "Sissy had to go to the doctors for a treatment." Instead of battling against the disease as if it were an intruding army to be defeated, she made friends with Sissy. She was caring for Sissy like a relative who moved in and needed her attention 24/7.

I marveled at Sally's story. Every time someone would tell me their story of disease and pain, I wanted to share Sally's story with them. But I was usually afraid the story wasn't appropriate, if only because everyone's journey is different. The day came, though, when I knew I had to share Sally's story with someone who needed it.

April was a young friend of mine whom I'd known almost her entire thirty years. At the time, we lived in a small town just outside Phoenix, Arizona. My wife and I were very good friends with April's parents. Her dad had been the pastor of the church Cathy and I attended before we became Episcopalians. April's parents, Cathy and I, and two other couples, all about the same age, spent a lot of time together. Our kids went to the same school, were friends, and hung out together. We adults shared many interests. We liked the same books, and we loved to talk about denominational church politics and progressive Christian theology. Those twelve years were formative in my family's life. As time went on, circumstances changed, though. Our children went to college, got married, and established their own lives. Then my wife and I moved from the small town into the Phoenix metroplex. April's parents moved to another state, while she stayed in Arizona.

April had some extraordinary gifts. She was outgoing, creative, intelligent. She had a gift for thinking theologically. For generations on her father's side, men had been pastors in Southern Baptist churches. But women, for the most part, could not be preachers in the Southern Baptist world. April also had a keen gift in the spiritual realm; she saw and heard things most people didn't. Like her theological gifts, her spiritual gifts were often misunderstood or simply not appreciated by the Southern Baptist church.

April suffered through some very trying times her final year in high school. Her college experience was unexpectedly interrupted. She got married and that seemed to bring a stable pattern to her life, but the marriage shortly ended in a painful disaster. During those times, April continued to rely on her church community, which supported her. She was doing her best to put her life back in order. Then she was diagnosed with lupus. She called me and asked if she could drop by my office for a visit. One visit turned into a series of spiritual direction appointments. About a year later, April wrote about her experience in those sessions. She gave me permission to share her story.

> I felt lost, angry, hurt, sick, hopeful, anxious, and depressed all at once. I blamed my lupus for a lot of the things I felt were wrong with my life. I desperately wanted and needed to feel like I could stand on my own. I didn't want to move in with my family, who all lived out of state. I hated thinking how hard it would be on them and that produced feelings of guilt. So, I took all those emotions and fears and worked through them with my spiritual director. Mostly I talked and he listened. He provided me with some tools to help me find myself in God's story and to bring that reality into my relationships with other people.
>
> Once he suggested that I try to be friends with my lupus. His suggestion made me very angry. I'm not sure what I said to him, but I know internally I was saying all the foulest things I could think of. I called my dad afterwards and completely freaked out. How the heck was I supposed to be friends with a disease? The concept was totally foreign to me. It was easier for me to be friends with people I could empathize with. Even people who had done awful things to me, I thought I could find it easier to forgive and love than I did my own disease. How do you do that? What would that look like? I had no freaking clue.
>
> So I simmered. Letting the truth of my spiritual director's words swirl in the depths of my being while I placed myself in front of God and felt Him molding me into something new. This was not some beautiful soul experience. It was painful and very

messy. I'd sit silently and wait to be molded. I'd rage loudly at my body that I felt was poorly designed.

Very slowly, though, I started to understand how to be friends with my disease. My Creator was gracious enough with me to let me act as broken as I felt.

We often think of friendships as bringing joy and love into our lives. This is accurate but not the whole picture of true friendships. Friends allow us the space (and even go so far as to prepare a space for us) to be who we are. In doing that, we find joy and feel loved. It's hard work to be a true friend. It takes intentionality and forgiveness, and goes beyond the acceptance of a partnership. The same goes for being friends with my disease. Grace must be continually extended. I have even found that I must prepare a space for my lupus to do what it is going to do. I'm not going to lie and tell you that I'm always happy with my friend Lupus. In fact we frequently fight, but somehow I am reminded of how my friend has shaped me. I love who I am. Some of that is due to my good friend Lupus.

I can't change my disease. I *can* change how I live with it. I'm no longer in a battle against it. In some very real ways I am fighting beside it. I know that seems counterintuitive but what isn't counterintuitive in Kingdom-of-God living? As with all true friendships, it requires you to sacrifice parts of yourself that you may not want to give up. However, as with all true friendships it can bring you joy and a deeper love than you've known before. Let the friendships bloom.

April's pilgrimage continues. Eventually, she had to leave Arizona to live with her parents. For the moment, at least, the move seems to have stabilized some things for her, though her lupus is still very present. I've witnessed April gaining wisdom by walking with her disease. She has been willing to process her senses, thoughts, and feelings so that she might imagine a future for her Self. She has worked through several stages of the fire of alchemy many times. April has melted some of the hard metals of her life, both a lifetime disease and the loss of her independence, in the alchemist cauldron. She has heated it, sometimes too much, sometimes not enough. But at least for now, she seems to have found the right temperature to work her transmutation. April is working at becoming what she thought she would never be—April. An April she didn't know existed but is now discovering.

This isn't a happy ending to a sad story. This is real life. This is not God's will—turning-lemons-into-lemonade-make-you-feel-better stuff. April is still working through her physical, emotional, psychological, spiritual pain every day of her life. She has decided to also walk the pilgrimage of life every day, especially on the days she feels like she just can't take another step.

Some pilgrimages we take because we want to. Some are forced on us. But living life as a pilgrim is something we intentionally decide to do. We make a conscious decision to absorb whatever wisdom we can from the journey and then we apply it as we walk in the world. April has embraced her friend Lupus. That was not an easy decision. She fought against the idea. Even now, she still struggles with the daily implications of her journey in the world. She will always struggle with lupus. Yet April has named her path. She is walking it only as April can. Knowing April, being a witness to her courage, being blessed by her wit and wisdom, has encouraged me to walk my own way through whatever I will face in life. She has also encouraged others. Her writing, her presence, her honesty, have inspired others to live their lives to the fullest. April is using the alchemist's tincture of her friend Lupus to heal others.

Hi, My Name Is John, and I'm Drunk on the Pilgrimage of Life

April made friends with her disease Lupus. John had to make friends with his disease, addiction to alcohol and drugs. Both April and John are making their own pilgrimage in their own way.

To live as a pilgrim is to live each day with mindfulness. Pilgrims are always looking at life through the lens of imagination. They watch others with a playful curiosity. Pilgrims pay close attention to nature, because she has much to teach us. Pilgrims listen, especially to others telling their stories. They also listen to the stories of the ancient pilgrims. A pilgrim listens to his own soul. Pilgrims are always ready to acknowledge that they are on a journey—even if they're walking on a path they may not have intended.

John is one of those guys who walked a path he never imagined would be his. He introduced himself with bluntness: "Hi. My name is John. I just turned fifty-seven. I am a drunk and a junkie." John spoke with practiced ease, he told me, because he's said the same words so many times to so many people. He's been in a lifetime, multiple lifetimes, of Alcoholics Anonymous and Narcotics Anonymous meetings. He's been in recovery for over twenty years. John and

I have been friends for ten years, and his story just rolled out of him as we sat in a coffee shop.

> I can't remember a time in my life when I wasn't scared. My early life was filled with worry, anxiety, and abject fear. I have no idea why or where it came from—just lucky I guess. Because of the fear, I learned early to hide my feelings. I was like a chameleon. I was an expert in wearing masks. I discovered alcohol and pot at fourteen. Later I would use just about every substance known to man. Being high released all my inhibitions. It was only years later I realized that I was medicating myself from the fear. I was the trapeze artist, flying through life with the greatest of unease.

I love being with John. He's funny. Knows the lyrics to hundreds of songs. He's introduced me to lots of rock-and-roll musicians I somehow missed when I was growing up. John is kind and generous. But he told me of the other side of his personality, the side he had to come to terms with.

> Before recovery, I was a world-class narcissist, liar, thief, manipulator, and all-around messed-up individual. I've hurt more people than I can remember—family, friends, and really anyone who crossed my path. I lost everything people consider important: jobs, money, houses, cars, and every other material possession. No big deal because all that stuff is replaceable and ultimately disposable. But what I really lost was the love and respect of a spouse, children, family, friends, and peers. I lost my dignity, my word, my personality, my ethics and morals, and the ability to tell the difference between what was real and what was false. I was incapable of being honest with anyone, including myself.

John's story sounded so familiar, much like the story I've heard from others who'd gone down the same path towards self-destruction. But fortunately, he had worked hard to find himself. He's worked even harder to stay on the path of recovery. His story was also filled with family tragedy.

> I buried my oldest brother, who was murdered. Truth be known, it was just a long, drawn-out, drug-fueled suicide. I knew the feeling. I once overdosed. They told me that I'd been dead for almost two minutes. I was resuscitated. Now I say that I was resurrected. I feel like Lazarus. That's probably what turned me

around. I kind of figured out I was living out Bruce Springsteen's lyrics. "It's a sad man indeed, living in his own skin, who can't stand the company."

During the time I've known John, he has become an Episcopal priest. He now spends his life helping others who've found themselves walking the path he'd been down. He's also heavily involved in encouraging churches to do more than just supply a room for the local AA group to meet. John believes the local church should be involved in the daily work of recovery, because all of us are recovering from some form of addiction. Still, in all of John's process of recovery and individuation, he continues his pilgrimage in progess. He has a spiritual director. He continues to confront those parts of his life that he had stuffed into his shadow. John does the daily work of imagining a new possibility for himself, becoming who he really is—the Self of John.

Warning: This Pain Is Too Much to Bear

The kind of walk that Cathy, April, and John experienced, that kind of pilgrimage, always comes with a price. Sometimes, a cost that feels like it's too great. Surely not one we want to imagine possible.

On a Sunday morning in the summer of 2008, Rob Groover visited St. Augustine's Episcopal Church in Tempe, Arizona. I pastored that church for nearly ten years, and visitors were easy to spot among the small congregation. I introduced myself to Rob. He forced a smile. Later we met for coffee. Rob was fifty-five years old and had divorced some years earlier. He had lived in Tucson, ninety miles south of Tempe, until his company transferred him to our area. He had had a long, reliable career as a major claims adjustor for a national insurance firm. Rob said he had lived a normal, ordered life until a few months before our visit. His story is one no parent wants to imagine, and it was horrifying to hear.

> The phone call replays over and over in my head like a reoccurring nightmare. April 7, 2008, changed my life forever. It was Monday, 5:37 PM. My cell phone woke me from an afternoon nap.
>
> "Is this Mr. Groover?" The voice on the other end of the line was emotionless.
>
> "Yes, I am Robert Groover."
>
> "Are you the father of Andy Groover?"
>
> "Yes."

The Tucson police detective told me my son was found in his apartment, dead from a self-inflicted gunshot wound to the head. He confirmed Andy's death as a suicide. I was in shock, disbelief, denial; I was numb. The week leading up to Andy's funeral was a blur. I don't remember much. My brother had come to be with me. But after the funeral, I sent him away. I thought I wanted to be alone. The next two weeks I found myself wandering every art gallery and museum in Phoenix. I realized I didn't want to be alone, at home, with my thoughts and memories.

Andy Groover was twenty-six years old. He was the older of Rob's two sons. He had owned a gem and mineral business, which was popular in Tucson. He was engaged to his business partner. Life seemed normal. But obviously it was not. At the time Rob had no idea why his son would take his own life. Even today, he's left with only his own conjectures.

Rob had tried to return to work a few times but could stay only a few minutes at a time. He hadn't been ready to go back to work, back to a new normal. He knew he needed time and space to heal, but he didn't know how to do that. Fortunately, the Human Resources Department at his work helped him find a Survivors of Suicide (SOS) support group. They also directed him to a psychologist, who helped him deal with his depression so he could begin functioning again at what Rob called "a basic level." Rob told me:

I attended my SOS group religiously. I was depressed. I cried often. I wanted to die but didn't want to die at my own hand. I listened to the stories of the first-timers at the SOS meetings. I understood their pain to be as real as mine. The more experienced group members knew the devastation that invades when a loved one dies of suicide. They had much to teach. And I listened.

After attending three months of SOS meetings, something began to change for Rob. He started to realize that he was going to be on this pilgrimage for the rest of his life. He continued:

Listening to the story of a newbie, I realized I was no longer new to this club that no one asks to join. Though my grief was still very real, horrible and nearly intolerable, I realized the chasm I was being forced to leap over was no longer quite as deep.

That's when Rob showed up at our church. I listened to him. The small congregation welcomed him. They embraced his pain like it was their own. Rob kept seeing his therapist and attending Survivors of Suicide. The raw, open wound slowly began to scar over. The therapist who led his SOS group invited Rob to begin taking on small leadership roles in the group. He became more involved in the association that operated his local chapter. Rob and another parishioner became leaders in Walking the Mourner's Path, a non-denominational faith-based program to support those suffering from grief. Rob gave a talk at a national gathering of suicide support groups. He has volunteered to work one-on-one with dozens of suffering families. Still, Rob is engaged in a lifetime process of healing. The grief will never completely be assuaged. The longing for his son will not be loosed. The hole that pierced his heart from the tragic loss of his son will always remain. Rob has been walking the pilgrimage that parents fear in the darkness of their nightmares, in the shadow of the eclipsed sun.

No parent would ever choose to suffer Rob's pain. But through the worst kind of fire, Rob has created the tincture of the alchemist's healing stone. He has leaned over the cauldron and sweat drops of blood into the alchemist's brew. The process that creates the gold of healing began when he found support at work. Then he did the hard work of attending regular meetings with other survivors. He talked about his pain. He listened to those who shared his suffering. Responding to others' encouragement, Rob began to share with other survivors what he had learned. He had the courage to be vulnerable about the gaping hole in his soul. The fire of his horrific tragedy has slowly transmuted Rob, as it burns constantly through the alchemical stages. Rob encountered the black sun, that place where we learn to see in the dark using the luminescence of darkness to light our way.[66] The experience of the black sun is a paradox: the integration of the pain of grief with the positive energy found in healing others. What kills us heals us. Like heals like. Rob has been working his way through the darkest shades of grief. He travailed the hottest fire, which would turn dreams into a pile of ashes, the place of raw vulnerability. He emerged from the roaring flames as the phoenix bird rising. Rob Groover's soul has become the golden stone that brings healing to the suffering of broken hearts.

The Art of Watchful Waiting ASAP

I tried to read while I was waiting in the urologist's office. But I knew that whatever I read I wouldn't remember. My mind was fixated on something else, the only thing I could think about. Cancer. I didn't want to think about all the possible outcomes. The image of my mother dying from radical chemotherapy was replaying over and over in my head like a nightmare. I kept telling myself not to run to the end of the story. Catastrophizing was useless. Besides, my imagination was giving me a migraine.

"Gil, the doctor will see you now." I about jumped out of my seat. Nearly peed my pants—something men with my condition fear.

Sitting in the examination room, waiting for the doctor, I found myself staring at the wall, eventually realizing my glazed-over mind was looking at an anatomical diagram of a man's genitalia. Seen enough of that. The doctored knocked at the door. What's the point of knocking? What would I be doing that the doctor thought he would interrupt?

"How are you?"

Stupid question, I thought. *Get to the point.*

"Good news. You don't have cancer. However . . ."

So it's the old good news/bad news scenario? He handed me a copy of the biopsy report. It might as well have been written in a foreign language.

"You'll notice about a third of the way down the report that it says you have atypical small acinar proliferation, suspicious for, but not diagnostic of, malignancy. What that means is that you don't have cancer right now. But there is a 60 to 80 percent chance that those ASAP cells will turn into cancer. So, we're going to watch and wait. We'll do regular PSA testing and see what happens. You have any questions?" he said as he turned to walk out the door. "If you think of something else you can always call me. Hope you have a nice weekend." And he was gone.

Hope you have a nice weekend? Excellent bedside manner. A bad joke told poorly. I couldn't laugh, but I could've peed my pants. In the parking lot, I didn't know whether to punch the air in celebration or throw up in the bush next to my car. At home, I went back to the internet. I had plenty of questions. I trolled for answers but didn't find too many. I guess this is what's known as watchful waiting ASAP? Bad joke, I know. I did find some answers regarding the removal of the prostate. Most likely the surgery would result in incontinence and impotence—adult diapers and no sex. No thank you. Yep, we'll wait to do surgery until either I was officially diagnosed with cancer that might escape the prostate or I'd get too old for anyone to care. You know they say that if a man is going to get cancer, prostate cancer is the "best" one.

Typically, men who are diagnosed with prostate cancer die with it, not because of it. Death comes if the prostate cancer leaks out—into the bones.

My naturopathic doctor, who helps me with my depression and migraines, which roared loudly within hours following the visit with my urologist—gave me a referral to someone who specializes in holistic men's health, a naturopath who also has a medical degree. The men's specialist encouraged me to become proactive about my situation. Participating in one's own health, he said, requires more than passive waiting. Health is, after all, a holistic endeavor. I wasn't quite ready to walk the cancer pilgrimage, but. . . what else could I do? Jung wrote in *The Red Book*, "If no outer adventure happens to you, then no inner adventure happens to you."[67] Damn it, Carl! A little pep talk here would be helpful. Unfortunately, that is not the methodology of depth psychology. The work is all in the question. And the question for me is, "What inner adventure will this outer adventure bring to my soul?" How are the outer life and the inner life connected?

My naturopathic doctor suggested that my question was not, "Do I have cancer?" I already have prostate cancer, he told me. Instead, I need to discover within myself how I will live with cancer. Living with cancer is counterintuitive. But fighting against it won't make it go away. Okay, so what name do I give my cancer? Freddy Krueger? Dark humor probably wouldn't be helpful at this point. The masculine soul is feminine, the anima. A woman's name maybe would be best? My naturopathic urologist said that there is a possible feminine hereditary link to prostate cancer. My mom had breast cancer. So did my paternal grandmother. My maternal grandmother died of ovarian cancer. Maybe my cancer's name should be Leigheasoir, a Gaelic healer? Or Nathair, the serpent? I feel like I have had to learn a new language, the language of cancer. Like I'm starting another pilgrimage, another alchemical process, all over again. I thought I had worked through the phases of alchemy. I thought I had evolved up the dynamic spiral of transmutation. Now I find myself feeling like I'm at the beginning again—the dark storm of chaos all over again.

"Always we shall have to begin again from the beginning," Jung wrote.[68] Singer and songwriter Amy Winehouse (1983–2011) called dealing with difficult consequences "Back to black,"[69] the place of debilitating depression. We are often being confronted with yet another alchemical cycle in our lives, back to the first phase all over again. How do we live with cancer? How do we live with chronic pain? How do we live with lupus? How do we live with being an alcoholic? How do we live with the constant grief of losing a child? We begin again at the beginning, always again. When we feel like we're at the end, when we can't walk anymore, that's when we have to begin again. More gold has to be made—more wisdom has to be discovered in the Self. Jung said, "The experience for the soul is always a defeat for the ego."[70] In learning to gain wisdom, we must accept that we will have to go through the alchemical process again and again and again. We will have to acknowledge, each time, that we will never arrive at the destination. We will have to believe that life is indeed a pilgrimage that repeats itself—that it is truly an experience of humility, the defeat of the ego. I must begin again, at the beginning, and experience the beauty of suffering, the defeat of the ego. That is not the way I thought life would turn out, not the way it is becoming. Cancer. Another new pilgrimage into the eclipsed sun of chaos.

:

Interlude
Greg's Transgendered Pilgrimage

Greg and I became friends when he moved his family to Phoenix, Arizona, in 2006. He was the pastor of a neighboring church. He and his wife loved each other and were committed to their relationship. They were outgoing and hospitable. Involved in the community on many levels. I knew both of them well. Greg and I talked about lots of personal things in our lives. We talked about our work and our families, conversations people have every day—but our sexuality was never one of the topics.

Then, in 2010, Greg told his wife he was transgendered, something he had known since he was a young boy. As a child, he began dressing as a girl, something he did secretly throughout their married life. As a teenager, he hung out with the guys, played football, and tried to fit into a world in which he felt he was an outlander. After college, he went to seminary, where he met his wife. He kept trying to "be normal." To be anything else, he was told, was to be a sinner, or something worse. He spent years in therapy. Finally, he couldn't take the secrecy, the fear, and the frustration. He had a bag packed, ready to leave his wife. He fully expected her to kick him out. She didn't. Instead, she was compassionate and understanding, remaining his best friend. They kept their secret to themselves.

Within months, his wife took a job in another state. (She too is a pastor.) Shortly after arriving at their new home, Greg began hormone therapy. At the same time, he took a part-time pastorate at a local church. From the outside, life seemed okay.

After they had moved from Arizona, I stayed in touch with Greg and his wife. In late February of 2014, Greg called to tell me what the world would soon know.

On March 1, 2014, Greg announced to the world that she was now Gwen, a transgendered woman. Within four months, shortly after they celebrated their twenty-fifth wedding anniversary, these two friends decided to separate. Greg's wife had married a man who was now a woman, and that had changed everything. Gwen was heartbroken because she had hoped the two would stay married. She was losing her best friend. But Gwen understood because she knew that everything had changed.

Gwen has hopes for the future, but she is realistic. While her denomination has passed resolutions ensuring she will not be discriminated against, she doesn't believe the local parishes are ready for a transgendered pastor. She has filled in for a vacationing pastor or two, but full-time work in the church seemed out of reach. At the time I am writing this, Gwen has taken a job using her leadership skills, working for a local nonprofit.

Gwen's pilgrimage, like all pilgrimages, has been long and yet, simultaneously, just beginning. She told me:

> I hope I can continue my evolution and growth of knowing and understanding more about myself as a person. I see myself as a voice for the transgender community. I am also discovering a new depth to my spirituality, my relationship with God, which has surprised me. I feel a real closeness to the sacred divine that I have never felt before. I see beauty in things I have not noticed before. I have also discovered a new level of compassion for others. I know now what it means to love those who hate me. I can pray for people who say terrible things about me. If others could learn to love those who hate them, the world would be a better place. When we put others first, we fall into the hands of an awesome God. You can't do anything on your own. You can't pull yourself up by your bootstraps. It takes a village to live in our world. Up until now, I didn't know the true depth of those ideals—right now I am totally reliant upon others. That is a huge, humbling thing.

I have deep respect for Gwen and her family. They have all been on a trying pilgrimage, one none of them expected.

.
.
.

Beginning Again, Always

*The principle of the art is the raven,
who flies without wings in the
blackness of the night and in the
brightness of the day.*

Carl Jung[71]

*The black sun is a paradox. It is
blacker than black, but it also shines
with a dark luminescence that
opens the way to some of the most
numinous aspects of psychic life.*

—*Stanton Marlan*[72]

Life as a pilgrimage is a continual process. Every day we begin again. The day begins in the darkness of night. Sometimes when the sun rises, it's not the bright morning star, but instead the black sun of depression that hangs in the sky like the burning smell of melancholy—the moment when the presence of the divine would seem only a faint memory. "The earth quakes before them, the heavens tremble. The sun and the moon are darkened, and the stars withdraw their shining" (Joel 2:10). This was my family's life. In alchemical terms, our darkness of suffering would be healed when we poured the purifying salt into the wound.[73] In other words, we would have to embrace the alchemical idea that suffering heals suffering, like heals like. The darkness of the storm would be found in every phase of alchemy.

I share this family story with you because it reveals how I intuitively learned that life is a pilgrimage. I am able to tell you our family story because my mom left her legacy in her journals, which my dad gave me after she died, and the book she wrote about our life together, *Dinah's Story*.[74] The story I am about to tell you is the culmination of years of my family's storytelling. A family learning from each other—my dad focused on rational thinking, my mom trusting her feelings, my sister using all of her six senses, and me relying on my imagination—each gaining wisdom from the other while we walked the pilgrimage of life together.

I began to find a way to make meaning from our life experience through the art of alchemy. Jungian psychologist Sanford Drob wrote a commentary about Jung's *Red Book,* saying that "the value of chaos, the reality of meaninglessness, and the soul-making potential of madness" can be found in our own lives.[75] My family knew those experiences all too well. Somewhere in the repeated alchemical spiral my family acquired the creative healing force found within the dark night of the soul. Our story has had many beginnings and endings; it's a simultaneous spiral upward and a spiral downward.

When Birth Is the Darkest Night

My sister, Dinah, was born in 1955 with Prader-Willi Syndrome (PWS). PWS is a genetic disorder, passed down through the male, that occurs somewhere in the region of chromosome-15. The genetic problem results in various degrees of mental and physical retardation. I know that word is not politically correct, but PWS (and all other forms of mental and physical disabilities and handicaps) should not be sanitized. Suffering is not easy to look at, but we must not turn away, thereby denying the presence of the pain. Typically, people with

PWS are small like my sister, who is barely four feet tall. Beyond their mental and physical handicaps, they also suffer from an eating disorder. Food is their death drug; at first too little, then too much. At birth they have neonatal hypotonia, floppy-baby syndrome. They can't suckle and have little appetite. If they survive, they will succumb to the opposite problem, an uncontrollable, voracious appetite, leading to morbid obesity. People with PWS also suffer from violent anger outbursts, almost always self-directed.

Due to the complications of obesity and temperament, the average lifespan of a person with Prader-Willi Syndrome is thirty-three years. Presently, Dinah is sixty-one. I'm writing this in 2016, and she is the oldest known living Prader-Willi in Arizona. The oldest on record lived to be seventy-one. My sister is stubborn and it's easy for me to imagine she will one day hold the record. Still, as strong as my sister is, she didn't make her way alone. Dinah's story really needs to begin with my mom and dad.

My mom, Loretta Young Stafford, was born September 9, 1930, in Weleetka, Oklahoma. At birth, she was missing one kidney and one clavicle. Such was the beginning of her endlessly long medical history of one trauma after another. She had always been afraid she would pass her deformities and insecurities along to her children. She and my dad, Finis Stafford, went to a rural high school outside of Elk City, Oklahoma. Though their families were poor and uneducated, my dad wanted to go to college. He has always had a plan—a rational, logical, practical plan. He would be a teacher and coach. My mom would stay home and take care of their children. By the age of twenty-four, Loretta had lost two pregnancies. Four doctors had told her that she had a malformed uterus, that she could not and should not have children. Dreams were hard to come by. But she had sensed from God that she should have a child.

Finis completed his undergraduate degree. Then he had a stint in the Air Force. They moved to Cheyenne, Oklahoma, where he was a high school teacher and coach. When they arrived in the small rural town in western Oklahoma, my mom was pregnant for the third time. Her doctors told her she would never carry me to full term. She vomited and bled almost every day for nine months. She prayed desperately that God would let her keep the baby. There were days that seemed impossible. Years later she would admit that she bartered with God. If the baby were born healthy, she told God, the child would be given over to God's service. A boy would be a preacher and a girl would be a missionary.

I was born on All Hallows Eve, October 31, 1953. Within minutes after delivery, the country doctor gave my mom a transfusion directly from my dad's arm. The doctor told Finis he believed Loretta would most likely die that very night. But even in his doubt, somehow Dr. Buster was able to stop her bleeding and save her life. Two miracles on Halloween. Seems so ironic. Death came knocking but the Dark One was cheated. Twice. God got a preacher. My mom got a son.

Six months later, my mom was pregnant again. This time her joy turned to grief. Worse, regret. She wrote later that she was angry with herself for getting pregnant. But she felt guilty for feeling that way. Maybe the doctors were right? Maybe this time she wouldn't survive the pregnancy?

For nine months my mom knew something was wrong with the baby inside her. With me, I had moved every day, constantly. Pushing, shoving, kicking. She knew that her son was fully alive. But, that was not the case with my sister. Rarely the slightest movement. Fear gripped my mother. Terror overwhelmed her. Everything smelled like death. Christmas was heavy with foreboding. The new year brought no hope. January 24, 1955, came as if the one who was cheated on Halloween had come for payment due.

Nature knew the child should be born. The child knew it was better off in the womb. With mighty force, three doctors fought to bring my sister into this world. Lifting my mother off the bed. Push, not scream, they sternly told her. As she raised her head she could see the blood-covered floor. The child gave way to the world that would never understand her. The doctors tried to get my sister to cry, but she would not on the night she was born, nor for years to come.

For days the doctors focused on my mom's survival, never mentioning the child to her. My dad saw the baby, but he would not speak of her to my mom. The doctors told my dad there was little hope the baby would survive. My mom knew something was wrong because no one was talking to her about the baby. Finally, the doctors had no choice. The baby defied the odds.

When the nurses first brought my sister to my mom, she couldn't believe what she saw. "Surely there was some mistake?" she wrote in her book. "Was this human? Not mine! A drowned cat. Misshapen. Alien. Tiny. Wrinkled. Scales. The back of her head was flat. She couldn't last much longer, they said. And I was afraid to pray she would live."[76]

The baby girl had no sucking reflex. The nurses used an eyedropper to ease milk into her mouth. They taught my mom how to feed Dinah. She couldn't swallow. The nurses said to pinch her nose. Close her mouth. Force her, they said. The child wouldn't cry. Couldn't cry. She didn't move. She was a floppy rag doll. But she was alive. Living would be her battle and helping her to live would be my family's life.

Round two with death came much too soon. No rest for the weary. Within weeks Dinah fell ill with a fever that was unwilling to release its grip on her. The devil seemed relentless in his efforts to collect his overdue payment. Cool baths. Baby aspirin. More cool baths. No more aspirin, that was too much, too risky. The temperature was out of control. Surely the thermometer was wrong, the doctor said. 108 degrees. Is she alive? She couldn't live. Rush to the hospital. Did the doctor say, "Before she dies?"

My dad sped to the hospital, which was sixty-five miles away. My mom was breathing for my sister. My dad kept saying, "Don't give up." When they arrived at the hospital the doctors told my parents what they would become accustomed to hearing: "Your baby won't survive the night." Yet somehow Dinah survived. Another battle won. Our life continued.

Within twenty-four months, death had come calling too many times. Was this to be my family's life? To live with death? Grief. Disappointment. Despair. Fear. Anxiety. Darkness. The reality of having a handicapped child began to settle over my family like living with a 24/7 migraine. One doctor told my mom that she needed to accept the fact that her daughter was retarded. He told her to go home, stand in front of the mirror, and say, "My daughter is retarded." He told her to keep saying it until she could look deep into her own eyes and accept the truth. It took her ninety days before she could say it and not look away.

My mom's daily routine was barbaric by any standard. The doctors told her she had to spank Dinah once, twice, three times a day, every day, in order to stimulate her body. My mom could hardly bring herself to spank Dinah, but she desperately wanted her to live. Even though it seemed cruel, my mom was not going to give up. And so it was, every day, a few spanks, hoping for some reaction. Never a sound. But finally one day Dinah's legs stiffened. My mom said that she never knew something so insignificant could cause so much joy. And that's the way the next three years went. Doctors constantly told my parents the things Dinah would never do—suck, swallow, roll over, sit up, stand on her own, walk, talk, be a living human being—and as each birthday passed, somehow, some way, Dinah overcame another never. At twenty-seven months Dinah took her first steps. While it would be years before she talked, at least by three she could make sounds.

My parents came to understand that this was our family's life—a life filled with difficulty, a pilgrimage that felt like it was almost always uphill. My mother's health played hide-and-seek with her. Her mother had died at age thirty-five from ovarian cancer. Now my mom's doctor was telling her that she needed another surgery; this one a hysterectomy. Given her poor health and history of bleeding, the surgery would be extremely risky. But, she survived once again. It took months for her to recover. My dad worked around the clock to financially support us. From the stress, he broke out with shingles. Misery loves company. Back to the beginning of chaos—always.

My parents knew something had to change. Oklahoma didn't have resources for Dinah. They knew they needed to move, but couldn't afford it. My mom decided to go to college to become a teacher. She spent four years commuting seventy miles one way. Two children—one handicapped, one wild little boy. A husband working three jobs. They rarely saw each other. But, somehow, as my mom said, "with the help of God, it worked." She graduated and they applied for jobs in Denver and Phoenix because both states had educational services for my sister. Two schools in Phoenix offered my parents teaching jobs. They loaded up what little they had and packed us off to the desert.

I was five and Dinah was just turning four when we moved to Arizona. Dinah could live at home while receiving specialized schooling and services. Somehow that sounds all nice and tidy, but that was 1959 and special schooling and services meant my sister was piled into a room with children and adults of all ages with every kind of syndrome and handicap imaginable. Educational services consisted of someone making sure the people in the day care were fed and cleaned when they soiled themselves, and that they didn't run off. My family was in a collective phase of living in a dark storm. Life felt chaotic. Everything had changed and everything was still in a constant state of change.

The Transmutation of a Six-Year-Old Boy

I was a six-year-old boy who loved playing baseball, being a cowboy, and riding his bike. These were the most important things in the world. Probably like most older brothers, playing with my little sister was definitely not on the top of the list. I thought she was goofy, silly, and just plain. . . well, different. I didn't notice that anything was *wrong* with her; she was just my little sister and every six-year-old boy would rather take out the trash than play with his baby sister, right? Although I did have to admit that she was better at convincing my parents to buy us ice cream than I was. That was kind of her saving grace.

The summer before I started second grade was when my family had moved to Phoenix, Arizona. I didn't understand why my parents would move the four of us what seemed to be a million miles from our home in Oklahoma. When we arrived in Arizona it was so hot my mother would rub Dinah and me with ice for fear we'd die of heat stroke.

We didn't know anybody in Arizona. We left all my friends and cousins behind. I couldn't imagine how I would survive without all my buddies. My mom said I would just have to make new friends. Unfortunately, those new friends didn't come easy. Everything in my life seemed like it was turned upside down.

School didn't start so swell either. Not only was I having trouble making friends, I also wasn't gaining any brownie points with the teacher. My parents were school teachers and my lagging success in school was troubling to them. In addition, Dinah went to school with me every day. We were in the same class. In Oklahoma she hadn't gone to school, but now I had to put up with her being in my classroom. That didn't make sense to me. Life seemed impossible.

Somewhere in the first few weeks of school I got sick. I'm not sure if it was the stomach flu or the school flu. Either way, I spent a miserable night being friends with the toilet. My parents had new jobs and couldn't afford to miss a day of work, but my projectile vomiting convinced my mom I couldn't go to school. She got up the courage to trouble a new friend she had made at church to babysit us. Mom didn't want to send Dinah to school alone so Mrs. Jones agreed to keep us both that day.

I spent the morning sleeping on Mrs. Jones's sofa. Dinah sat on the floor watching her favorite television shows. By lunch I was munching on soda crackers and slurping chicken noodle soup. It was a miracle how fast I recovered when her son, Billy, and the rest of the neighborhood gang got home from school. After persuading Mrs. Jones I was feeling better, I got to go out in the backyard and play. Here was a chance to make some new friends.

Dinah was standing at the edge of the yard, watching. We hadn't been outside too long when the game of tag turned rough. Out of nowhere Billy shoved Dinah to the ground. He stood over her taunting, "You're retarded! You're retarded! You're retarded!"

Some force of nature I had never experienced before came over me. I dropped him with a hard right hook to the nose. My granddad had taught me to never start a fight, but if I had to, to be sure and land the first blow on the other guy's nose. "He won't be able to see through his tears," Granddad said.

From the ground Billy was screaming, "You broke my nose!" He was just repeating a line he had heard in a movie. I was certain of it, though I did hope I had crushed his miserable nose.

His mother came sprinting out of the house. Everyone was pointing at me. "He did it. For no reason, he punched Billy in the nose." Mrs. Jones believed them and not me. I had to admit, the blood on his face was pretty convincing. What I needed was for my little sister to stick up for me. She couldn't. She did what she always did—kept quiet.

I was marched into the house and banished to a corner. "Wait until your mother gets here," she said, wagging a finger in my face. She said she knew without a doubt my mother "would punish me severely. Probably with a whipping."

When my mom arrived from work, Mrs. Jones was animated in demanding my mother teach me a lesson.

We headed for the car. I knew I was in big trouble. Before Mom could ask for an explanation I told her every detail.

"We were playing nice, in the yard. And then, for no reason, Billy started laughing at Dinah. And then, he shoved her down, on the ground, real hard." Then I said with great emphasis that "he called her retarded, over and over again. I couldn't help myself. I punched him as hard as I could, right in the nose. All the others kids said Billy didn't do anything wrong. But he did!"

My mother began what I now imagine was the difficult task of explaining to me that Dinah was, indeed, mentally and physically handicapped. Vividly, I remember my mother telling me Dinah's story, a story she would repeat many times. It was a miracle Dinah was alive. She had endured a difficult birth, a high fever her first weeks of life, and she was what the doctors had diagnosed as a floppy baby.

As Dinah's family, my mom said, we would have to work hard to ensure Dinah had every opportunity to enjoy life. My mother explained that she and Dad moved us to Phoenix so Dinah could attend a special school. The reason Dinah had been going to school with me was so my teacher could attest that Dinah was mentally challenged. My parents were educators and they knew better than anyone what Dinah required. But they had to follow the rules. That wasn't the first, or the last time, my parents would suffer frustration from a bureaucratic and underfunded education system in Arizona.

Mom trusted, even though I was six, that I could understand. That was a pivotal moment in my young life. My loving, gentle, and compassionate mother told me I would be defending Dinah the rest of my life. Maybe, sometimes, I would indeed have to use my fists (she turned out to be right). But hopefully, more often, I would use my brains, wit, and courage. Just like my parents.

On that day, as best as a six-year-old could, I stopped looking at the world through a child's kaleidoscope. My worldview shifted. My role in the world changed. My sister became a treasure who needed protecting. From that moment I began to judge people by how they treated my sister. If they were considerate and accepting, then they could play in our world. If not, well they risked Billy's fate.

During those early years, Dinah painstakingly began to create her own special language, a word and a sign at a time, a dialect with love at the center. Using very few words, she developed a fascinating gift of art—demonstrating a resiliency that let a bit of light out from behind the darkened sun that shone over our life. My family stumbled through the days, figuring out by trial and error how to help Dinah without really any guidance. Simple things like my dad putting locks on the refrigerator and pantry helped keep Dinah's weight under control. Oddly though, as far as Dinah's doctors knew, her problem didn't even have a name.

Not until 1956 did three Swiss pediatricians—Andrea Prader, Alexis Labhart, and Heinrich Willi—write about their observations on the multisystem genetic disorder known as Prader-Labhart-Willi Syndrome. It wasn't until 1970, when my dad was reading an article in the local newspaper, that my parents were able to put a name to my sister's malady. Dinah was fourteen years old. She had survived against all the odds and was living with PWS. She also suffered two major back surgeries for severe scoliosis of the spine. And she endured the poor educational programming that was available for the handicapped. Somehow she and our family maintained a positive spirit. Both my parents have told me countless times that they relied on their faith in God to help them through the many fires of their life's pilgrimage. Those fires, however, never seemed to die down for long.

Am I Awake or Is This a Dream?

While Dinah was recovering from the second surgery on her spine, my mom started suffering from pulmonary issues. Early in my senior year in high school my mom was diagnosed with one aneurysm on the abdominal aorta and another on her renal artery. The prognosis was bad. The doctors predicted that the aorta aneurysm would rupture in less than a year. Basically, that doctor gave my mom a death sentence. Someone recommended Mom check out a surgeon at Houston's Methodist Hospital, Dr. Michael DeBakey (1908–2008). He would become world renowned for pioneering several cardiovascular procedures. After several consultations with Dr. DeBakey, my mom decided to risk the surgery. My parents told me before the surgery there was some danger in it, but they never mentioned she might die. Given my mom's health history, though, I suspected things were worse than they told me. I'm sure they were trying to protect me, but I could always fantasize the worst ending to any story.

In the spring of 1971, just before I would graduate from high school, my mom would spend more than a month in Houston, and my dad spent most of that time with her. Dinah was constantly upset and confused. I never knew what questions to ask my dad or what to say to Dinah. All the while, I was being recruited to play college baseball and being watched by professional scouts. The Vietnam War was at full tilt and I would turn eighteen in 1972. I was confronted with the possibility of being drafted by a professional baseball team and the United States Army. Honestly, I wasn't that stable of a teenager anyway. My head was a mess and my dreams were wild. Over the years I have revisited my teenage journals while processing some unresolved issues from that time in my life. I felt like I was living in a waking dream. On reflection, my experience was alchemical—almost like I was living what Jung wrote about in his *Red Book*, which was his journal of psychic exploration while he was under great distress.

The day my mom and dad flew to Houston, I was left trying to be normal in my weird world. I had baseball practice every day on top of the schoolwork that had to get done. I had a major paper in my English class that was weighing heavily on me. I wrote in my journal most every day. Being a Southern Baptist at the time, my daily prayers went something like this:

> God, I pray mom's gonna be okay. So far away. I'm at home in the desert. They're in Houston. I've never been there. I don't feel like I'm here. Am I going to get a chance to play professional baseball? And Vietnam. Ah!! Dinah's not gonna be okay if something happens to mom. She's only fifteen. God, you know what Prader-Willi Syndrome is, don't you? Did you create that? She can't make

it without mom. She'd probably survive without you, but not
without our mom.

At the time, I felt like I needed to remind God of the situation every day.
As a child I had been taught not to question God, but instead to accept that
God's will would be done. And if I prayed hard enough and if I had the right
amount of faith, God would answer my prayers—hopefully with the outcome
I wanted. All the while, I watched my parents accept what had been handed
them almost with a sense of fatalism. Things were the way they were because
that was life. I felt like life was too complex, and those feelings manifested
themselves in my dreams, sometimes like this:

> Down! Down! Down! Sniper! Up Left! In that tree. . .the sound
> was ripping through me like a bullet—the phone—dad—your
> voice is trembling—are you crying—Gil. . .I. . .don't know how to
> say this. . .mom. . .she's gone—I'm dreaming—I know it—floating
> over my bed—looking down on myself—wrapped in mom's
> quilt—Gil—are you still there—dad—be my rational father—
> yea—I guess I'm here—what did you say—your mom died during
> the surgery—I'm dreaming—right—this is a dream—dad—for
> sure—this is a dream—Gil—your mom is dead—listen to me—
> she's dead—what about Dinah—what do I tell her?

Thinking about my dad's words in the dream cracked against my head
like a ninety-mile-per-hour fastball off my helmet. Was I asleep or awake? I
thought I heard my mom's voice. Her perfume lingered in the house.

Dinah's presence was a constant reminder that life is filled with uncertainty. If the worst happened to my mom, my dad and I would be left with
the helpless feeling of trying to fill Mom's void for Dinah. That task would be
impossible. And explaining the situation to Dinah was not allowed, although
I had a good idea she knew something serious was happening to our mom.
I never thought about my sister dreaming. But I found out that she did. The
conversation went something like this:

"Gi?"

"Dinah. Why are you up?"

"Momma?"

"Mom's gonna be okay."

"Seep."

"You were asleep."

"Momma. Ba dre."

"You had a bad dream?"

"Gi."

"Dinah? Go back to bed. Everything will be okay."

"Sca."

"Don't be scared. It's okay. Come on. Let's get you back in bed."

"Yu."

"You want me to sleep in your room? Okay. You get in your bed. I'll sleep in the other twin."

"Gi. Han." Her hand came drifting across the space between the beds. I held her hand in the thin line that separates loneliness and love, fear and relief, life and death. In a moment her hand slipped from mine. I matched my breathing to the rise and fall of my sister's dreamland. I could smell my mom's perfume on the pillow. She had slept in the same bed, comforting my sister the night before she left for Houston. My worries about Dinah appeared in my dreams like this:

> Dinah, you had a dream about mom—tell me your dream—
> Dinah's never had a dream—she can't dream—can she—she's
> never told me she had a dream—I must be dreaming about my
> sister having a dream—am I awake—I gotta throw up—am I
> dreaming about puking—I can't move—Gi—Dinah—I'm sick—
> you go back to bed—sorry—don't be sorry—not your fault I
> smoked peyote—just go back to bed—the darkness enveloped
> her—Gil—is that you, mom—can't be—you're dead—that's your
> voice—I'm dreaming—the phone's ringing—dad—Gil—sur-
> gery went okay—mom had a rough time—but she's going to be
> alright—I'll be home in time for Easter—when's mom coming
> home—I didn't finish my thesis—was it a poem or an essay on
> Shakespeare. . . *To die—to sleep—To sleep! Perchance to dream! Ay,*
> *there's the rub; For I that sleep of death what dreams may come.*

In the space between the dream world and being fully awake, night's dark-ness and the daylight, is the space between life and death. Life is lived fully in the dream. Death lurks about in the daylight. My thoughts were muddled. The black sun of melancholy would rise once again, day after day. What magic could the world's soul deliver in the moments in between the confusion of "thisness" and the fear of what might happen next? War might be an uninten-tional suicide. The experience and my journals of the time reminded me of a poem by seventeenth-century Anglican priest and metaphysical poet George Herbert (1593–1633): "Therefore we can go die as sleep, and trust Half that we have Unto an honest faithful grave; Making our pillows either down, or dust."[77]

I was having trouble imagining a future. Life was safer in my dreams. I wondered if I could live in the constant motion of flowing from one dream to another? I didn't need drugs. Wisdom words came from the saints in my soul dreams. I began to wonder if I could control my dreams—lucid dreaming. Hovering over the dream space, I thought I would be able to stay in dream sleep before my brain switch would flip me into wakefulness. Life was all a dream anyway, wasn't it? That month seemed like it would never end.

My mom had survived the surgery. She had spent a little over a month in Houston and she returned in time to see me play the final game of my high school baseball career. She was at my graduation, too, but never saw me receive my diploma. During the ceremony my dad had to rush her to the hospital for emergency surgery, due to complications from the aneurysm operation. She survived that surgery as well.

After that time, my sister had an acute awareness of the fragile nature of our mother's health. And once again I was transmuted by Dinah's presence in my life. Our spirits spoke to one another across the absence of words, motivated by the creative force of death. We no longer fretted over death's breath whispering, but instead gave it a place to sit at the table of our family council.

Shortly after graduation I was drafted and signed by the Houston Astros Major League Baseball organization. A year later, the United States Army drafted me. Fortunately, the Astros didn't give me a physical exam, but more importantly, the Army did. Ironically, I failed the military physical exam due to a heart murmur. I was classified 4F by the military while I went on to play five years of minor league baseball. The Astros only paid me $2,500 a year. Heart murmur or not, as long as I showed up, I was cheap labor.

After high school, my sister and I never lived under the same roof, but we have stayed closely connected in all ways. She still frequently shows up in my dreams and she's always in my prayers. Our parents taught us by their example the importance of prayer. Now, many years later, I imagine my parents as having been alchemists who prayed fervently over the cauldron of Dinah's life, hoping against hope that some impending disaster wouldn't blow up in their face. But while we prayed for Dinah and supported Dinah and gave her every opportunity to learn and grow—in truth, she was the teacher and we were her students.

Dinah the Teacher

Through the more than sixty years with Dinah, I have learned and experienced that she lives with God in the thin place, between this world and another. A glimpse into her world is rare. I've learned to expect the unexpected when I'm with her. Dinah dances the waltz with God. She has these little *koans*, cloudy windows into her hidden world. She's like a druid priestess reciting rituals from another world. When I ask her what she thinks about God, she'll say, "I not not know." Hmm, I could say the same thing. What do I know about God? Nothing. I could say, the Bible says, or this guy I heard said, or my mom said, but what do I know? Nothing. What do I honestly, intellectually, know about God? Nothing, as in "I not not know." Still, Dinah's intimacy with God is palpable.

We were walking in the mountains of Arizona on a summer day. The clouds rolled in. Rain was threatening. The rapidly moving purple sky readied a downpour. Thunder crackled through the trees. We jumped at every bone-rattling explosion. We walked quickly, holding hands, trying to get back to the cabin.

Out of breath, still a ways from the cabin, Dinah stopped. She glared up at the storm. "God," she hollered out, "dat nuff!" She waited, as if God would say, "Oops, sorry about that," and humbly halt the storm. Instead another battery of lightning rippled across the sky. Dinah shrugged her shoulders as if to say, "I said my piece and that's all I can do."

In those moments with Dinah, I think I get it. I can say whatever to God, as long I realize God's not Santa Claus. Not everything is going to work out the way I planned. In fact, God may not be in control of the thunder and lightning. Still, I can say my peace, good enough. Then, I keep walking. I keep talking to God, like Dinah. She uses about fifty words and hand signs, and that seems to be more than enough for her to communicate with God. I keep thinking I should pare down my vocabulary when having God talk.

As children, we went past the Dairy Queen each week on our way home from church. My dad never stopped at the Dairy Queen. One Sunday, out of the blue, Dinah started saying "I-Cee." She curled her index finger up and down. My parents always strained their ears and intellect to clue into Dinah's vocabulary. It didn't take too many times for us to drive by the Dairy Queen listening to Dinah's insistent "I-Cee" to discover she wanted my dad to stop for ice cream. Her little finger signal mimicked the curly swirl of ice cream on top of the Dairy Queen sign. Thanks to Dinah, after the linguistic breakthrough, I got a lot of chocolate-dipped cones. I wonder if God has soft serve?

As with Dinah, I rarely understand what God is trying to tell me. All the clues and signs in the Bible and the cosmos have left me baffled. And as with Dinah, I cannot give up. There is something about the mystery of it all, luring me to continually strain to get a glimpse, to hear a whisper, and maybe find a drop of understanding falling on my tongue. I don't get it very often, but the few times the code is broken, the revelation is intense, worth the monumental effort, which requires years of constant presence and perseverance.

Instead of sweet ice cream, though, life sometimes smells like, well, you know. When a horrible day gives off the aroma of a four-day-old rotten egg, Dinah will hold her nose and say, "Keyqankey." Try it. Hold your nose and say, "key-qank-key." You got it? No? Hold your nose harder, like it really smells bad. "Key-qank-key." Her word sounds more true than saying, "Life really stinks."

When life goes south, I use Dinah's word. "God, keyqankey." I feel like God might be getting the picture. When I pray, it is all I can do to hope, from the depths of the pit I am in, that God can smell the putrid pain of life. Dinah paints a picture with her sounds. The nasal sound she utters tells me, and (I am fairly confident) tells God, that life can be disgusting. For Dinah, there is no excuse for boring and emotionless prayers.

We used to have a Thanksgiving Day tradition. My mom would ask me to say a word, something spiritual. Then it was my dad's turn to offer thanks for the food. Several years back my mom said she wanted to start a new tradition. "Oh God," I thought. "Here we go, change." I'm not fond of change, especially when it entails the treasured traditions of the holidays. The day is supposed to go like this: I say a word, my dad says a prayer, we eat, and we watch football. Right? Not, not.

Mom told us the girls were in charge. Well, I was okay at that point, sort of. My mom had it all lined out. First, my daughter read a poem. I liked it. Good so far. Then my wife read something from the Bible. Okay. So I figured my mom was going to pray. Not, not.

My mom pointed to Dinah. My sister was going to pray. From before memory, my parents had taken us to church. Truthfully though, up to that moment, I'd not heard, or seen, or even thought about Dinah praying. She bowed her head, as I imagined she had seen us do before a thousand meals. Out of an automatic response, I wanted to bow my head and close my eyes, but

I couldn't. I had to drink in the experience. I had to suck that moment deep into my soul. Now what?

"God!" she said. It was stunning. I sensed God was there, present, at attention, and listening with attentive ears. God was bent forward, straining to hear my sister's every utterance as if she were speaking the holy words God needed to hear.

"God!" she repeated. There was a long, yet comfortable and healing silence. I could tell she was gathering every ounce of intellectual and spiritual energy within her being. She connected with her soul. Then it gushed forth like the joy of a freshly popped bottle of champagne. "I thank."

Thankfulness? What was Dinah thankful for? Not only had she been dealt a bad hand, someone had dealt her cards from the wrong deck. While we hope for a Royal Flush, she was stuck playing poker with a deck of Old Maid cards. She will never experience the things that bring the sigh of a smile to this life. Yet, I heard her say, "I thank you God." For what?

"God, I thank. Mom, Dad, Gi [me], Cafu [Cathy], Nee [our son, Neil], Esika [our daughter, Alicia]. . . " What came after our names was a flood of emotion from every heart in the room. We were the objects of her prayer and we were now the thankful ones. We had been blessed by Dinah's beckoning God into our midst. I was pretty sure I had even seen a tear stroll down the face of God.

Dinah put her prayer out into the cosmos for everyone to hear. No begging or pleading for rescue from the inconveniences of existence. She did not want anything to be magically made better. Nothing to be fixed, or protected, or made right. She only offered thanks in what appeared to be the cold absence of the reasons to be thankful.

Still, more often than not, Dinah is silent. When we go to dinner at her favorite restaurant, we spend the evening unlike most siblings. I ask questions and she responds with "I not not know," a shrug, a smile, or a laugh. I talk about our parents. I tell her how my wife and kids are doing. I ask her about her friends at the day program. After a while, to her relief, my questions cease. We sit there, quietly. She becomes the one in control of the evening through her peaceful silence. She draws me into her silent space. She has the gift of allowing all thoughts to drift away like fragrant incense. She bundles the thoughts and sets them aside for a while. Her silence is restful. I wonder if that's what it's like sitting with God?

I have no idea what to say to God most days. I struggle trying to get the right words. At times, it seems nearly impossible to communicate what I'm sensing, what I'm thinking, what I'm feeling, and what I'm imagining. Dinah has taught me to be comfortable with silence, and when I can't stand the silence any longer to just blurt out whatever is on my heart. She does the best she can. She says what she can and, evidently, she trusts God will understand her. When I'm with Dinah I feel like I'm observing God and my sister watch the polar icecaps melt. What they see is profound, though rarely a comment is made. What word or two might be exchanged, though, feels vital to knowing what they witness together and their mutual experience of one another.

Yet Again, Another New Normal

In the introduction, I told the story of our mother's death and Dinah telling me, "Momma no more." Leaving Dinah that day, I wondered why she said, "Momma no more" instead of "Momma gone," or "Bye-bye momma," which she said to our mother at the viewing. I had heard a few people tell her that our mother is with God and in heaven, but she didn't say any of those things. She simply said, "Momma no more." She repeats the phrase, now years later, in those moments of her grief revisited, especially at the holidays.

I still wonder what she really meant; what was behind her words? Was she acknowledging the hard, cold, existential reality of death? Was she making a comment on the absence and loneliness we were both experiencing without our mother? Or does she know something about the afterlife? Can she see the other side? What I heard from Dinah was that our mother had shaped our souls and has now set us free to live into our own identities. Now our guide is no more. While we are on our own, however, death may be the most creative experience of our life—the paradox of life and death.

I have come to realize over the years that talking to my sister is like doing dream work. The dream is full of images, strange messages, unfamiliar characters, the things of life and death. I believe listening to Dinah is a conversation with the collective unconscious, a conversation of archetypal importance. Dinah communicates words and archetypal images from the unconscious; words like "Momma" and "death."

I can't know with confidence what she is fully trying to tell me. I can only do the hard work of listening and reflecting, hoping I will uncover some bit of wisdom. I can't know what she knows, or feel what she feels. I can only know what I feel when I listen to her. When she reminded me that Momma was no more, I was overwhelmed with grief and sadness. Indeed, my mother is no more. Yet, I am also humbly thankful that I can dine at my sister's table of wisdom and listen to what she has to say. Everything I really know and understand about God has come from my little sister. Were it not for her, the only thing I would be able to say is, "I not not know."

Someone once asked my mom if she had just one wish, would it be that Dinah was normal. Mom's quick humor had sustained her sanity through those years and it arose then. "Maybe Dinah's the normal one?" she said with a laugh. "I'll admit," Mom said, "our life has been difficult, seemingly impossible at times. But, I must say, none of us would be who we are today were it not for Dinah's love. It's Dinah who gives us courage and strength. It's Dinah we aspire to be like. We want to be as loving and forgiving as Dinah." Living with Dinah is always being ready to live into another new normal—another alchemical transmutation. Dinah has become a living alchemist's philosopher's stone, the stone that brings healing to the lives she touches. My parents discovered their own new normal. They were healed by Dinah's presence. And like my sister, they beat the odds. Nearly 70 percent of couples with a PWS baby divorce. When my mom died, my parents had been happily married sixty-four years.

When I reflect on my life, I scroll down through a long list of beautiful memories. A long, happy marriage, the birth of two healthy and beautiful children, multiple graduations, career success, the day I was ordained as an Episcopal priest, and now two holy grandsons. These are mileposts in my life's pilgrimage. Yet when forced to declare one day as the single most important day, it had to be the afternoon I broke Billy's nose. That day my worldview was transmuted in order to make all the subsequent days imaginable.

On that September day in Phoenix, as a six-year-old boy, I began to see my sister as beautiful, wise, and holy. On the warm desert ground in a neighbor's backyard, I became passionate about protecting my sister. Because of that day, I have learned over time to treat others with that same compassion. From the events of that day, I began to learn how to care for the vulnerable and defenseless. The way I would play with others for the rest of my life had been rewritten. Because of Dinah, my life's story has continually been one of an alchemical state of transmutation—I've spent life walking on Dinah's pilgrimage path.

:
.

There Will Be Days Like This

The uncertain way is the good way.
Upon it lie possibilities.
Be unwavering and create.

Carl Jung[78]

Van Morrison's song "There'll Be Days Like This" was playing on the taxi radio as Cathy and I made our way from the bus station to our B&B in Dublin. It seemed like a year since I was last in Dublin, but it had been only eight days. The night before, we had finished walking the hundred miles of the Wicklow Way with the Saint Brigid's group. Cathy was in excruciating pain but she felt jubilant in her triumphant completion of the pilgrimage.

Riding in that taxi, I couldn't distinguish the overwhelming afterglow (having walked for days in the quiet of the forest) from the hangover (having been on pilgrimage with our group). While you might think I had too much Guinness in celebration with my companions, I did not. My heart was overflowing with the light of joy that came from being with twelve other people who had completed the walk. Seeing them shout in jubilation, leap into each other's arms with gratitude, share tears of satisfaction, and beam with a newfound confidence from accomplishing something they feared not possible, still, years later, makes my heart flow with love for what the experience had brought them. The hangover feeling came from my own sense of having worked hard to create pilgrimage space for them and from knowing that the soul work would continue for years to come in their lives and mine. The hangover also came with the depression of leaving something I love so much—walking Ireland—not knowing if I would return to walk another day.

Too much reflection the day after the walk would be too draining on a weary mind, body, soul, and spirit. Holding spiritual space for others while they do their work had exacted a toll on my soul energy. I felt like I had during those days when I was a new parent—ecstatic about being a father, exhausted from too little sleep. Like most first-time parents, I was both excited and frightened for the future for my child. I knew that each of my fellow pilgrims would have to spend a considerable amount of time negotiating with themselves about how they would live their lives after making such a soul trek. And I was not their parent; I was their shepherd. Van Morrison's song was in the background of my every thought. There will be days like this over and over again; days filled with both grief and celebration. Such is the way of wisdom walking and the path of living life as a pilgrimage.

The Saint Brigid's group would return home to family and friends, changed from the work of pilgrimage. Each would have left part of themselves on the trail, while at the same time they would have gained a bit of new wisdom. The experience of unpacking the pilgrimage would take weeks, months, maybe years. I know for my part, I am still working through my Ireland coast-to-coast walk I made two years before the Saint Brigid's pilgrimage. The Vox Peregrini walk was yet to come. Pilgrimage was becoming a way of life. Each person who has walked with me has been affected in a different way. While we have shared the same path, we have walked alone with our own burdens. What we each learned was unique to our own experience. Still, at the same time, walking together, we gathered new insights from one another. Pilgrimage is complicated in that way. As in the rest of life, you are alone and at the same time, not alone.

Of course, there are some things on life's pilgrimage we wish we could have left behind on the metaphoric trail, but didn't. These are issues in our lives that will never be completely resolved, only managed; things we've spent a lifetime living with in the dark, like anger, depression, fear. The morning after the Saint Brigid's pilgrimage my wife and I took a train from Dublin to Limerick. I'd made that trek before, been to the train station dozens of times. While I was trying to purchase a train ticket, I became very frustrated and angry at the machine that would not take my credit card. After several failed attempts to use my credit card, the ticket dispenser demanded the exact amount in cash. I got so flustered that I made the costly mistake of buying two same-day round-trip tickets to Limerick when I only wanted one-way passage. Unfortunately, I didn't realize I had bought the same-day round-trip tickets until the train had left the station. When I asked the conductor if I could get a refund, he told me it was too late. If I had asked before the train had left for Limerick, I would have been given a refund. You would think after five trips to Ireland and several train trips, I would have had enough experience not to make such a blunder and especially not to get so upset. Yet, as the Irish are fond of saying, "Wherever you go, there you'll be." Okay, so then what's all this talk about pilgrimage transformation? Was all that walking for nothing? Had I not changed one bit?

I have learned that part of the transformational work is to be transparent and vulnerable with myself, and with others. Not hiding my frailties is the result of having been changed by the work of living life as a pilgrim, a life of trans-mutation. In other words, instead of covering up my mistakes, I own them. The alchemical process of pilgrimage has allowed me the opportunity to leave behind my self-created persona, which I have used to hide my true Self. I have tried to project to others that I'm a priest, and the mask I wear says that I'm always calm and in control of my emotions. That's only a defense mechanism, though; it's not who I am. The reality of who I am must be exposed so that I can work on it in the fiery light of day, as well as in the darkness of the night.

After the pilgrimage, we spent ten days on the western coast of Ireland. There I could begin to enter another process of reflection, journaling, talking about the pilgrimage experience with my wife. I had gone back through the alchemical process, back to the beginning of the first phase, which allowed me time to rein-tegrate those parts of me that I hide from myself. The part of me that exudes too much confidence when I feel like I know what I'm doing—that's when I don't look at the lay of the land and I don't ask for help. As an integrated person, to use my example of the train station, when I go to the station to buy a ticket, I must walk slowly, read all the instructions before me like a map, and ask for help before making a decision. Then, on our return trip from the western coast of Ireland back to Dublin, buying a one-way ticket seemed so easy.

What I have learned in years of reflection on my experience of pilgrimage is that simple lessons can be the most profound. When I go on pilgrimage, I don't care how I look. I don't shave. I wear the same sweaty, dirty clothes for days. By letting go of my projected persona, somewhere in the pilgrimage, my natural Self emerges. The days of carrying a heavy pack strain my social tolerance. The pain in my knees brings out my complaints. Somewhere along the way, I am who I am—there is no hiding me from myself or anyone else. There, at that moment, I can truly see myself. Then the work of pilgrimage begins. I must look in the mirror and begin to accept myself. Like when the doctor told my mom to look in the mirror and say, "My daughter is retarded."

As odd as it sounds, I must look at my reflection and say to myself, "Gil, you're a mess, but it's okay to accept that truth as long as you're working on your Self." I can do my work only if I keep walking. The pack has not gotten lighter, nor the road smoother. I must still deal with all the walking still to come, all the knee pain, all the weight of the pack, all my frustration with other people, all of me. Such is the reality of life; wherever I go, there I will be. And after the pilgrimage, even though the walking is over, the pilgrimage still continues; it never ends. That's why the work of the pilgrimage, the work of transmutation, individuation, is extremely demanding. For me, this kind of work is worth the payoff because it brings a systemic change to the mind, body, soul, and spirit. After doing the work, over time, in small increments, a significant transmutation begins to happen and a new part of my Self begins to emerge.

But for this kind of change to happen, the pilgrim must continue his or her personal work long after the walking has stopped. Patience is required for the days ahead. The Self must confront the ugly truth about who I am day after day. There in the light and heat of the day and the cold reality of the night, change can and most likely will take place—however, we have to continue moving through the spiral and re-enter the fourfold phase process of alchemy countless times. We must begin again at the beginning, always over and over again, but at a higher level of the spiral, because there will always days like these, days of afterglow and hangover.

A Disorientating New Normal

On my first walking pilgrimage in Ireland I was with my son, Neil. We walked from Dublin to Glendalough, which is about forty miles through the Wicklow Mountains. Then we turned west to walk about fifty miles along Saint Kevin's Way to Kildare, the home of Saint Brigid. By the fourth day of the walk we had been turned around, lost, and off the path so many times that whenever we weren't absolutely sure we were on the right path, we would look for someone and ask for directions. Toward the evening of the fourth day we were walking to where we had hoped we would find our B&B. Unsure if we had walked too far, we stopped to double check our map. We had taken off our packs and sat down on a low rock wall. There was a house about fifty yards back off the road down a driveway. I told my son I didn't want to take any chances that we'd get lost that late in the evening, so I started to walk down the driveway toward the house to ask if they knew the location of the B&B. Within a few steps I felt light-headed, like I had just gotten off a whirling ride at the fair. Halfway down the driveway, I had to stop for a few minutes in hopes the dizziness would subside before I continued walking. Fortunately, my head stopped spinning long enough to make it to the front door of the house. The man who answered was very gracious and told me our B&B was just another mile in the direction we had been walking.

Heading back to my son, I was still a bit off-kilter. When I got to him, I sat down on the wall and I told him how weird I felt. He's a psychologist and he told me about having read a study in which people were asked to wear goggles that made the world appear to be upside down. After three days of wearing the goggles, their brains adjusted and the world again appeared to be normal. Then, after a week, they took off the special glasses. Without the glasses, the world once again appeared to be upside down; it would take another three days for their brain to re-orientate their vision to right-side up. His point was that my body had adjusted to carrying the thirty-pound pack. I had found a new normal. So when I took off my pack, my body had lost its balance.

The experience highlighted a simple principle: after walking any kind of pilgrimage our perspective, our vision of life, our sense of balance, will change—as if we're finding a new normal for how to walk.

One of the more difficult experiences of this new normal after a pilgrimage is returning home—back to the routine of our life—where we'll be learning how to walk and see all over again. I've been changed by my pilgrimage, seeing the world through a different lens. But often, those around me don't notice. The changes are about how I see the world and how I am beginning to see myself. Normal has moved ever so slightly. Experienced pilgrims say that for however long we've been on pilgrimage, it will take four to six times that amount of time to reorient our self to our new normal. I've talked to friends who've gone through cancer treatment and they use the same language: after treatment they must learn to live with a new normal.

Upon returning home, the first hurdle most pilgrims face is answering the same question multiple times: "How was your vacation?"

"Well, I wasn't really on a vacation. I was on pilgrimage."

"Didn't you see any sites while you were in Ireland?"

"Yeah. Lots of forest."

"I don't understand why anyone would spend so much time just walking around in the Irish woods. If I had a chance to go to Ireland, I would want to see everything. Do you have any pictures?"

This is when I say to myself, "Be gentle with yourself, Gil, and especially with the person asking about your trip." I tell myself to go slow. Breathe. Like walking uphill. Like walking into the train station. Stop, take a breath, process. The person asking you the question means well. So, be well. Remember that you're loved by all of creation. Unless the person asking the question understands life as a pilgrimage, my answer will be lost on ears that cannot hear. I didn't go on a vacation. I walked the back woods of Ireland in days of downpour, lost, hungry, struggling to carry my pack, weighed down with my questions, doubts, fears. I am the same person I was before I started walking, yet forever different. I see the world like it was upside down. My imagination has expanded. I have connected with the Self. I have moved higher up the spiral and deeper into alchemy. But that's too much, too soon, to tell the person asking to see my pictures. They're only asking an innocent question. How could they understand? They could, if I can just find the right words to connect my experience to their experience.

I pull out my phone. "Sure, here's a few pictures." All will be well. There is life after pilgrimage, and there will always be days like this.

The Pilgrimage Afterlife Begins Now

Telling my story is often difficult. The first question I ask myself is, "Will the other person listen to me?" Then I turn to "How transparent should I be?" Or, I wonder, "Does this person really want to listen to the dark side of my story?" And my stories are usually laced with my ideas about the mind, body, soul, and spirit. Too often I find myself starting off a story by saying, "I know you'll find this weird, but. . ." So, why should this story be any different? I know you'll find this weird, but I think the afterlife begins now.

My mother died a month after my first grandchild, her first great-grand-child, was born. Mom loved my sister and me. She adored her two grandchildren. She had healthy, loving relationships with each of us. I was never sure if her desire to have a great-grandchild was about her wanting our children to experience the joy of having their own children, or if she wanted me to know the deep love of being a grandparent. Because my sister has Prader-Willi Syndrome, she couldn't have children. (My sister's life is truly a paradox of opposites—so much pain and so much joy.) My children were the only chance for my mom to see her dream of great-grandchildren realized.

I have many loving memories of my mom, but I think the one that burns with the brightest light was when I watched her hold my grandson, her great-grandson, for the first time. She was so happy. She held him only a few other times. I am sad that my grandson won't have any memories of her. Well, that may not be true. He will know his great-grandmother as well as I knew my maternal grandmother, whom I never met. She died at the age of thirty-five of ovarian cancer long before I was born. Still, I know her well through my mother's stories, which were compounded by the vivid stories my granddad told me a hundred times over. I also knew my maternal great-grandmother, who had survived her daughter. My great-grandmother loved me like her daughter would have. She was the daughter of a Cherokee family. Little is known of them because so many died on the Trail of Tears, a forced pilgrimage of death. But their tradition still lives in our family.

The part of my family that I have not met appears to me in my dreams. They come to me in moments of lucid imagination. At times, I feel like I am one with them and they have become the many voices of my multicolored soul. They speak to me like a circle council, offering sage advice distilled through alchemical timelessness. The essence of family and our traditions is passed down to us through the ages. Our families have been on a genetic pilgrimage, and we continue the journey as if our destiny depends on walking together. When we open our Self to our own past, we are opening the mouth of the dead,[79] for they have much to teach us.

My mom and my grandson represent the spiral nature of the cycle of life, birth and death, that mirrors the double helix of our DNA. Our traditions, way of life, our very DNA, is spiraled down and through us, generation to generation. The image of the spiral reflects the vast number of genetic possibilities that the typical flow chart of a linear family tree misses. We share so many similarities with our ancestors. Yet, we might also be the one person of our family to carry on a tiny genetic detail passed down from a single family member of a time long forgotten. We do have differences that seem to defy explanation. We are individuals unique to our own self and still, we are a product of people we have not known. And so, for those far in the future, past our comprehension, they will evolve as the results of how we live our lives. Our responsibility is to be caretakers of the genetic and historic stories of the past for the sake of the future. We are the stewards of our family's living afterlife.

For sure, the generations who have lived before us have affected who we are—our Self. For Jung, the generations yet to come also have a role in shaping the core of our being—the yet unborn are intertwined with the past and with us now in a state of timeless presence. What was, and is, and will be, is present now, in this moment of the Eternal Now; a living afterlife is now in this very moment, present. While Jung never suggested a clear theory of time, over the course of his work he did provide us with images of timelessness, like the World Clock and the Uroboros (the tail-eating serpent). Jungian scholar Angeliki Yiassemides, in her book *Time and Timelessness*, writes that these images "can help us appreciate his theory since they emphasize the idea that in a unified reality the past, present, and future co-exist and can be observed simultaneously. Through these amplifications we will grasp an essential element of Jung's 'time theory': beyond its temporal bidirectionality, it relies on non-linearity and multidimensionality."[80] In other words, our present state of existence is the only moment we truly have, the now—what we call "the age of the now," the aion.

In one of Jung's last works, *Aion: Researches into the Phenomenology of the Self*,[81] he explored the nature of the wholeness of the Self within Christian symbolism. Jung constructed a complex web of time—the past, the present, and the future—which exists only in this present moment, ever now, still ever becoming.

Aion is a word whose roots are found in Hebrew, Greek, and Sanskrit. Judaism, Christianity, Buddhism, Hindu, the Gnostics, and some pagan religions share the concept of aion—the idea that the present is connected to the beyond, the eternal where time does not exist. The meaning of aion encompasses the vast meaning, both the time of an age of human understanding, and the beyond, which we struggle to comprehend but yearn to know. Various concepts of aion include a very long period of time, an age, eternity, forever, or an age yet to come. Homer conceived of the aion as the unified concept of the psyche, the soul, the inner water of life. Aion has captured the imagination of humanity's spiritual mind in such a way that aion has been viewed as a deity; the god of boundless time, master of the four elements, the kaleidoscope of destiny.[82]

Time is a human construct that, unfortunately, limits our ability to live fully in the presence of this moment. We feel defined by the past and also captivated by what might happen in the future. Both distract us from living in the now. But the reality is that in this moment we are living, there is neither past nor any future. God exists in this present moment of timelessness with us, where all that was is now unified with all that is now. To exist in this state of time is to exist in the timeless unity of the divine, the aion of now. This state of timelessness is to live in *unus mundus,* which is living within the unified reality from which everything emerges and to which everything returns (God). This is the blissful moment of timelessness that can be found in meditation, where we are one with the great everything.

Jung's conceptual understanding of *aion* and *unus mundus* allows us to consider the notion that pilgrimage is more than a long walk that comes to an end. The concept of aion allows us to see that pilgrimage is the past, the here and now, and the future being lived in this moment. In other words, pilgrimage is a way of life that experiences all of life—our past, the present, the future of our death and the afterlife—simultaneously in this single moment. Aion provides a way of thinking about pilgrimage as a timeless adventure— a journey into the realm of the life after pilgrimage, life after life all in the present moment. This is what it means to live a non-dual life, a life of unity.

Jung taught us to work toward the integration of the two halves of our earthly life. The first half of life we are in the process of acquiring a structure, a framework. We play the game of our culture, society, and family long enough to know the rules and how to survive them. In the second half of life, we realize there is more to life than the rules others have projected onto us. We start to ask the more important questions of life. Hopefully, we begin the individuation process, discovering the Self. We start to live with the Self in the center, the conductor of the symphony of our life, while the ego plays the appropriate role of travel manager, figuring out how to get us from one point to another. Somewhere in the second half of life we start asking the questions about the end of life. We are confronted with the death of our family and friends. We begin to accept the reality that we will not live forever. We might ask our Self the question, in relation to the aion, am I already dead (metaphorically) in the grandest scope of time? And if so, how does that affect how I live now, in this moment?

For Jung, the second half of life culminates in the preparation for death. In his essay "The Soul and Death,"[83] he considered death not as the end of life, but instead the goal of life.[84] Jung considered the psychological process of alchemical individuation, working with one's Self, affected by the unconscious, to be an experience of a transmutation that exceeds our concepts of this life—timelessness. The transmutation, he says, begins after the first half of life, producing a satisfying change in the person's focus, so that "consciousness is no longer preoccupied with compulsive plans but dissolves in contemplative vision."[85] This place of contemplative vision is the intersection of the conscious and the unconscious. The center is where the Self resides, the heart of the mandala and the cross. This is the mystical moment when the rising solstice sun streams like lava down Newgrange's light box. Jung goes on to say, "I have reasons for believing that this attitude settles in after middle life and is a natural preparation for death. Death is psychologically as important as birth, and like it, is an integral part of life."[86] Death then, like birth, becomes a creative act. According to Jungian depth psychologist Stanton Marlon, in his book *The Black Sun*, metaphoric death (symbolically represented by the black sun) is "at the heart of the alchemical experience."[87] Death is always present in life, whether in the first half or the second half.

Jung's concept about the two halves of life is extraordinarily important for the individuation process. Wouldn't life be sad if at the end of my fortieth year I simply stopped evolving, changing, maturing, being transformed? Yes, it would be, and that's why I keep walking wisdom's way. Such is the point of Jung's lifetime of work—we continue to psychologically mature and individuate throughout life. But what if, instead of the middle of life being forty, the whole of life (maybe eighty years) is the first half of life? What if the time we walk this earth before we step through the veil from this life to the next is the first half of life? And what if the afterlife is the second half of life? What if we are living simultaneously in this aion (the age of our life) and the new aion (the age of timelessness)? What if there is life after pilgrimage, and that life is now a series of moments strung together in an experience of timelessness? In other words, life continues by virtue of this moment existing and my full awareness of it. And whatever exists next still is the next present moment because there is no next moment—only now, only this.

If such is the case, I want to live constantly in the now of being in the process, so when this life is over and the second half of life, the afterlife, or the next present moment, begins, I know how to be continually on pilgrimage in a constant state of transmutation. I know some religions teach that the after-life is a place of sudden transformation into something perfect, heaven. Those religions teach that the afterlife is dependent upon the divine doing the work and the human soul simply accepting whatever God hands out, perfection in heaven or something worse, a damaged existence in hell. But what if that is not what the divine had in mind? What if the afterlife is like the second half of life, a pilgrimage, a process of learning, growing, developing, asking the bigger of the biggest questions? What if on the other side of the veil we continue the pil-grimage of soul evolution, maturing into who we have been called to be from our beginning. What if the work is not finished? I think that prospect is good news.

My real fear is that who I will be in the afterlife is the person I am at the end of this life. In other words—that formation ends at death and I am frozen in eternal time the way I died. That's a horrifying thought. Evangelical writer Dallas Willard put those thoughts in my head in his book, *The Divine Conspiracy*. He writes:

> I often wonder how happy and useful some of the fearful, bitter, lust-ridden, hate-filled Christians . . . would be if they were forced to live forever in the unrestrained fullness of the reality of God . . . . What if death only forever fixes us as the kind of person we are at death?"[88]

Yikes!

I don't think that is the case. But if it is, I am even more motivated to open my mind, body, soul, and spirit to the transformational work of life before death. If I am going to be stuck in the afterlife as I am now, I still have a tre-mendous amount of work left to do. Jung said that it would take him ten life-times to process all his stuff, to individuate. If it would take him ten lifetimes, mercy, how many would I need—ten thousand? And if there isn't any life after death, I for sure don't want to leave my family and friends with the eternal image of Bitter Gil frozen in their minds. Save me from such a horrible ending. Fortunately, I don't sense the work is done when we step through the veil into the next life. Either way, I'm still on pilgrimage so I can be shaped, formed, and transmuted into a new being. Pilgrimage continues her soul-shaping work in our lives as we walk the road of life—in this world and the next. There is, however, I pray, a lot of walking still to do before I pass through the veil. But losing a dear friend has caused me to keep my attention intently on the cyclical spirals of life and death.

A New Imagination of Life and the Afterlife

Between my finishing the previous chapter and my beginning to write this one, two unrelated events happened within days of one another. Both have had a profound impact on the spiritual alchemy of my life. (The second event I write about later in this chapter.) In the introduction, I talked about my Jungian mentor, spiritual guide, and sometimes therapist, Scott Haasarud. I was supposed to have an appointment with him on April 13, 2016. After a very brief stint in the hospital, he died that very morning. Scott completed his pilgrimage on this earth, and I was asked to organize his memorial service.

Scott Haasarud (1940–2016) was a healer of the soul. He healed with golden love from the giant cauldron of his heart. I have been a recipient of the healing from Scott's philosopher's stone. But even the best healers have only so much tincture to give away.

I met Scott on December 1, 1995. He was the energy behind bringing his friend Marcus Borg (1941–2015) to Phoenix for a two-day presentation. I had read and reread Borg's *Meeting Jesus Again for the First Time*.[89] Borg's wisdom and his gentle willingness to answer my many emailed questions, inquiries from a person he had never met, kept me within the Christian world. When I saw the flyer about his presentation in Phoenix, I knew I *had* to meet Borg. Little did I know, though, that I would meet the man who would later help me keep my life together.

From that first handshake with Scott, I felt there was something unique about him. At the time I couldn't wrap my arms around it, but from that point on, everything Scott invited me to attend, I did. Scott invited me to attend an Enneagram seminar. I went. Scott invited me to a dream seminar. I went. Scott invited me to apply to the spiritual direction school where he taught. I applied. Scott invited my son and me to a father-son retreat. We went. From that retreat, Scott would have a major influence on my son's decision to become a psychologist. Scott taught. I soaked it all in. He and I had this long, ongoing, never-ending, life-giving conversation.

Then nine years after Scott and I met, my world was turned upside down. For months, I could barely leave my house, and never alone. One morning, before my wife left for work, she gave me a task. Make an appointment to see Scott. That was April of 2004. From then on, I met with Scott once a month. I met with him for 144 sessions—12 × 12, (3×4) × (3×4)—those numbers represent the pureness and the messiness of the alchemy that was done on my soul—the incomplete three struggling to become the fullness of the four, over and over again. Those numbers are the symbols of a long and fruitful pilgrimage of two people companioning in life together.

A friend, who also saw Scott regularly, said that he filled a void in her life that was larger than Scott himself. He was a big man in every way; it was hard to get your arms around all of him. Wise and gentle. Subtle at times, yet straightforward when necessary. Scott was a complex man, paradoxical, yet in many ways uncomplicated. At times, I was confident he was channeling the larger force of Carl Jung. Yes, some people call themselves Jungian, but Scott breathed Carl Jung in and out, like tobacco from an ancient pipe. He had placed the tea bag of his life into Jung's alchemical brew and then he ladled it out to the rest of us, one sip at a time. Scott and I sat within his endless library. He listened no matter how long I talked. Then he would tell a story. Sometimes he would quote Jung at just the right moment, reach for the appropriate book and hand it to me. He never gave instructions, only offerings. I could wisely take it, or foolishly leave it.

You could call Scott a Christian, though you'd have to clearly define what you meant by "Christian." Scott understood Jesus through Jungian eyes. Jung said in *The Red Book* that, "Whoever possesses wisdom is not greedy for power. Only the man who has power declines to use it."[90] Scott Haasarud had a power that seemed to arise from the unconscious. He never used it, but I felt it. Now that he is among the dead, I still feel his power healing me. I think that's what Jung meant by listening to the lament of the dead—timeless listening and living in the present moment.

In *The Red Book,* Jung told of a vision he had.[91] He was hanging from the Tree of Life, wrestling with the rational and irrational, his thinking and his feeling. He asked his anima, his soul, to cut him down from the tree, but she said she couldn't reach that high. So the *anima* became a serpent and slithered up the tree. The serpent, in an attempt to get Jung out of the tree, then became a bird and flew high into heaven. She brought back a golden crown for Jung. The inscription on the crown read, "Love never ends."

He asked the bird, "What does the riddle of the golden crown mean?"

"It means," said the bird, "that the crown and the serpent are opposites, yet one. Did you not see the serpent that crowned the head of the crucified?" Jung's vision, through his active imagination, was a way for him to accept that the purpose of his life was to be a loving healer in the archetypal image of Christ, sometimes serpent, sometimes dove. Scott was that same kind of healer.

Scott was both the serpent and the dove, a voice of poison (hard words to hear) and a voice of salvation (salve for the soul). We are all called to be healers in the image of the Christ. We need not be like Jesus. Instead, we must do the unthinkable. We must become Jesus, through our own internal work, for the sake of others. Scott Haasarud became Jesus, healing others with love. Scott did his own soul work. He modeled for us, with us, in us, around us, the way to become who we are all called to be: our own Self, the Christ within us all, within every human being, within every creature, every stone of creation. "Love Never Ends" because in a paradoxical way, death creates the healing love of life that never ends.

Scott Haasarud has left the world of the seen to reside in the realm of the unseen. He has been grafted into the Tree of Life. He has become the bird that flies upward to retrieve the crown. No longer encumbered by earthly limitations, he is now free to meet us in the collective unconscious. Scott's life and work lives, infused into the essence of the mind, body, soul, and spirit of his family, friends, and clients. While we may not see Scott every day, or once a month, we will now encounter him in a better realm, in our dreams, in our creative imagination as a part of the collective unconscious, who speaks the wisdom of the dead to the living. I still wonder how my relationship with Scott will continue to shape my life in this one moment of time that I live in. And in living in this time of grief, oddly enough, there can be celebration in "days like this."

Living into Our Own Personal Legend

The long days after a pilgrimage is over can become drudgery. Whether the pilgrimage was walking Ireland or grieving the loss of friend, we must still keep living life as a pilgrimage. The metaphoric daily work of lacing our boots, putting on our pack, and walking the road of life are spiritual practices that help build the capacity of our soul, the container of transmutation. By creating more inner space, we can move closer to fulfilling what author Paulo Coelho calls in *The Alchemist* our "personal legend." He writes, "Whoever you are, or whatever it is that you do, whenever you really want something, it's because that desire originated in the soul of the universe. . . . And when you want to do something, all the universe conspires in helping you achieve it."[92] But we have to continue on the pilgrimage trail in order to envision and create our personal legend. Even though we are worn out and exhausted, we can't stop walking. But such work, indeed, can be a mundane grind.

In the daily-ness of life, our spiritual practices of pilgrimage will require the same one-step-at-a-time steadiness needed to walk up a long hill in solitude. What sustained us on those hours of walking will now carry us through the sometimes mundaneness of the new normal we experience after pilgrimage. Life is different now after wisdom walking. I rely on what I had learned on pilgrimage to carry me during the times when I feel like no one understands what I have experienced, whether the experience was the pilgrimage of walking, grief, pain, disease, or transition. I do the things that are required—go to work, clean the house, pick up the dog poop in the backyard, buy the groceries, and deal with the complexity of life in the twenty-first century. While enduring the mundaneness of life, my prayer is that the divine, the universe, and whoever walks beside me will help me through whatever I encounter, mundane or otherwise.

I depend on the spiritual guides, like Scott Haasarud, who have walked with me through so many rough trails. Wise guides through the centuries have taught us proven practices to help us defend ourselves against things like projections from our family or from culture, our lack of confidence, the struggles of daily life, and acedia—a malady of listlessness convincing us tomorrow is a better day to walk the road. While some spiritual traditions practice rituals that are unique to them, there are practices common to most traditions—such as prayer, meditation, and silence—that could help us in our work toward the fulfillment of our individuation process.

Prayer, meditation, silence, memorizing sacred texts, chant, music, dance, the physical acts of ritual, and having a spiritual companion can be found in the spiritual practices of ancient pagan religions, the most fundamentalist or liberal of any of the three Abrahamic faiths, and the Eastern religions of Buddhism, Hinduism, and Sikhism. The theurgic practices, the rituals of divine-working, that are common to so many religions are fertile ground for living life as a pilgrim.

Prayer as a Pilgrimage Practice

The alchemist, both ancient and contemporary, begins his or her *opus* (work) with prayer. As the work proceeds, he or she will heat each stage of the vessel with prayer, like breath warming cold hands. In every phase the alchemist pours prayer gently over the contents of the cauldron as if it were a fragile egg.

Much like Teresa of Avila's journey through the seven-storied castle of the soul, the alchemist's pilgrimage relied on prayer to carry the spiritual art of life upward. The prayer is not for the sake of some divine miracle. Instead, we pray to encourage the Creator to work with us in the natural world. In vigil, the alchemist hovers over the cauldron of the psyche. We cry out to God, like Job, hoping to influence the divine to listen to our petitions, questions, and challenges. Prayer is essentially a co-creative act of the alchemist's soul and the work of the divine. Without our work and our prayers and the divine's partnership, the pilgrim's healing stone will not develop. Our healing tinctures can take many forms, both materially physical—like stones and prayer beads—and in forces of energy—a prayer being spoken aloud by a faithful friend.

In telling the story of Scott's death, I mentioned two unrelated moments of synchronicity. That second moment is the story of Justino's pilgrimage. I met Justino five years ago. At the time he was a friend of Jillian's. In chapter 2, I told you about Jillian's pilgrimage. She had walked the Santiago de Compostela (the Camino) as a dare. Upon returning, her community washed her feet as a sacred symbol of her holy pilgrimage. Knowing Jillian as I do, I think there was a lot more to her willingness to walk over five hundred miles than simply to prove to a friend she could accomplish the feat alone. Jillian has a passion for life, for spirituality, and for a life among Spanish-speaking people. After she finished the Camino she began her senior year in college at Northern Arizona University in Flagstaff. She graduated and stayed in Flagstaff to teach elementary school. She finished her master's degree and excelled as a teacher, being awarded Arizona's Teacher of the Year in 2016. During her years in Flagstaff she met Justino, a bright, hard-working, kind man who dances with the same passion he has for all of life. He was in the United States illegally. The two of them became fast friends and eventually started dating. In October of 2014, I performed their wedding and immediately Justino and Jillian started taking the steps to get him a visa.

Justino's pilgrimage from Mexico into the United States started years before he met Jillian. He is from Mexico City, Mexico. His brother had arranged for a coyote (illegal human trafficker) to meet Justino in Los Algodones, a small Mexican village about seven miles south of Yuma, Arizona. For a lot of money, the coyote would lead a dozen men and women across the desert in February.

Justino, and those traveling with him, came unprepared for their journey. While the daytime temperatures were mild, the nights were freezing. Without water, carrying nothing but the clothes on their backs, the thirteen people moved stealthily through the desert. Justino had worn black loafers, not anticipating the rough desert terrain and the long hours of the journey. After the first six hours his feet were so blistered he wondered if they would ever be normal again. During the night they huddled under bushes, trembling from the windy, cold desert nights. They were warned to remain absolutely silent in the darkness. The coyote told them that the border patrol would call out in Spanish, "I met your sister and she gave me a message for you." The officers were counting on a response from the desperate immigrants that would give away their hiding place.

After a few days of literally crawling through the desert, the group arrived at a location north of Yuma. There, Justino was told to get into the trunk of a stranger's car. He was covered with a blanket behind some luggage in case the trunk was searched. The coyote told Justino that the driver would take him to Mesa, Arizona. He rode for six hours in a hot, suffocating trunk just hoping to survive one more day. I've wondered what was going through his mind in the darkness of that mini-tomb, trapped in the trunk of that car.

Finally, in the middle of the night, the trunk was opened and Justino stepped out into a new life, in a new land, frightened. He was alone. He didn't know anyone. After hanging out in Mesa for a while, he left and headed north to Flagstaff, where he thought he could find work and be farther away from the border. He did find a job, first in hospitality and then in construction. In the shadow of being deported, he began to create a new life for himself. And then he met Jillian at a dance. Justino has worn dress shoes only once since crossing the border. That day was at their wedding.

When he told me his story, I asked if he considered his journey across the border dangerous. He was hesitant to say it was. I asked him if he thought his walk across the border was a pilgrimage, and he was very unsure of that. At the time I interviewed him, he didn't want me to use his name (though later he changed his mind), but he also wanted me to understand that many people had died making the journey across the desert—and he was sad for them and their families. He was lucky, he said. He had made it, and now life is good and for that he is very thankful. I had interviewed Justino after their marriage, and they were still working on getting him an immigration hearing, hoping he could acquire a visa and permanent residency in the United States.

A month before Scott died, Justino's immigration lawyer called to say that he had been granted a hearing in Juarez, Mexico. Then, a few days after Scott's death and before Justino and Jillian headed to Juarez, my wife and I met with the couple in Flagstaff. They asked if we would pray with them. I pulled a small rope of prayer beads out of my shoulder bag. I had used the beads at the baptism of both my grandsons. I also held the beads in my mom's hand as she was dying. The beads had been with me every step of three pilgrimages in Ireland. I carry the beads with me every day. There were a lot of prayers and sentimental meaning attached to that eight-inch rope of wooden beads. As Jillian and Justino held hands, I wrapped the small rope of beads around their wrists. Then we prayed for their safety and that they would return from Juarez, together. A voice within me said to tell Justino to keep the prayer beads with him on his pilgrimage across the border. I wanted the beads returned one day—but only after he was safely back in the United States. The prayer rope, I told him, had power, for it had become a talisman. He wept. We all did.

Jillian was confident (as she is always wont to be) that the hearing was just a matter of formality. While I didn't say so, my skepticism was on red alert. I couldn't imagine that something so important would be routine. And, besides, I could see the fear in Justino's eyes. I doubted that he thought getting a visa was a done deal. He knew once he crossed the Mexican border, he might never be able to return to the United States. Jung said that uncertainty would be the good way. At that moment in Justino and Jillian's life, it was the only way.

As Cathy and I drove home from our prayer time with Justino and Jillian, I could feel the absence of my prayer beads. Those beads have a material presence of the divine within them—their matter has been infused with the spirit. Within a week, that presence would be making another pilgrimage, this time with Justino across the US–Mexico border.

Justino took the risk of walking across the border at Juarez. He had two long interviews over the course of a week. At the conclusion of the second interview he was granted a visa. Jillian immediately sent us pictures of Justino as he came out of the immigration building. His face was awash with smiles and happy tears. As in dealing with any bureaucracy, they had to spend another week in Juarez waiting for his official documents. During that time Jillian sent me pictures of my prayer beads in various churches where she and Justino used them to pray prayers of thanksgiving.

A month later, Justino and Jillian met Cathy and me for lunch in Phoenix. With an embrace of thanks and tears of joy, Justino dropped the prayer beads into my hands. There's a palpable energy in those beads, now more than ever. The presences of my mom, my grandsons, Ireland, Justino, and Jillian reside with the divine in those beads. In "days like this," even in my grief of losing Scott, I could celebrate with my friends in their new life of liberty—a pilgrimage of the timeless spirals of life, death, and rebirth.

Exercise as a Pilgrimage Practice

As important as prayer is to the work of the pilgrim's soul, daily exercise is a key to the health of our body. Both must be practiced for the sake of relationship with the divine and with other people. The obvious practice is to walk every day. Nothing mimics the pilgrimage path better than walking. As I walk, I pray. My daily walk becomes like praying a labyrinth through my neighborhood. Admittedly, walking through my community has its limitations. But given the weather, location, or other obstacles, I have to make a committed effort to find ways to keep my body healthy through exercise. Walking is only one choice.

Another practice that has been borrowed by many people, religious or otherwise, as a daily way of connecting to earth, self, and the divine, is yoga. The Hindu practice of yoga has become a part of millions of people's daily routine to improve their physical, psychological, and spiritual well-being. The purpose of yoga is that the practitioner, using a disciplined set of physical postures, will become one with their deeper nature through a daily ritual of death and rebirth. The Dalai Lama wrote in the introductory comments to *The Tibetan Book of the Dead*, "Particularly in Highest Yoga Tantra, the methods for utilizing the processes of death, the intermediate state and rebirth are specifically taught as the basis for achieving liberation from cyclic existence."[93] Yoga integrates the mind, body, soul, and spirit through its practices, much like the process of alchemy.

Like yoga, most forms of exercise done in a prayerful manner can replicate walking the path in Jung's concept of preparation for death. The process of death arises throughout each phase of alchemy. Pilgrims need a daily practice that will turn up the heat, the dis-ease and discomfort, in their life to begin brewing what's in their personal cauldron—enough to move them past those mysterious forces, whether internal or external, that keep them from accomplishing the dreams of their personal legend. Regular, systematic exercise and prayer establish a rhythm for our psychic, spiritual, and physical health. I cannot imagine living a life without prayer and exercise. Otherwise, in the new mundane, I can suffer from long bouts of melancholy. And acedia is always just a whisper away, with excuses like, "It's too cold to walk" or "I can pray tomorrow." Unfortunately, one day of avoidance turns into a week of lost practice, and suddenly I'm not prepared to walk an unexpected pilgrimage or offer intense prayers in a time of someone else's need. At those moments, the fire under my alchemist's cauldron has cooled to faint embers. The work inside my soul has subsided. Then when the call of the unintended pilgrimage appears in forms like cancer, I might not be capable of turning up the heat, or making the walk, or sustaining life. One of the ways that helps me stay faithful to my spiritual practices is having a companion who will hold me accountable to my commitments.

Spiritual Companions as a Pilgrimage Practice

Having a spiritual companion is vital for our life after pilgrimage. In my book *When Leadership and Spiritual Direction Meet*, I go into detail about the practice of the spiritual director and the person he or she walks with as a companion. I used the term "spiritual director" because Christians, especially Catholics and those in the Mainline Protestant traditions, are often familiar with the practice. My trepidation, however, in using the term arises from the baggage the word "direction" carries. Today, the spiritual director should never tell the companion what to do. Instead, the director, as a companion, walks with the pilgrim as a partner in prayer and silence and as a resource in times of discernment. We need a wise soul to sit with us as we seek to hear what the divine is whispering into our soul. We need a companion, a guide, to assist us on our way.

When I have walked a pilgrimage with a group, I've taken on several roles, including that of spiritual companion. Most of the time, when the road we traveled was fairly well marked, I walked at the back of the group. Every once in awhile, though, the markers were missing or the directions were confusing, and that's when the group needed my experience. But even with my knowledge of the path, I can get turned around. As the guide, I do rely on my maps and compass, but I also depend on the abilities of my fellow travelers. We work together, as partners. Guide I can be, but I cannot walk another person's pilgrimage. I can only walk alongside them. This is the role of a spiritual companion in the life after the pilgrimage.

During the last twenty years, I have had two spiritual companions. Both men have listened to my problems. They helped me sort out my dreams and encouraged me in my daily practices. Asked me questions I was afraid to ask myself. Most importantly, they have prayed with me and for me all along the way. Scott has now walked through the veil into his life as a pilgrim after pilgrimage. My other friend, Mike, has returned to Ireland. What's next for me? I don't know the answer to that question. I'll have to live in the uncertainty of this moment. I'll have to be unwavering in walking my life as a pilgrim and creating a new imagination for my personal legend.

Prayer, exercise, and having a spiritual companion are the trinity of spiritual practice in the life after the pilgrimage. Remember, though, alchemy is a practice of wholeness represented by the number four—four directions, four elements, the four quadrants of the mandala, and the four points of the cross. We must discover on our own the fourth unique practice that will sustain us through the days of the new mundane. Possibly we could read Tarot cards as a way of accessing the universal archetypes present in our psyche. Or we could study the mystics such as Meister Eckhart. Maybe we could become an herbalist, using our craft to heal others. We might study the Kabbalah of Jewish mysticism as a way of connecting to the divine. Whatever it might be, the practice must come from an authentic expression of our Self.

The Opposites Will Not Leave Me Alone

Even in the afterglow of life beyond the pilgrimage, during days of the quiet new mundane, when we might think life is simply flowing along nicely, at the moment we're feeling so good—those pesky pairs of opposites make an untimely appearance: good and evil, dark and light, masculine and feminine, or even the less complex but still troubling opposites of thinking and feeling. All of a sudden, we're confronted with an unexpected tension, caught between two poles. The afterglow spirals into a nasty hangover. According to Jung, that means we're one of the lucky ones who have a "sufficient range of consciousness to become aware of the opposites inherent in human nature."[94] Some people don't like to hear this kind of language because it sounds elitist. Frankly, most people don't want to engage the unconscious. Such work seems too risky. There is too much pain involved. The work is too difficult. While we will naturally go through the maturation processes as we get older, there is no guarantee we will metaphorically move from the structured first half of life into the ambiguous second half where the work of individuation is fully engaged. We have to be willing to take the risk, embrace the pain, and do the work. In those times, when I'm especially feeling in the conflicted middle of the opposites, I find myself yearning to see my sister. I told you about her wisdom in the introduction and in chapter 5. She is a wisdom walker, and I am her student.

June 12, 2016, was one of those complex moments of trying to manage the opposites—in this case, it was my anger-filled rage that was held in the tension of broken-hearted compassion. On that Sunday morning a shooter killed forty-nine people and injured fifty-three others at Pulse, a gay nightclub in Orlando, Florida. It was the largest mass shooting by a single gunman in the United States and the deadliest attack against LGBTQ people in the United States.

That Sunday morning I had to preach and found myself struggling for words that didn't sound like a violent retaliation against a government that permits nearly free access to assault rifles. Like so many others in this country, this particular mass shooting was a profound instance in which to once again ask the question, "Was this senseless violence enough for our legislative body to take some action of gun control?" Even while I tried to be rational, I knew deep under my righteous reflection of cold anger, the flaming rage was boiling in the dark corners of my soul.

In 1979, one of my first acts as the pastor of a small Baptist church in Coolidge, Arizona, was to conduct the funeral of one of three teenage girls who were senselessly murdered while working at the local Dairy Queen. Robbery was not the motive, and the killer or killers were never found. Then, in 1999, as the incoming president of a small college in Phoenix, Arizona, I sat at the funeral of Sydney Browning, a personal friend and an alumna of our school, who had been killed in a mass murder at her church in Texas. In 2001, as president of the university, while weapons of any kind were banned on campus, a man living in student family housing accidentally shot his young child while cleaning his gun. Then in 2009, when I was pastor at St. Augustine's Episcopal Church in Tempe, Arizona, a parishioner's adult son was murdered while working as a photo enforcement officer in Phoenix. These events have stoked the fire of my position on the need for gun control. Even though I feel justified in my ideals, I often translate them through the voice of anger—I know that is not helpful in the debate. I knew I needed to hear my sister's wisdom. So Cathy and I headed to Tucson to visit Dinah.

As I have written before, Dinah has a very limited vocabulary. When we sit at dinner, Dinah is mostly silent. When I ask her questions, I have to watch for answers that are found in a raised eyebrow, the tilt of her head, a smile or a frown, a gesture, and if I'm lucky, a word or two, some of which are impossible to understand.

That evening the conversation turned to Dinah's friend. He has multiple-sclerosis and is a paraplegic who can't speak. Jo, Dinah's beloved caregiver, filled in the gaps of my sister's story about this man who lives in a nearby house for handicapped guys. When Dinah goes to his house, she sits with him, holds his hand, strokes his arm, and says, "I luv ou." She knows what he needs—human touch, a kind face, and the words of love that heal.

Dinah doesn't see the color of a person's skin. She doesn't care about their ethnicity. It doesn't matter to her if someone is religious or not. She's not concerned with how someone identifies their sexuality. I've watched Dinah interact with the diversity of humanity and she treats everyone the same way—a smile, a big hug, and pure love.

I've wondered a thousand times what it would be like to get inside Dinah's head, to walk around in the world in her skin, to be Dinah. I've witnessed her frustration at not being able to tell her story. I imagine that's why she connects so well with people who have been marginalized—people of color, people of various religions, people who are lesbians, people who are gay, people who are bisexual, people who are transgendered, people who are queer. They know what it's like not to be able to freely, openly, and safely tell their story. Dinah knows that feeling because she lives in the borderlands of unique difference. Listening to her that night, I once again was reminded that but for a twist and turn of a tiny piece of chromosome-15, Dinah and I would trade places. But, then again, I could say that about everybody I meet—we're all just a breath of fate away from being in some other circumstance, living in someone else's skin.

Dinah taught me that if I really want to love someone, I have to touch them, imagine myself being them, walk around in this world as if I am them. I have to let go of the idea that I am different from anyone else in the world, for by the very twist of a sliver of DNA, I could be that person. Maybe that's what "love your neighbor as yourself" and "respect the dignity of every human being" really mean. That night I think Dinah was asking me if I could live my life like she lives hers: in a state of love, even, as Jesus said, "to love our enemies."

Dinah has changed her friend's life with unconditional love. Dinah has changed my life with her love. Indeed, Dinah's kind of love could change our world if we could love ourselves, our neighbors, and our enemies. Maybe that love starts by holding hands?

Dinah is a pilgrim of wisdom's way, and I believe to do the work of transforming lives, both ours and others, we must live life as pilgrims. To live this life means we'll always be on pilgrimage, some walking, some metaphoric, some with words, some in silence.

By going on pilgrimage and seeing life as a pilgrimage, we activate the heat of transmutation, the discomfort that brings about systemic change, which is needed for the work of alchemy. Then after we stop walking, we have to accept the reality that there will be days when we are confronted with a pair of opposites that we thought we had already dealt with in days past.

One partner of the pair has been hiding in the shadows, waiting for us to acknowledge its presence. It emerges at the point when it has lost patience with having been ignored too long, usually appearing in a dream, sometimes in an undesired behavior, or when provoked, such as in the Orlando shooting. As I wrote about in chapter 4, the serpent confronts us. The pair of opposites —both the archetypal symbols of the poison and the healer—held within one iconic figure, the serpent. I face the powers of my compassion co-mingled with my anger, which is the chaos of my alchemical individuation. Do I embrace the part of me that lurks in the shadows of the Tree of Life and Death (anger)? Or do I suppress it? If I deny that part of my Self, then I will project the poisonous serpent onto someone else, a boss, a spouse, a parent, or someone who owns an assault rifle. To embrace the reality of my shadow and the darkness where it resides is hard work. But darkness produces its own light, and in that moment the light of the shadows heals the storm.

There is no symbol of the light of the Cosmic Christ without the equal symbol of the darkness of the serpent. Jung wrote in *Alchemical Studies,* "One does not become enlightened by imagining figures of light, but by making the darkness conscious."[95] The pairs continue to show their faces to us if we work on improving the range of consciousness in our life. Why? So we can stop projecting our weaknesses, failures, and self-expectations onto others, and embrace who we are—allowing the Self to be in the center of the psyche, instead of our ego, which is very happy to blame everyone else for what befalls us, frightens us, paralyzes us. The choice is ours: do we live into the heat of our alchemical work of wisdom walking, or do we fall back into the old way of living, denying, avoiding, projecting, and hiding behind a mask? My mentor sister keeps teaching me about the better way to walk in this world.

Never Let Them See You Sweat

Pastor Amy Wiles reminds me of my sister in many ways. She walked the Wicklow Way and was a part of Vox Peregrini. She has a lovely voice and is married to John Wiles, founder of Vox Peregrini. Her pilgrimage was a difficult one. On the walk she encountered several physical hardships along the way. Still, she was able to finish the walk on her own terms. She wrote the following devotion, which I believe is a beautiful expression of what it means to find a way to live a life of pilgrimage after you stop walking.

> A pastor's life is very public, and I often feel a little like I am performing. People project a lot of expectations onto pastors, and it is difficult not to let other people's expectations become your own. I try to make the right decisions, make the best impressions, deliver the most moving sermons, develop the most innovative ministries, lead the most efficient meetings, and contact anyone who might have a pastoral need. These are very high expectations to live up to. But I try . . . for better . . . or perhaps more times than not . . . for worse.
>
> In her book *Daring Greatly,*[96] university professor Brené Brown says that many women have a mantra running in their head: "Do it all and never let them see you sweat." For me, this mantra had come to define performance. I try to hide away the imperfections and fret over the mistakes here and there. I work hard never to let people see me sweat.
>
> But that proved impossible on the pilgrimage. People saw me sweat. I was stinky and physically raw, without makeup or the kind of clothes that hide the parts of my body that make me insecure. But people saw me sweat in other ways, too. People saw me struggle from day one. I packed more than I could carry, and had to let others help me. I always felt like I was at the back of the pack. My ankles and knees gave me trouble. I was constantly borrowing supplies. The second-to-last day, I nearly had to quit. Even musically, I wasn't ever fully confident in my skills. I was always relying on another voice to guide me. Even worse, I often wore my emotions on my sleeve, crying at the drop of a hat. On the Wicklow Way, my imperfections, my mistakes, and my vulnerability were wide out in the open. I couldn't hide them. People saw me sweat, and it was hard.

But then I had a revelatory moment. It happened during a closing interview with Ian Goldsmith, who came on the trip as our documentarian. In my final interview he asked, "You have had a lot of struggles on this trip, and you have been an inspiration to me and several others. What will you tell your two-year-old daughter one day about what you've learned from your pilgrimage?"

I was absolutely floored. The last word I would have used to describe my pilgrimage was "inspirational." But there it was, hanging in the air. Inspirational.

After a few moments, I responded with what I will tell my daughter.

You may try to do inspirational things with your life. But don't expect experiences of inspiration to *feel* inspirational in the moment. Don't expect to feel like you've got everything under control or that you are doing an awesome job. Don't expect to feel like you are impressing people or living up to standards of perfection. Don't expect the kind of performance that you would want spotlighted center stage. Life's going to be scary and you will probably feel more like a weakling than Wonder Woman. There will be moments of difficulty and even sadness. You might even wonder if you can keep going.

But don't ever be *afraid* of those feelings and certainly don't try to prevent them because of what other people may think. Vulnerability is the place from which inspiration comes. When you try to hide and cover up the stuff that you would rather people not know—when you try to cover up the things that you're embarrassed of or ashamed of, it's then you're only half living, you're only half experiencing the world around you. And shockingly, sharing those things that you'd rather hide is what enables us to connect with other people in amazing ways.

There are two ways to live life. One path would be to try and put on the best show possible. The other is to let down your guard and share who you really are, even the parts that you'd rather not be plastered on the marquee.

Life after pilgrimage is so messy, so complex, at times the kind of life we might regret having started. But there's no turning back, because the work is so vital to living a fully integrated life, a life of wisdom, a life of imagination. Amy will have more than something to tell her daughter about how to live life—Amy Wiles will have lived that life as an example for her daughter and she will know it without Amy ever having told her child one thing about the pilgrimage of life. Those who matter the most to us will see that we live our life differently because we walk wisely in the world. That's the way of Dinah Stafford, that's the way of Pastor Amy Wiles, that's the way of a wisdom walker.

A Natural and Queer Revelation

Anthropologist, educator, and author Loren Eiseley (1907–1977) wrote in *The Star Thrower,* "The World, I have come to believe, is a very queer place, but we have been part of the queerness for so long that we tend to take it for granted. . . .One must seek, then, what the solitary approach can give—a natural revelation."[97] My queer pilgrimage through this book has been a natural revelation. Over the course of my work on this book, my mother died, two grandsons were born, and I walked three pilgrimages. We moved. I changed jobs. I'm learning to live with the prospects of cancer. And my Jungian mentor and friend, Scott Haasarud, died.

Writing this book has been a long alchemical pilgrimage. The higher I climb into the world of Jungian thought and alchemy, the further I plummet into the depths of my soul and the unconscious. Spiraling higher, spiraling deeper. This book has taken years to write and during that time, it has become a living thing; the book is speaking to me every moment of my life; it speaks to me from my computer screen, from the paper it's printed on, in my dreams, when I wake up, when I go on my morning walk.

The book has its own voice, the husky depth of age that cracks with emotion every time it tells another story. My relationship with this book has and is still transmuting me, doing alchemical work on me. Working on this book has caused my writer's voice to age with its own raspy rattle. I've heard wisdom calling my name in ways that would drive me into simultaneous grief for the dead and celebration of new life, the crying and the laughter, and to beg for forgiveness for what I have done while I swear vengeance for what has been done to others and to me. And through the work of my imagination, I continue to see old visions cast by the ancients that create within me the hope for new possibilities.

The cycle of death and rebirth has heated the cauldron of my life, and from the ashes of alchemy the raven with the peacock tail would peek her head above the cauldron's rim, tempting me with her resurrection—but not yet. Then I would start all over again. Part of me wants the alchemical work of writing this book to end, so that the pilgrimage will end. But I know that's not going to happen. Life keeps moving. The pilgrimage never ends. Wisdom continues to emerge, because I will keep walking, from this queer life into the next queer life, one natural revelation into another. What we dare risk writing about becomes the way we will live our fragile life—on dangerous terms. Writing about wisdom walking and the work of an alchemical pilgrimage has made available to me the symbols and images with which I write. And so, as Hillman said, I have been transmuted by the work, the images, and the symbols of writing this book.

On my life pilgrimage I have gained wisdom.

I have learned not to think first, but instead to trust my senses, then think and feel, and finally to let my imagination have a definite power in how I interpret my experiences.

I have learned that to be authentic, I must let others see me sweat my way through the alchemical phases, over and over again.

I have learned that the chaotic feelings of the first phase actually linger throughout all the other phases, for constantly we are always returning back to the beginning, up the spiral of higher consciousness and down the spiral into the unconscious.

I have learned that living with the eclipsed sun of melancholy is not a bad thing; it's just the way life is for me—but not for everybody, and that's okay.

I have learned that absolute darkness has its own light, and that to truly see I must walk into the temple tomb with only the irrational midnight light of uncertainty.

 I have learned that there is creativity in the darkness of death—the creativity of life, death, and rebirth, happening over and over again in everyone's life.

I have learned that in the grand notion of timelessness, I am living in this present moment already dead; for in that prospect, I am fully alive and fully present to what I am experiencing.

I have learned that the healing of the soul lies in the archetypal figure of the serpent, both poison and healer.

And I have learned that God, the divine, YHWH, the ground of all being, the unspeakable name, whatever name you call the eternal one, loves me, you, and all creation, both in presence and in absence, as we walk our muddy, mist-covered, uncertain, and yet creative pilgrimage. The natural revelation continues as long as we are willing to never take this queer world for granted. Please keep walking the wisdom way.

Epilogue

Three times I had walked the Wicklow Way starting from Dublin, walking south to Clonegal. I was familiar with the trail and I knew the landmarks. I knew where I was and where I was going. Then, when I decided that Vox Peregrini should walk in the opposite direction so they could finish in Dublin, I knew, rationally, I would see things differently, even see parts of the way I hadn't seen before. But I didn't expect to walk right past an important signpost the very first day. I kept an eye on my map and phone, which was marking the miles we had walked. I knew we were near the landmark where we needed to stop and call for our ride that would take us to our hostel in Shillelagh. But I missed the sign. I hadn't seen it from that direction. We walked almost three miles before I realized that we had walked too far. Not a very good way to prove that I was up to being a good trail leader, especially on the first day. I was embarrassed and I felt so badly that I had caused the group to walk an extra six miles; especially those who had struggled so much that first day.

Unfortunately, I was familiar with those feelings. It wasn't the first time I had led a group past an important marker. But with Vox Peregrini, I had committed myself to not let that happen again. It did, though, and I kicked myself for it. But I made no excuses. I simply missed the turn as if it was the first time I had been walking the Wicklow Way. I was back in the first phase of chaos. I was at the beginning of the alchemical process, but I wasn't starting over again at the same place. I hadn't walked in a circle. My life as a pilgrim had taken me many levels up the spiral of consciousness and down into the spiral of my soul, the unconscious. I was a different person because of my many outer and inner adventures. And I could handle the mistake with much better grace and self-forgiveness. The group laughed it off—it was the first day after all.

You have walked with me through the pilgrimage of this book. While I have done my best, I imagine we might have gotten off the path, even lost, a few times—but hopefully not too often and definitely not on the last day.

We have explored the work of Carl Jung and his ideas of personality type preferences and alchemy. I have outlined what walking through the world would look like if we used the process of wisdom walking: relying first on our senses, then on our thinking and feeling, and finally opening our soul to the experiences of a new imagination for our life. We have dared to be alchemists, lowering ourselves into the cauldron of chaos, then hoping for the fire to create a cracking in the egg of our consciousness, praying more intently for the rising of the raven with a peacock tail; and then finally, in our imagination beyond imagination, we turned the heat up enough for the phoenix to rise and create our philosopher's healing stone of gold. And then we learned that we must always go back to the beginning, consciously and unconsciously.

I admit, I've taken you on an exhausting, long pilgrimage. You've walked farther than across Ireland—you've walked across the vast expanse of your mind, body, soul, and spirit. I offer this blessing to you: the blessings of the great raven, the standing stone, and the One whose name we cannot speak; as you walk your pilgrimage of life, I pray that you will be blessed with visions, hear the voice of the universe, grow in wisdom, and be comfortable living with uncertainty.

Truly, I do hope to meet you someday at a crossroads in Ireland. We can walk the day and finish the night in a local pub. We can share our stories of wisdom walking while we down a pint. And we can know we have something in common—we are pilgrims on wisdom's way. Until then, *slainte* and good walking.

⋮

Appendix

The Pilgrim's Companion: A Guide for Wisdom Walking

Gil W. Stafford

This guide is the result of having taken several walking pilgrimages across Ireland. While walking alone, in moments of being speechless, I found the silence to be my best companion and teacher. Still, there were moments when a few words felt comforting. When I walked with fellow soul travelers, there were times when words could be a container for our emotions. Words were also a means of supporting us while we did the hard work of leaning into the language of silence—the words of the world of the unseen. The words here are not meant to intrude. The intention is to hold the tension between inner silence and external sound.

Pilgrimage is more than an international vacation. Pilgrimage is something beyond a long hike. Pilgrimage is soul work, challenging, adventurous, transformative—we are gaining wisdom as we walk. While on pilgrimage, there were those tiny instances when I felt my soul being fetched into a deeper inner path of becoming one with the Other, with other people, with myself, and with all of creation—one with the *anima mundi* (the soul of the world). At times, these words helped articulate my experience. Other times they got in the way. My work, your work, is to use these prayers and rituals at the times most helpful.

Pilgrimage is wandering with a purpose—the exterior work. Pilgrimage is also to wonder into the imagination of the soul—interior work. Pilgrimage is an opportunity to let go of what you want to leave behind, both interior and exterior work. Pilgrimage can be permission to set down the burdens that are too heavy. Pilgrimage is a challenge to pick up what you need for each day. Tomorrow may bring something new to consider. The goal is to walk with intention and reflect on your purpose while not missing the unexpected.

To support walking your pilgrimage with both intention and the surprise of spontaneity, I have included a few ways of exploring the inner world as well as means of encountering the outer world. You will find prayers, offerings, and practices to help you create ritual, and ways to approach the seen and the unseen. My hope is that this tiny book of prayers and rituals will support your work of integrating the mind, body, soul, and spirit.

These prayers, practices, and activities could be done individually or in community. Any instructions offered are given only to support you, the explorer, in your search for connection with the *anima mundi*. Care must be taken when approaching the natural world. Caution must be exercised when beckoning the unknown. Our inner world can be troubled by the transmigration of movement from the unseen into the seen. I write only of what I have experienced.

Prayers, Practices, Activities for Pilgrimage

A bidding for the daily journey

Holy One, hold us safe within the sacred circle;

Holy One, walk with us on the Way.

Holy One, guide us into the four directions; carry us wisely
across Mother Earth.

Holy One, walk with us on the Way.

Holy One, we implore Father Sky to be gentle with us this day.

Holy One, walk with us on the Way.

Holy One, may we be willing to offer our reverence to what we see;

Holy One, walk with us on the Way.

Holy One, to what we do not see with the eye,
may we chance a curious stare;

Holy One, walk with us on the Way.
Holy One, may we listen to what we hear;
    Holy One, walk with us on the Way.
Holy One, for what we do not hear, we give thanks for the silence.
    Holy One, walk with us on the Way.
Holy One, be above us, below us, around us, and in us.
    Holy One, walk with us on the Way.
Holy One, we pray that we may experience the pilgrim's path this day
      as a way to learn about the world, each other, and ourselves. May
      the pilgrim's path be our teacher and may we be her students.
Holy One, may we know you and may we be known by you this day.
Holy One, walk with us on the Way.

Day One of Walking
(A seven-day pilgrimage)

As we begin our pilgrimage, we give thanks to you, Holy One. Walk before us. Walk behind us. Walk with us. Walk in us. We give thanks to you, Holy One.

As we begin our pilgrimage, we give thanks for those we have left behind and how they have enabled us to be here this day. *(You may speak those names to creation and her creator.)*

As we begin our pilgrimage, we give thanks for all those who have walked this path before us. May we hear their voice of instruction and see their soul of guidance. *(You may speak their names.)*

As we begin our pilgrimage, we give thanks for our equipment, our packs, our boots, our clothes. May we work together as we walk together.

As we begin our pilgrimage, we give thanks for one another; for what we mean to each other, what we will learn from each other, and what will irritate us about each other.

As we begin our pilgrimage, we give thanks for those who prepare a place for us this evening. May we be gracious guests. Amen.

Day Two of Walking

On this second day of our pilgrimage, we remember that we walk upon Mother Earth's hallowed ground. Our steps are our prayers. With our bodies and our feet feeling the ache of the first day's journey, we ask Mother Earth to be gentle with us through the forest, up the mountain, over the river, across the hill, and down the valley. We ask that all the way markers send us a true message. We ask that we may see the message and understand her directions. Grant us the knowledge we need this day. Ensure us the strength we need this day. Bless us with the courage we need this day. May we walk on sacred ground, see sacred space, and know the sacred experience. Amen.

Day Three of Walking

O Holy One we give thanks to you for bringing us to this moment in our pilgrimage. Speak into our souls this day that we may feel your presence as we walk towards the ancient world. For in the heating of the soul comes new imagination. Holy One, grant us the inner wisdom to know what we need to place in the spiritual cauldron of new growth. Give us the courage to make our sacrificial offering of what we hold, what we carry, what we treasure. As we drop each personal element into the womb of new birth, let us do so in confidence that what emerges will indeed be our own transformation. Amen.

Day Four of Walking

O Holy One, today we offer our prayers in hopes of having the strength to continue climbing the mountains of our pilgrimage. Grant us air to breathe. Lighten our load. Empower our legs. Keep our hearts open to the signs you bring us. Might we hear the words of pilgrims who have traveled before us. Keep mindful of those who have sought refuge in these mountains. May we commune with the spirits of this place. Bring us safely through this day. Amen.

Day Five of Walking
(A prayer for the midpoint of a pilgrimage)

O Holy One, today we offer our prayers of thanksgiving. We are at the halfway marker. Our lives have many midpoints. May we be mindful of those brought into our soul vision this day. We have experienced much; for this we give you thanks. We still have much to see; for this we give you thanks. Grant us strength for what lies ahead. Amen.

Day Six of Walking

O Holy One of all that was, and is, and is to come, the divinity of timeless-ness, hear our prayers and know our hearts. Keep us present to the moment. Let us walk the way mindful of why we came. Breathe in our souls your vision for our imagination. O Holy One, hold the thoughts of our return to reality at bay for a few more days. Let us walk and breathe in the grace of this sacred earth. Amen.

Day Seven of Walking
(A prayer for the final day of a pilgrimage)

O Holy One, Mother and Father of us all, we pray for our final day of pilgrimage together. May this day be one of presence—to you, to ourselves, and to one another. To you, may we be satisfied with what we have experienced, and not disappointed in what we have not. To ourselves, may we accept ourselves for who we are and be hopeful that what we have learned will travel with us. To one another, may we be thankful for those who have shared their pilgrimage with us, forgive if need be, let go if need be, take up if need be. For this day we pray your blessings of completion be gently poured upon us. Amen.

Sabbath Day
(A ritual of blessing for a day of rest)

On this day of Sabbath, we gather in this sacred place remembering your work is most profound in the deserts of our lives. We give thanks your spirit is not confined within the official walls of any institution. We give thanks your work is not restrained by the expectations of our community. We give thanks you bring life even when the world sees death. Today, we gather in this space humbly seeking your blessings on the desert we have experienced in our own life.

Prayers in community:
(A ritual of bread and wine)

We give thanks for the beauty of the world we live in and especially for this sacred ground. We pray that through our experience of pilgrimage we may grow ever more mindful of our responsibility to care for our island home.

We give thanks for those who have come before us in this world. We give thanks for those who have been stewards of this place. We praise you for the women and men who served this community, for their courage of risk, their gentle love, their willingness to hold weeping grief in their arms.

We pray for those who are buried in the hallowed earth. We pray that all souls may remember us kindly as we worship in their space.

We pray for those we have left behind. Be present to them. Let them feel our love for them this very moment. Embrace them as we would.

We pray for each other this day. We pray for each other's physical needs. We pray for each other's spiritual needs. We pray for each other's emotional needs.

We pray for ourselves this day. We pray for our physical needs. We pray for our emotional needs. We pray for our spiritual needs.

O Holy One, of all that was, that is, and that will be; who holds us in the timelessness of this moment; grant us peace of soul, healing of body, and refreshment of life. May we know you this day in a manner yet to be experienced. Transform us in the way of the pilgrim.

Gathering around some bread and wine:

O Holy One, in whom we live, move, and have our being, hear our prayers. In the beginning of time, you created this earth, this island, this ground, these stones. Millennia ago, you brought people to this earth. People have worshipped you in the ancient ways of the sun. And people have worshipped you here in the ways of the child of all humanity. We humbly stand here remembering you have brought us to this holy space. We give thanks to you that you love us. We are grateful you continue to move in our lives because we are a part of your creation.

O Holy One, we remember that in the light of your love, we, your creation, have not always loved you as you love us. To teach us how to love, you sent us many guides to show us the pilgrim's way. You also sent wisdom, that she would be our spirit guide. Together they shine your light on our path towards wholeness.

In this moment, we offer to you this bread and this wine. We ask wisdom to pour the spirit of creation into these elements, that they will become for us love and wisdom. Bless us as we partake, that we may become the love we eat and the wisdom we drink.

In this moment we pray to you (together):
Creator of all that was, and is, and will be;
We praise you as the Holy One.
You have created the path,
The pilgrim,
And this holy space.
In this place,
At this moment,

Humbly, we ask for your love,

We beseech your forgiveness.

May we love as you love us,

May we forgive as you forgive us.

We give you thanks for this our bread and wine,

So that daily we may be sustained and transformed by your nourishment.

For you are the creator, the child, the wisdom, and the spirit.

(Alternative Prayer: Our Mother by Miriam Therese Winter)

Our Mother who is within us,

We celebrate your many names.

Your wisdom come,

Your will be done,

Unfolding from the depths within us.

Each day you give us all that we need.

You remind us of our limits,

And we let go.

You support us in your power,

And we act with courage.

For you are the dwelling place within us,

The empowerment around us,

And the celebration among us,

Now and forever. Amen.[98]

This is the Bread of Love.

This is the Cup of Wisdom.

(*After the sharing of the bread and wine.*) Let us pray together:

Strengthen us this day to be love and wisdom in the world. May we have the courage to share this love and wisdom with others. Walk before us, walk behind us, walk above us, walk below us. Let us walk in the world as transformed pilgrims. Amen.

Prayer for the end of the pilgrimage

O breath of the holy soul of all, we give thanks for the strength, courage, and will that has brought us to the completion of our walk. We thank you for our boots, packs, clothes, and equipment. We ask you to bless them for their service. For all we have seen, we give thanks. For all we have not seen, we give thanks. For all we have heard, we give thanks. For all we have experienced, we give thanks. Grant us acceptance that our pilgrimage continues now as we walk back into our lives. May we have the courage to renegotiate how we will live our life. Bless us now as we continue our travels, that we live within your safe arms. Amen.

Prayer for the end of the day

O Holy Mother, hear my prayers at the end of this day. I have walked. I am weary. Thank you that I am here. Thank you for this place. I especially thank you for what I have experienced this day (*name what you are thankful for*). Grant me refreshment and rest this evening that I may walk again tomorrow.

Prayer before water

O Holy One, thank you for this water. Here at this (*lake, river, well*) . . . I see and know you are present in creation. From this water you sustain my life, brighten my face, refresh my feet, and cleanse my soul. Without you I could not experience the fourfold blessing of water. Without water, I would not know you. I touch this water seeking you. Touch me as I touch this water.

Prayer before a tree

O Holy One, thank you for creating this sacred tree who represents the Tree of Life. I bow before you, majestic tree. May I touch you? Would you hear my prayers? Would you speak to the creator for me? This is what I need to say. . . . O Great Tree, thank you for listening. Please keep my words with you. Amen.

Prayer before a stone

O Creator, I give thanks for this stone. I still myself in quiet reflection so that I might listen to this stone. Stones on the ground, stones standing, stones in the circle, stones alone, and stones in community—all stones have a word. O Creator, may my soul hear the word of the stone. Amen.

Prayers for the spirit animal, bird, fish

(*Caution, do not pray this prayer unless you have a true and deep sense that the animal, bird, or fish is indeed to be your spirit guide. If you pray the prayer in uncertainty, the animal, bird, or fish will reject you out of graciousness, not malice. Consult with a wise sage before praying this prayer.*)

O Holy One, power of the spirit, I give all my thanks for this (*animal, bird, fish*) of power. If it be the will of the (*animal, bird, fish*), let them be my guide. I bow in humility. I commit my spirit ears to listen. I pledge my soul(s) to be faithful. Creator open my spirit to the spirit of the (*name the animal, bird, fish*).

Prayer for strength on the pilgrimage

O Holy One, Creator of all that was, is, and will be, hear my prayer for strength in my weakness. Refresh my feet, ease my aches, lighten my load. Give me courage if my feet must endure this pain. Grant me comfort if I must tolerate this ache. Empower me if I must carry this burden. Raise my head, straighten my back, pump blood through my heart, breathe your air into my lungs. Hear my prayers for strength. Grant me strength. Grant me power. Grant me grace to endure. (*Repeat with rhythm of your breath and heart.*)

Prayer for healing

O divine healer, I need you to pour your healing salve over my (*name your pain*). Touch me with your healing presence. As I touch my body may I feel your healing touch. Heal me in the timelessness of the world in which the spirit lives, moves, and has her being—there may I be healed. Amen.

Asking someone else to pray the prayer for you

O divine healer, empower me as I pray this prayer for (*name*), pour your salve over (*her/his*) (*body*). Touch (*name*) with your healing presence. As I move my hand (*lightly move your hand over the area without touching them*) may (*name*) feel your healing touch. Heal (*her/him*) in the timelessness of the world in which the spirit lives, moves, and has her being—there may (*name*) be healed. Amen.

Soul Work

Mandala

Creating a mandala is one form of soul work. The process is simple. The work is illuminating. There are no limitations because the imagination is limitless. Draw a large circle. Ask your soul (or souls or spirit guide or the divine) to speak to you from the unconscious. Look beyond the space in the circle. What do you see? Colors? Shapes? Figures? Be open to whatever appears. Begin to draw and color as your imagination experiences your soul.

A mandala is a work in progress. Carl Jung would work with one circle for months, others only a day. Those that spoke deeply to him he would create drafts of until he felt the mandala expressed his emotion. Over a lifetime he drew hundreds of mandalas. Many of them can be found in *The Red Book*.

Listen to nature

Modernity has convinced us that our human minds are superior to animals, birds, fish, and lizards. The advancement of science, enlightenment, and modernity has left us without the mythological ears to hear our walking, flying, swimming friends, much less the souls of all creation: stones, trees, small plants, the earth. Speak out loud to the world around you. Then listen to what they have to say. To listen to the sound of nature is to learn. To hear what the world has to say is to be a sentient being. Conscious awareness is to expand the mind, body, soul, and spirit.

Ask

Ask the world of creation and all its inhabitants to allow us to move within their world. To humble ourselves and acknowledge our vulnerability before the sky, the earth, the mountain, the path is to become one with creation. To ask creation is one way to love creation. Love heals both creation and our soul.

Ritual work

What is the purpose of your ritual? What words will you incorporate in your ritual? What movements will you use to symbolize what your words cannot say?

Ask the four elements—air, earth, water, and fire—to give you their symbol of presence in the ritual.

Create a circle. Ask the element symbols what direction they should be placed within your circle (N,S,E,W). From the center of your circle, name your purpose and call upon your guides, spirits, god(s), and goddesses to be present. Speak or sing your ritual words. Enact your movements. Be your ritual.

At the end of your ritual, while still in your circle—What did you sense? Think? Feel (experience)? What did you imagine? What are you imagining?

Build a nest

What new thing or idea would you like to birth into the world? Imagine your nest. Gather what you need to build the nest. Imagine that new thing or idea as an egg. What color is the egg? How small or large is the egg? How strong or fragile is the shell?

Place your egg in the nest. How long will it be before the egg hatches? What will feed your idea once it is born? When will you push it out of the nest to fly?

Prepare a Tomb

What must you let go of? Is there a person, thing, idea, time of life that you must symbolically bury? Write a letter about the event you want to bury. Or find an object that symbolizes that which you are going to bury.

Find an appropriate stone or stick for the "headstone." Search for the perfect spot for the tomb. Ritually dig the hole. Spend some final time with your letter and object you are going to bury. Have a wake. Give a eulogy. Then, with care and respect, bury what needs to be let go. Cover the object with the dirt. Set the headstone. Say a final word. And depart leaving what needed to be left behind.

Endnotes

⋮

1 Steven Charleston, *Hope as Old as Fire: A Spiritual Diary* (Oklahoma City, OK: Red Moon Publications, 2012), 56.

2 Karen Hering, *Writing to Wake the Soul: Opening the Sacred Conversation Within* (New York: Atria Paperback, 2013).

3 James Hillman, *Alchemical Psychology* (Putnam, CT: Spring Publications, 2014), 73.

4 C. G. Jung, *Psychology and Alchemy* (Princeton, NJ: Princeton University Press, 1968); C. G. Jung, *Alchemical Studies* (Princeton, NJ: Princeton University Press, 1967); C. G. Jung, *The Archetypes and the Collective Unconscious* (Princeton, NJ: Princeton University Press, 1959); C. G. Jung, *Aion: Researches into the Phenomenology of the Self* (Princeton, NJ: Princeton University Press, 1969); C. G Jung, *Mysterium Coniunctionis* (Princeton, NJ: Princeton University Press, 1970); C. G. Jung, *The Red Book: Liber Novus* (New York: W. W. Norton and Company, 2009).

5 Daniel J. Siegel, *Mind: A Journey to the Heart of Being Human* (New York: Norton, 2017), 162.

6 Ibid., 56.

7 Ibid., 126.

8 Eligio Stephen Gallegos, *Animals of the Four Windows: Integrating Thinking, Sensing, Feeling, and Imagery* (Velarde, NM: Moon Bear Press, 1991), 21.

9 C. G. Jung, "Psychology and Alchemy," in *The Collected Works of C. G. Jung*, vol. 12 (Princeton, NJ: Bollinger Foundation, 1977), 89.

10 Jung, *Red Book*.

11 C. G. Jung, "Everyone Has Two Souls," found in *C. G. Jung Speaking: Interviews and Encounters* (Princeton, NJ: Princeton University Press, 1977), 57.

12 Sheryl A. Kujawa-Holbrook, *Pilgrimage—The Sacred Art: Journey to the Center of the Heart* (Woodstock, VT: SkyLight Paths, 2013).

13 Phil Cousineau, *The Art of Pilgrimage: The Seeker's Guide to Making Travel Sacred* (Berkeley, CA: Conari Press, 1998).

14 Paulo Coelho, *The Alchemist: A Fable about Following Your Dream* (San Francisco: HarperCollins, 1998).

15 James Hillman, *Alchemical Psychology: The Uniform Edition of the Writings of James Hillman*, vol. 5 (Putnam, CT: Spring Publications, 2014), 125.

16 Jung, *Psychology and Alchemy*, 28.

17 Gil Stafford, unpublished prayer book prepared for the pilgrimage groups going to Ireland.

18 M. Scott Peck, *In Search of Stones: A Pilgrimage of Faith, Reason, and Discovery* (New York: Hyperion, 1995), 213–16.

19 Paddy Dillon, *The Irish Coast-to-Coast Walk: Dublin to Bray Head* (Milnthorpe, Cumbria, UK: Cicerone, 2005).

20 Jung, *Psychology and Alchemy*, 270.

21 Thomas Merton, *Mystics and Zen Masters* (New York: Noonday Press, 1967), 92.

22 Carmel McCaffrey and Leo Easton, *In Search of Ancient Ireland: The Origins of the Irish from Neolithic Time to the Coming of the English* (Chicago: New Amsterdam Books, 2002), 157.

23 Ian Bradley, *Columba: Pilgrim and Penitent* (Glasgow: Wild Goose Publications, 1996), 17.

24 Jung, *The Red Book: Reader's Edition*, 131.

25 Emma Jung and Marie-Louise von Franz, *The Grail Legend* (Princeton: Princeton Press, 1998), 127.

26 C. G. Jung, "Religious Ideas in Alchemy," in *The Collected Works of C. G. Jung*, vol. 13, second edition (New York: Princeton Press, 1953).

27 Ibid., 370.

28 Jung, *Psychology and Alchemy*, 315.

29 Ibid., 28.

30 Irene Gad, in the Jung Memorial Lecture at the Jung Society of Washington at the Embassy of Switzerland, June 2000. http://www.jung.org/gad.htm.

31 http://www.wicklowway.com/index.php.

32 Jung, *Psychology and Alchemy*, 79.

33 James Hillman, *Alchemical Psychology*, 128.

34 Ibid., 127.

35 John Shelby Spong, *The Fourth Gospel: Tales of a Jewish Mystic* (New York: HarperCollins, 2013), 198.

36 C. G. Jung, "Aion: Research into the Phenomenology of the Self," in *The Collected Works of C. G. Jung*, vol. 9, part 2 (Princeton, NJ: Bollinger Foundation, 1978), 109.

37 Richard Rohr, *The Naked Now: Learning to See as the Mystics See* (New York: Crossroads Publishing, 2009), 23.

38 Douglas Harink, *Paul Among the Postliberals: Pauline Theology Beyond Christiandom and Modernity* (Eugene, OR: Wipf and Stock, 2003), 26–27. Harink makes an excellent case for the mistranslation of the words "faith in Jesus Christ," which instead should be translated the "faith of Jesus Christ." This change dramatically changes how one may see their relationship with Jesus and understanding his life.

39 Richard Rohr, *Immortal Diamond: The Search for Our True Self* (San Francisco: Jossey-Bass, 2013), 150.

40 Ken Wilbur, *Integral Spirituality: A Startling New Role for Religion in the Modern and Postmodern World* (Boston: Integral Books, 2006), 95.

41 Daniel C. Matt, *The Essential Kabbalah: The Heart of Jewish Mysticism* (Edison, NJ: Castle Books, 1995), 10.

42 Matthew Fox, *The Coming of the Cosmic Christ: The Healing of Mother Earth and the Birth of a Global Renaissance* (San Francisco: Harper and Row, 1988), 1.

43 C. G. Jung, "Alchemical Studies," in *The Collected Works of C. G. Jung*, vol. 13 (Princeton, NJ: Bollinger Foundation, 1983), 107.

44 C. G. Jung, "*Mysterium Coniunctionis*: An Inquiry into the Separation and Synthesis of the Psychic Opposites in Alchemy," in *The Collected Works of C.G. Jung*, vol. 14 (Princeton: Princeton University Press, 1963), 249.

45 Craig Chalquist, *Terrapsychology: Re-engaging the Soul of Place* (New Orleans: Spring Journal Books, 2007). Chalquist makes a strong argument to support my belief that the history of a place lingers in the psyche of the geography.

46 Jung, *The Red Book: A Reader's Edition*, 344. See also James Hillman and Sonu Shamadasani, *The Lament of the Dead: Psychology after Jung's The Red Book* (New York: Norton, 2013), 120.

47 Mark Leviton, "Wrong Turn: Biologist Rupert Sheldrake on How Science Lost Its Way," *The Sun*, No. 446 (February 20, 2013), 4–12.

48 Bernd Heinrich, *Mind of the Raven: Investigations and Adventures with Wolf-Birds* (New York: Harper Collins, 1999), xvii. Heinrich's book is an excellent resource for understanding the profound characteristics of the ravens and the nature of their vast abilities.

49 C. G. Jung, ed., *Man and His Symbols* (New York: Dell Books, 1968), 49.

50 Ibid.

51 Robert Van de Weyer, ed., *The Letters of Pelagius: Celtic Soul Friend* (Worcestershire, Great Britain: Little Giddings Books: 1995), 91.

52 Lawrence M. Principe, *The Secrets of Alchemy* (Chicago: University of Chicago Press, 2013), 68.

53 Anonymous, *Meditations on the Tarot: A Journey into Christian Hermeticism* (New York: Putnam, 1985), 16.

54 Jung, *Mysterium Coniunctionis,* 536.

55 Ashenden Gavin, *Charles Williams: Alchemy and Integration* (Kent, OH: Kent University Press, 2008), 84.

56 Jung, *Mysterium Coniunctionis,* 290.

57 Gavin, *Charles Williams,* 58. Williams's views on the exchange of love are explored in his own writings in several essays. However, his work is often opaque, and Gavin's book shines some light through the murky window.

58 Jung, *Mysterium Coniunctionis,* 498.

59 W. B. Yeats, *Essays and Introductions* (New York: Macmillan, 1961), 43.

60 Principe, *The Secrets of Alchemy,* 209.

61 Jung, *Mysterium Coniunctionis,* 230.

62 James Hillman, *Alchemical Psychology,* 125.

63 Jung, *Mysterium Coniunctionis.*

64 Ibid., 496.

65 Jung, *The Red Book: A Reader's Edition,* 553.

66 Stanton Marlan, *The Black Sun: The Alchemy and Art of Darkness* (College Station: Texas A&M University Press, 2005), x, 5, 113. See also, Jung, *Mysterium Coniunctionis,* 98, and *Alchemical Studies,* 266.

67 *Red Book,* 225.

68 Jung, *Mysterium Coniunctionis,* 533–34.

69 "Back to Black (Song)," *Wikipedia,* www.https://en.wikipedia.org/wiki/Back_to_Black_(song), accessed May 4, 2016.

70 Jung, *Mysterium Coniunctionis,* 546.

71 Ibid., 43.

72 Marlan, *The Black Sun,* 5.

73 James Hillman, "The Suffering of Salt," in *Alchemical Psychology* (Putnam, CT: Spring Publications, 2014), 54.

74 Loretta Stafford, *Dinah's Story: The Struggles and Triumphs of Parenting a Child with Prader-Willi Syndrome* (Fairfax, VA: Xulon Press, 2002).

75 Sanford Drob, *Reading the Red Book: An Interpretive Guide to C.G. Jung's Liber Novus* (New Orleans: Spring Journal Books, 2012), 265.

76 Loretta Stafford, *Dinah's Story,* 32.

77 John N. Wallace, Jr., "Death," in *George Herbert: The Country Parson, The Temple,* ed. John N. Wallace, Jr. (New York: Paulist Press, 1981), 313.

78 Jung, *The Red Book: The Reader's Edition,* 468.

79 Hillman and Shamdasani, *Lament of the Dead,* 1.

80 Angeliki Yiassemides, *Time and Timelessness: Temporality in the Theory of Carl Jung* (New York: Routledge, 2014), xx.

81 Jung, "Aion: Researches Into the Phenomenology of the Self."

82 Edward F. Edinger, *The Aion Lectures: Exploring the Self in C. G. Jung's Aion* (Toronto: Inner City Books, 1996), 15–18.

83 C. G. Jung, "The Nature of the Psyche," *The Collected Works of C. G. Jung,* vol. 8 (Princeton, NJ: Princeton Press, 1975), 404.

84 Mary Ann Mattoon, *Jungian Psychology in Perspective* (New York: Free Press, 1981), 183.

85 Jung, "Alchemical Studies," 44.

86 Ibid, 46.

87 Marlan, *The Black Sun*, 79.

88 Dallas Willard, *The Divine Conspiracy: Rediscovering Our Hidden Life in God* (San Francisco: HarperCollins, 1998), 302.

89 Marcus Borg, *Meeting Jesus Again for the First Time: The Historical Jesus and the Heart of Contemporary Faith* (New York: Harper Collins, 1994).

90 Jung, *The Red Book: The Reader's Edition*, 439.

91 Ibid. 439–47.

92 Paulo Coelho, *The Alchemist*, 23–24.

93 Graham Coleman and Thupten Jinpa, eds., *The Tibetan Book of the Dead* (New York: Penguin Books, 2007), xx.

94 Jung, *Aion*, 247 footnote.

95 Jung, "Alchemical Studies," 265.

96 Brené Brown, *Daring Greatly: How the Courage to be Vulnerable Transforms the Way We Live, Love, Parent, and Lead* (New York: Gotham, 2012).

97 Loren Eiseley, *The Star Thrower* (New York: Hartcourt, 1978), 27.

98 http://www.patheos.com/blogs/carynriswold/2014/01/our-mother/#.